Women

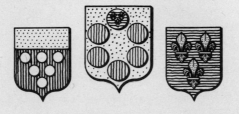

# of Power

ALSO BY MARK STRAGE

Cape to Cairo: Rape of a Continent

MARK STRAGE

WOMEN OF POWER
The Life and Times of
Catherine de' Medici

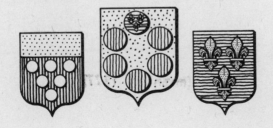

A HELEN AND KURT WOLFF BOOK

HARCOURT BRACE JOVANOVICH

NEW YORK AND LONDON

Printed in the United States of America

Library of Congress Cataloging in Publication Data

Strage, Mark.
Women of power.

"A Helen and Kurt Wolff book."
Bibliography: p.
Includes index.
1. Catherine de Médicis, Consort of Henry II, King of
France, 1519–1589. 2. Poitiers, Diane de, Duchess of
Valentinois, 1499–1566. 3. Marguerite de Valois, Con-
sort of Henry IV, King of France, 1553–1615. I. Title.
DC119.8.S75 944'.028'0922 [B] 75-35771

ISBN 0-15-198370-4

First edition

B C D E

Inadequately, for Tanya

Contents

Illustrations

ILLUSTRATIONS

Between pages 242 and 243

Catherine de' Medici in her middle forties
The weighing of the Bible, a Huguenot drawing
Jeanne d'Albret
Gaspard de Coligny
Philip II of Spain
The Massacre of Saint Bartholomew's Eve
Marguerite de Valois, prior to her marriage
Charles IX
Mme Charlotte de Sauves
The Duke of Alençon
Henry of Navarre as bridegroom
An evening at the Valois Court
Three of the Valois tapestries
    The Procession
    The Assault on the Island
    Combat at the Barrier
Henry III
Henry III's reception in Venice
A performance by *I Gelosi*
The Ball for the Duke of Joyeuse
Henry of Navarre
Henry, Duke of Guise
The cover page of *Les Hermaphrodites*
Marguerite de Valois on her return to Paris
Catherine at the age of 66
A procession of the Holy League in Paris
Henry IV and Marie de' Medici

Prologue

This is the story of three women—Catherine de' Medici, Diane de Poitiers, and Marguerite de Valois.

The first was Queen of France for twelve years and Queen Mother to three of her sons for another thirty. A historian has called her "a serpent born of tainted parents in the charnel house of Italy"; another said she was "the most infamous she-devil ever to hold royal power." One of her compatriots, diplomatically ambiguous, summed her up as "a true Florentine if there ever was one." These are opinions. The fact is that while she lived, during most of the sixteenth century, she was the most important woman in Europe.

The second was her husband's mistress, today and in her own time a legend of icy mystery and remote, eternal beauty —a spurious legend which she herself deliberately fabricated.

The third was her daughter. Superb, accomplished and anything but remote, she was described by an unsuccessful suitor as being "more divine than human, but created to damn and destroy men rather than to save them."

Each was animated by her own private passion—love of power, love of self, love of love—and pursued it in full measure and to its natural end. Together, through circumstances and the impact of their personalities—and the character of the men around them—these women helped to create an extraordinary period.

Without benefit of rights, for they had none, nor any claim or pretension to any, without the spur of feminism or emancipation, for neither existed as even a hazy abstraction, these women came to dominate the times as their sisters have never done since. One after another they troubled, corrupted, soothed, and civilized their century. They shaped it to the rhythm of their own design, their sometimes unbridled aspirations, their needs, and their secret fears.

Part One

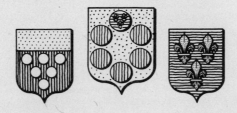

Preparation

I

It was by far the most magnificent wedding the sixteenth century had seen.

The bride's uncle and guardian, Pope Clement VII, and his retinue had departed from Leghorn aboard a fleet of sixty vessels. As was traditional when the Holy Father undertook a sea voyage, the lead galley carried the Holy Sacrament. Trailing off behind it to both flanks was a Genoese squadron under the personal command of Admiral Andrea Doria; immediately behind the military craft rode the papal ship itself, the *Servant of God*. It had been built expressly for this occasion, entirely draped with crimson and gold brocade that trailed over the side to the water. The principal salon, hung with silk and shaded by purple awnings, extended from mainmast to rudder. The rowing benches were outfitted with silver chains, and the crew of three hundred which occupied them wore satin uniforms in the papal colors of red and yellow.

As soon as the lookout posted on the tower of the Château d'If spotted the approaching ships, on the morning of October 12, 1533, a welcoming flotilla of fishing boats and pleasure craft sailed out of Marseilles Harbor to greet them. Bells from all the city's churches rang out in unison, only to be drowned out by the three hundred heavy cannons of the fortifications and the returning salutes from Doria's warships. Flame and smoke so filled the air that, according to an observer, "the water itself seemed to be on fire."

Ashore, His Holiness was greeted by Anne de Montmorency, Grand Master of France. Wearing his full pontifical robes, he was hoisted onto the *sedia gestatoria* and carried

3

on willing shoulders through the narrow streets, followed in pairs by a train of fourteen cardinals and thirty-six bishops. Then as now a busy, utilitarian, maritime city, Marseilles was poor in accommodations, but adequate lodgings had been prepared for the Pope in a large town house facing the Place Neuve. Next to it, separated only by a small alley, another house had been set aside for the bridegroom's father, King Francis I of France. The two houses had been connected by means of a wooden covered gallery that would permit their occupants to discuss matters of common interest in absolute privacy—and with some measure of comfort as well because the gallery's appointments had cost the city 3,000 écus.

Francis had himself inspected the arrangements and found them satisfactory. Then, not wishing to detract from his guest's arrival—the first state visit to France by a reigning pontiff within living memory—he had courteously withdrawn. He made his own formal entry on the following morning, dressed from head to toe in gold-embroidered white satin, and bringing with him the entire Court. Immediately the round of parties, dances, pageants, and banquets the Grand Master had spent three months arranging began to unroll. A letter from a guest at one of these described the details: the graciousness with which the Holy Father urged the King to make use of his personal hand basin; the procession of rare dishes, each introduced and paraded to the sound of trumpets; the dress of the ladies—the Queen, it appears, was so heavily covered with pearls and jewels that it was impossible to determine the color of her gown underneath them. Between the courses, there was more music and a dwarf who was able to dance and perform wondrous things, which gave great delight to the King.

The bride arrived ten days later, traveling overland and preceded by a suite of papal pages escorting a contraption never before seen in France: an enclosed, four-wheeled carriage. She herself, the better to be seen by the people who

4

lined the roadside, rode mounted on a great roan caparisoned in scarlet and gold brocade and followed by twelve young ladies also on horseback. The crowds were large and curious because so little was known about her—just that she bore a celebrated name, that she was the niece of the Holy Father, and that she was coming to marry the Duke of Orléans, the second son of the King.

Once in Marseilles, she paid her respects to her uncle, then to her future father-in-law in front of whom, as befitted their respective stations, she prostrated herself, and finally to her fiancé whom she was meeting for the first time. Like herself, he was fourteen years old. Gifts of rare splendor were exchanged. Francis presented the Pope with a large Flemish tapestry depicting the Last Supper and received in return a "piece of the horn of a unicorn"—presumably an elephant tusk—mounted in a gold setting and possessed, it was said, with the power of detecting the presence of poison in food. The King had also received, and tried to press on the pontiff, a huge, live Nubian lion which, according to the historian Paolo Giove, was "marvelously tame."

At last the marriage contract was signed on October 27, and the actual ceremony, at which Clement pronounced the nuptial benediction, was celebrated on the following day. The great scene, as painted by Giorgio Vasari, is to be seen today in the Palazzo Vecchio in Florence. At the center stands the Pope, his posture and full, flowing, gray beard bespeaking patriarchal benevolence. To his right is the groom's family, Francis, of course, slightly in the foreground of the Queen and her attending ladies, and Henry of Orléans, handsome, solemn, and looking every inch the bridegroom. To the Pope's left are the Medicis and the most politically important of the cardinals who had journeyed from Rome. Although the artist was not present, he has recreated the solemn moment with accuracy. All but one of the principal human figures are readily recognizable, and the scene is enlivened by the inclusion in the foreground of both the dwarf, Gradasse, whose antics proved so diverting, and even the lion.

Only one detail mars the composition. Ever the practiced courtier, Vasari has placed directly next to the Pope a slender, elegant and self-assured young lady who bears no resemblance whatever to the real-life bride.

II

Her mother was Madeleine de La Tour d'Auvergne, a marvelous eighteen-year-old fairy-tale princess who rode and composed verse with equal grace, and could trace her lineage to the sainted Louis IX, and beyond him to Godfrey of Bouillon, one of the leaders of the First Crusade. Her father was Lorenzo, Duke of Urbino, and, of course, a Medici.

But two generations had, in a quarter century, drained most of the vitality out of this astonishing family. At the time of his death in 1492, Lorenzo the Magnificent had been an immense presence, the political arbiter of Italy. Within two years, his eldest son, Piero, contrived to have himself and his descendants banished from Florence in perpetuity. As an afterthought, the Signoria offered a reward of 4,000 florins for his head—an insulting sum which Piero saved his former fellow citizens by falling into a mountain stream and drowning. He left a single son, Lorenzo, who bore his grandfather's name, but in his own right was handsome, lazy, and worthless.

The family fortunes took a brief favorable turn in 1513 when Piero's brother, Giovanni, for whom their father had had the foresight to purchase a cardinal's hat, connived election to the papacy as Leo X. With apostolic blessing, young Lorenzo was reestablished in the massive Medici palace on the Via Larga. But even in his new position of eminence Leo did not have total faith in the Florentines' capacity to forgive and forget. Lorenzo, then just twenty-one, returned to his native city as a simple, private citizen. To provide him with suitable rank, the Pope sorted through the Church's nominal holdings and selected the Duchy of Urbino. After an unequal struggle, the incumbent Duke was dispossessed, and his title and estates were awarded to Lorenzo.

The next step would have been to find an adequately dowered bride, but happily this problem solved itself through the intercession of the same Francis I, then himself twenty-three years old and only three years on the throne of France. Ambitious, boundlessly self-confident, and innocent of the subtleties of Italian politics, Francis had been sufficiently impressed by the resurgence of the Medicis to write Lorenzo a letter, congratulating him on gaining his dukedom. "For my part," he had added, "I would dearly love to help you, and to this end would like to see you marry some fine young woman of quality connected with my household."

The reply, which arrived promptly, satisfied Francis's aspiration. And, as more concrete evidence of Leo's delight, when the bridegroom himself arrived he brought a token of Medici esteem reminiscent of older, better days: a pair of magnificent Raphaels (*The Holy Family* and *Saint Michael Slaying the Dragon;* they still hang in the Louvre).

The wedding of Lorenzo and Madeleine was celebrated on April 28, 1518, at the old feudal fortress of Amboise, looming over a wide reach of the Loire. Most probably it was graced by the presence of Amboise's most distinguished resident, the aged Leonardo da Vinci whom Francis had two years earlier, in exchange for an annuity of 700 gold *écus* and the use of a delightful manor house, induced to become "First Painter, Engineer, and Architect to the King." It is likely, too, that in this capacity Leonardo had taken a hand in devising the decorations which converted the castle's inner courtyard into an immense banqueting tent, brightened to

7

daylight with thousands of torches, and the still more elaborate preparations for the eight days of tournaments and jousts that followed the wedding. According to the *Journal* of Robert de la Marck, Seigneur de Fleurange, one of Francis's boyhood companions, they were in fact miniature and not wholly mock military engagements. He describes one contest for which a wooden fortress large enough to hold a hundred defenders had been erected in the center of a cleared field, complete with moat, drawbridges, and four cannons which fired wooden balls bound in iron hoops. The Duke of Alençon, brother-in-law of the King, was assigned the task of holding the fortress against a larger force led by the Count of Vendôme and equipped with artillery and siege pieces of its own. Just as the fortress was about to fall, a third force led by Francis himself, with Fleurange riding at his side, swooped onto the scene to rescue the beleaguered defenders and drive off the attackers. It all was, Fleurange observes with satisfaction, *"le plus approchant du naturel de la guerre"* ("most similar to real warfare"). He also notes that during this and the other exercises the Duke of Urbino took care to place himself away from the center of action. The reason, he states, is that the Duke was suffering from an attack of *grande vérole,* the sixteenth century's all-purpose term to describe the disagreeable diseases which had recently been brought into the rest of Europe from Naples. The diagnosis must remain suspect, however, because elsewhere in his *Journal* Fleurange betrays both his partiality and a pang of envy when he describes the bride, on her wedding night, as "too much more beautiful than the husband."

As an heiress, Madeleine owned enormous properties in France. Because Lorenzo showed great interest in inspecting them all, their honeymoon passage was leisurely, and his young wife was already pregnant and evidently quite happy when they finally returned home. A caller to the Palazzo Medici on December 24, 1518, wrote, "The Duchess is in good health and excellent spirits. She has taken to dressing in the Florentine style, which is extremely becoming to her." The Duke, however, felt unwell and had himself carried to a villa in the hills north of the city where, regrettably, neither medical attention nor the bracing air seemed to arrest his mysterious illness.

At eleven o'clock on the morning of Wednesday, April 13, 1519, the Duchess was delivered of a baby girl who, three days later, was christened Caterina Maria Romola. Neither of her parents attended the ceremony. Her mother, who never left her bed, died of puerperal fever on April 28. Her father followed five days later, and although they are not as explicit as Fleurange, all chroniclers agree that his passing was occasioned not so much by grief as by a young lifetime's strenuous dissipations.

Art, if not history, is wealthier for Lorenzo's existence. In 1525 another Medici Pope commissioned Michelangelo to erect a suitable mausoleum for the family. This project, like so many others demanded of the artist, was never completed. But what he did achieve, the New Sacristy of San Lorenzo in Florence, could well be the perfect single expression of the Renaissance. Because his patron had not specified which Medicis should be memorialized first, Michelangelo arbitrarily chose two who had died recently—Lorenzo, Duke of Urbino, who is represented as the contemplative thinker, and his equally unmemorable uncle, Giuliano, Duke of Nemours, who symbolizes the life of action. When it was pointed out to the artist that neither statue bore the slightest resemblance to its subject, he is said to have replied, "And who will care?"*

* Lorenzo, Duke of Urbino, was singled out for another unmerited distinction which was inadvertently to cause considerable grief to his daughter. It was to him that Niccolò Machiavelli dedicated his *Prince,* voicing in its final chapter the hope that Lorenzo would turn out to be "a new Moses to redeem Italy from the barbarians."

III

It is odd, and has proved both a frustration to historians and a boon to polemicists, that generations of assiduous searching have established very little about Catherine de' Medici's earliest life. Regarding her later career when she became the most important woman in Europe, in turn Queen of France and Queen Mother of three successive kings, there are mountains of documentation—diplomatic dispatches to and from every important capital, state papers, private diaries, and the more than seven thousand letters of her own which have been collected, many of them so naked in their frankness that they could scarcely have been written with any audience in mind beyond their immediate recipient. But about those formative years of childhood and young adolescence, which, one is told, forever shape character and help determine future behavior, virtually nothing exists.

It is known that her parents' death was a dynastic catastrophe, for with the exception of some bastard cousins she was the last of the elder Medici line. The prospect was not lost on Ariosto, who was commissioned by the Duke of Ferrara to compose a suitable elegy. The poet responded by invoking the image of a single, slender branch bearing a small, green leaf, and wondering whether the coming winter would kill it or spare it. His rhetorical question was nearly answered within five months when the tiny girl contracted a violent fever.

Recovered, she was brought to Rome where she remained for six years, first under the watchful eye of her grand-uncle, Leo X, and then after his death in 1521 under that of another "uncle," the Cardinal Giulio de' Medici. Giulio was, in fact, an illegitimate second cousin, a blemish which did not prevent him, after the brief pontificate of Adrian VI, from ascending the throne of St. Peter as Clement VII.

He was tall, rich, well-mannered, by training and inclination an informed patron of the arts. But beyond this he was not much of a man. One contemporary refers to him as "fearful of spirit, with a cold and dry heart." Another speaks of his "timidity, not to say cowardice, and habitual duplicity." Leo X, on assuming office, is reported to have said, "Since God has seen fit to grant us the papacy, let us enjoy it," and for the nine years of his rule had wholeheartedly obeyed his own injunction. Clement's first act was to distribute some of his own benefices among the cardinals in an attempt to buy their loyalty. He might have prevailed. But his fatal flaw was his inability to juggle with safety the rival ambitions of the growing national powers of Europe. His predecessors had managed to do it, through bluff, guile, agility, or even, in the case of Julius II, by strapping themselves into armor and leading armies into the field. Probably it was inevitable that the delicate balance they had constructed would fail some day. Clement's everlasting misfortune was that it happened during his tenure, in the fearful calamity of the Sack of Rome.

On May 6, 1527, through a chain of events for which the ultimate blame is still debated, a rabble of twenty thousand mercenaries, mostly Germans and Spaniards, breached the walls of the city and, under cover of fog, poured like ravening wolves into its streets. Months earlier, they had been a disciplined army in the employ of Charles V, the Holy Roman Emperor, who had given them the orders to march on Rome. Undoubtedly he had originally intended it as a bluff to match Clement's own diplomatic wriggling, for it is inconceivable that the first prince of Christendom should command the evisceration of the Eternal City. But in the intervening time the money to pay the men had run out, and with it whatever control their officers had exercised over them. Rather, to preserve their own skins, they promised the ragged, hungry troops that once in Rome they could themselves collect their pay many times over.

Cities had been taken by force before. Like epidemic and famine, the prospect was one of the hazards of contemporary urban life. But no city, not even Rome at the hands of the barbarians, had ever experienced more systematic ferocity. In the first rush, every man, woman, and child caught in the streets was slaughtered and their bodies either heaved into the Tiber or left where they fell. Then, every substantial house in the city was plundered and its occupants required to ransom their lives not once but again and again by every marauding party. Parents were encouraged to disclose the hiding places of their treasure by the sight of their children hurled out of windows or raped before their eyes. Churches were pillaged of their precious vessels and reliquaries. Many of the Germans, recent converts to Reform, conceived their new faith as license for atrocity. In St. Peter's, a mob proclaimed Martin Luther pope, then went back to its looting. What could not be carried away was destroyed, desecrated, or scattered into the streets. Horses were tethered in the Vatican apartments which Raphael had finished painting only sixteen years earlier. Numberless books, manuscripts, and archives were destroyed and the great pontifical Library itself saved only because Philibert of Orange, one of the army's commanders, had the presence of mind to take it over as his personal quarters.

The full tide of looting, rapine, and killing lasted eight days and nights; it was extremely thorough. No careful count of casualties was compiled, but in a city whose population had perhaps been fifty-five thousand, more than twelve thousand bodies were found and buried. Thousands of others fled, not to return for a long time. Nine months after the attack, a visitor to the city could report that thousands of buildings were in ruins, and four-fifths of the houses still abandoned.

As for Clement, he had tried at first to bribe off the attackers with a promise of 60,000 ducats—less than the value of one of the rings on his quaking fingers. With the first exchange of fire, he had scurried through the subterranean passage to take refuge in the Castel Sant'Angelo. From its uppermost battlements, against a sky filling with smoke and the acrid stench of spilled blood, he was heard to echo Job's anguished cry: *"Quare de vulva eduxisti me?"* ("Why didst Thou take me from the womb?"). Long after the troops had moved on, leaving only a small garrison, he cringed in his fortress, haggling through intermediaries the terms of his ransom. When this was at last settled, on December 7, he paid the agreed-upon amount of 112,000 ducats, which he raised by selling cardinals' hats, and prepared to leave. Afraid of reprisals from his fellow Romans, he took the precaution of disguising himself as a simple servant and sneaked humbly out of the city.

Young Catherine was spared the horror of the Roman disaster because two years earlier Clement had ordered her back to Florence. Ostensibly she was to begin her studies there, but a more likely reason was his desire to take advantage of the genuine sympathy that the little *duchessina,* as she had become universally known in Italy upon her sad birth, enjoyed among the Florentines. The Palazzo on the Via Larga had stood untenanted since Clement himself had moved to the Vatican, its empty chambers and loggias a mute invitation to any of his dozens of enemies. Here, with appropriate pomp, he installed Catherine with a tiny retinue including her governor, Messer Rosso Ridolfi, and her two illegitimate Medici cousins, Ippolito and Alessandro. Eight years older than Catherine, Ippolito was the son of Giuliano and an unknown woman from Pescara. He was a gay, handsome youth, good-natured and skilled, even at this age, at composing verses. Alessandro, dark and surly and given to "excesses no more controllable by human reason than those of a beast in the forest," was represented to be the son of

Lorenzo and a woman also unknown but long believed to be a Moorish slave. This fatherhood would have made him Catherine's half brother, but more recent supposition is that he was actually the natural son of Clement himself. It was the Pope's design to perpetuate the Medici dynasty in the person of one of the two boys, preferably Alessandro. The casual character of their birth, however, coupled with that of Clement's own, presented certain difficulties. As a female, Catherine was barred from ruling by the Salic Law, but her presence in the ménage provided a touch of legitimacy. That, at any rate, was the scheme, and it seemed to be progressing well enough when Clement's world had come crashing around him.

As soon as news of the fall of Rome and its Medici Pope reached Florence, the city rose up again and declared itself a republic—oddly, at the same time proclaiming Jesus Christ as its legitimate king. As bells pealed, joyous crowds set about destroying all vestiges of the loathed Medici name. Statues associated with the family were destroyed or mutilated; even the great *David,* politically innocent, had its left arm broken by a bench thrown out of a window of the Palazzo Vecchio; wherever it could be found, the familiar coat of arms bearing the six pills was smashed off the façades of monuments. Only the family's living symbols were permitted to survive by the Florentines, as ever too civilized for their own good. On May 15, 1527, Ippolito and Alessandro fled the city on horseback and made their way unharmed through Pisa to Lucca. On the following day, a mob appeared at the front gate of the palace on the Via Larga, demanding that it be turned over to them as a public building. As servants argued to delay them, Catherine, then eight years old, was hurried through a back door and into the nearby small convent of Santa Lucia. After some negotiations during which the French ambassador, in the name of her mother, interceded on her behalf, she was permitted to move into the larger, more secure convent of the *Santissima Annunziata delle Murate.*

The *Murate,* the immured ones, commemorated the name
of an ancient strict order of nuns which had once occupied
the buildings, and whose memory was symbolically preserved
in a ceremony during which a newcomer was required to
enter into the convent through a freshly broken hole in the
outer wall which was then immediately sealed up behind
her. Inside, however, the *Murate* had long since become more
of an exclusive school than a convent. Young girls of excellent family were sent here from all over Italy; in remembrance
of ancient kindness done for him, the King of Portugal
annually sent a gift of seven casks of sugar, and in Florence
the Sisters of the *Murate* were talked about because their
gowns did not fully cover their ankles, and because they
attended holy offices coiffed only in diaphanous white shawls.

Perhaps it is this mild display of worldliness, and the absence of evidence to the contrary, which has influenced a
school of her biographers, typified by the Victorian Thomas
A. Trollope in *The Girlhood of Catherine de Medici,* to conclude that "Catherine's educating influence left her active
and acute intellect wholly uninformed by any moral ideas
whatever. Right and wrong were practically words devoid of
sense for her."

A harsh indictment. The fact is that Catherine stayed at
the *Murate* for three years, and there is indication that they
were probably the happiest of her entire life. She remembered the Sisters after her departure, made gifts and offerings
to the order, and maintained an irregular correspondence
which lasted until 1588, the year before her death. She certainly would have chosen to remain at the convent had not,
in 1529, Clement's pernicious shadow again reached across
Italy to fall on her.

This time, it was his unexpected resurgence which
plunged her into the most acute peril of her young life.
Shortly after his departure from Rome, English legates who
had come to see him about King Henry VIII's divorce from
Catherine of Aragon reported finding him in a half-

abandoned, dilapidated house in Orvieto, a prematurely old and unkempt man—he had vowed never to shave again—dazedly sitting on a straw pallet. From the depth of this abasement and despair, he had managed to restore himself into the good graces of the Emperor Charles V and, indeed, to become his good friend and valued ally. It had required the Pope's agreement to place on Charles's brow the iron crown of Charlemagne, a symbolic act which cost Clement nothing in money or sentiment. In exchange, he secured the Emperor's permission to return to Rome, a promise that Alessandro de' Medici would be honored with the hand of Charles's daughter Margaret, herself appropriately illegitimate, and a further promise that the young couple would be given Florence as a wedding present. There was the minor matter that Florence was still in Republican hands, but with resources provided by his new friendship Clement had the means to deal with that problem. As the nineteenth-century German historian Leopold von Ranke wrote, "With astonishment did men behold Clement launch upon his native city the very army by which the horrors of the Sack of Rome had been perpetrated before his eyes."

On October 14, 1529, that army, which had been promised wealth and diversion beyond anything which they had experienced in Rome, appeared before Florence and established camp. They found that the Florentines had made preparations for their arrival. For the space of a mile around the walls of the city, the country had been swept clean; every tree, every garden had been cut down, every house and villa had been burned and demolished.* On the heights of San Miniato, dominating the approach to the city, new fortifications bristled; Michelangelo had interrupted his work—ironically, he had been laboring on the Medici tombs—to supervise their design and construction.

---

* One exception was made: the monastery of *Salvi Santi,* which contained Andrea del Sarto's fresco of *The Last Supper,* was spared. Art-loving Florentines had not the heart to destroy it.

PREPARATION

As a military exercise, the siege of Florence cast no credit upon the attackers. Softened and sated by two years of conquest, they were kept off balance and distracted from their goal by a far smaller force led by the Florentine Francesco Ferrucci, which picked at their flanks from the sanctuary of neighboring hill towns such as Volterra and Pistoia. Inside the city, however, hunger and disease could not be distracted. As the defenders' situation worsened, they began to consider what use they could make, against the Pope, of the young hostage which he had unwittingly placed in their hands. Suggestions were made (one can only speculate how seriously) that Catherine be chained naked to the city walls as a deterrent to the besiegers, or that she be cast out for the pleasure of the soldiery—or better still, that Clement be threatened with the prospect of her removal to a brothel, an experience which would seriously damage his matrimonial plans for her. On the evening of July 20, 1530, a deputation from the city's governing Council of Ten arrived at the *Murate* and requested that she be turned over to them. Upon being refused, they left but came back the following morning and this time demanded her surrender at the price of setting fire to the entire convent. According to the account of one of the sisters, Giustinia Niccolini, Catherine herself thereupon appeared from behind the group of nuns who had been barring the entrance with their bodies. She had cut off all her hair and donned the habit of a novitiate. "Will you dare remove me now," the eleven-year-old girl is said to have cried, "and show yourselves to the people carrying a nun by force from her cell?" A compromise was reached when Silvestro Aldobrandini, the senior member of the delegation, personally assured her safety and accompanied her to the site chosen by the Council, where none of the dreadful usages proposed were made of her.

Nor was she kept in suspense long. Michelangelo's fortifications held, and Florence was spared the fate of Rome. But unrelieved sieges can have only one outcome; on August

12, 1530, after ten months that had claimed the lives of some sixteen thousand of its citizens, mainly the old, the young, and the weak, Florence surrendered.

Clement had promised leniency and the preservation of the Republican constitution, but as soon as they could be carried out orders were given that the great eleven-ton bell, *"la vacca"* ("the cow"), which hung in the tower of the Palazzo Vecchio and which generations of Florentines had heard in moments of joy or alarm, be thrown down and smashed—"that we should no more," wrote the patriot Davanzati in his diary, "be able to listen to the sweet sound of liberty." Despite Clement's additional assurances of amnesty, the Republican leaders were arrested, tortured, and put to death. In recognition of his intercession on behalf of Catherine, Aldobrandini was treated more generously: his sentence commuted to exile for life.* Within six months, Alessandro de'Medici was reinstalled in the Via Larga, alone this time, to await the appropriate moment for his investiture with the new dignity of Duke of Tuscany.

As soon as the siege was lifted and it became safe to travel, Clement ordered Catherine brought to him in Rome. Here, on October 13, 1530, guardian and ward had a reunion which, according to one eyewitness, was at least one-sidedly emotional. "His Holiness," writes the French envoy Nicholas Raince, "received [her] with a true cordial and paternal welcome, his arms wide and his eyes full of tears with the great pleasure of seeing her, after her mistreatment, in such excellent countenance."

The two had not seen each other for five years during which Clement, through his most trying vicissitudes, had continued the task of trying to pollinate his lone sprig of greenery. The tears of joy he shed at seeing her intact may

---

* Fortune turned swiftly in the sixteenth century. Despite this sentence and the confiscation of the family's fortune, his son subsequently himself became pope, as Clement VIII.

well have been occasioned at least in part by the imminence of success for his efforts.

The search for a suitable bridegroom had begun in 1524, when Catherine was five years old, and had ranged as far afield as distant, misty Scotland whose reigning sovereign, James V, was proposed, evaluated, and adjudged to be of insufficient consequence. He subsequently married Marie of Guise, by whom he had a child who would one day become Catherine's own daughter-in-law. Other candidates who were considered, or who voluntered their services, included the Duke of Richmond, the natural son of Henry VIII by Elizabeth Blount, one of Catherine of Aragon's ladies-in-waiting, and the Duke of Vaudemont, of the powerful family of Lorraine. Closer to home, there was a clutch of Italian princelings who would gladly have consented to a papal alliance: the elderly Duke of Ferrara; Federigo, the Duke of Mantua; Francesco Sforza, the Duke of Milan, whose family pressed his suit with energy even though he was widely reputed to be impotent.

Catherine's preference, had she been allowed to express it, appears to have been for an undeclared candidate, her own cousin Ippolito. He was the companion of her childhood and probably the only human being save for the nuns of the *Murate* who had ever shown her any kindness. Furthermore, judging by Titian's portrait of him in the Pitti Palace, he had grown into a singularly attractive young man. The artist has captured a gentle, serious expression illuminated by inner intensity. It is also known that Ippolito was generous, loved sports and festivals, played the lute and the organ with skill, and had become good enough a poet to translate the second book of the *Aeneid* into Italian.

But Clement was not about to waste one Medici on another. Before matters between the young people could get out of hand, he elevated Ippolito, then not yet twenty years old, to the unwanted eminence of the Sacred College. In vain did an ambassador to the Holy See note in a report that "the Most

Reverend Cardinal de' Medici shows a very great reluctance to being a priest." The very clothes in which Titian posed him, a rich red velvet doublet and cape, was the uniform he wore on his first ecclesiastic assignment, hand-picked by Clement himself: to represent the Holy Father at the court of the King of Hungary.

Early in his search, Clement had conceived a secret ambition—secret most especially from his good friend the Emperor Charles. This was to match the coup scored by Leo X and marry Catherine into the royal family of France. Such an alliance would counterbalance his dependence on the Emperor and solidify his own position by permitting him, as the need arose, to play off one of the two most powerful rulers in Europe against the other.

There is evidence that Francis I did not find the notion absurd. The Vatican archives contain a letter which reads in part: "I have received the letter which it has pleased your Holiness to write me with your own hand concerning the marriage of my son the Duke of Orléans and of the Duchess of Urbino your niece, and also of the good feeling between us which has been and is a very singular pleasure and contentment to me. . . ." The document, regrettably undated, is addressed to the "Holy Father," and signed: "Your humble and devoted son, Francis."

The letter alone may have been a diplomatic response to an importune suggestion, but there are also reports which were sent back to Francis, clearly at his request, and which give more substantial proof of his interest. One of them is from Raince, the French representative in Rome, who describes favorably and at length the young duchess's "wisdom, prudence and self-control." A special emissary, the Vicomte de Turenne, was sent to meet Catherine herself in September, 1528, and relayed the impression that he had never seen "a person of her age more aware of the good or evil that is done to her."

The price for this paragon of precocity and, of course, for

the Pope's support of Francis's transalpine ambitions was high but not exorbitant; the Duke of Orléans was only the second of his three sons and therefore not likely to inherit much in his own right. Negotiations began in earnest during 1529, while Catherine was still trapped in besieged Florence, and were finally concluded with a lengthy, explicit agreement signed by Francis on April 24, 1531, and by Clement on June 9. For the present, Francis consented to keep the accord secret, because Clement persuaded him he had not yet extracted all the favors he thought he could get out of the Emperor Charles. Furthermore, there were some provisions in the agreement which neither the King of France nor the Pope were quite yet ready to make public. According to one of them, Clement was to bestow upon his niece, and in consequence upon her future husband as well, the cities of Pisa, Leghorn, Parma, Reggio nell'Emilia, and Modena, promising to deliver them "at an opportune and convenient time." According to another, he undertook to give aid to the King of France in recovering the Duchy of Milan and the city of Genoa, both of which, he ruled, still rightfully belonged to the French crown even though they had been usurped by the Emperor.

Catherine, it appears, learned of the agreement indirectly— when the study of French was added to her other lessons. She was living in the Palazzo Madama, the Medici residence in Rome and now the seat of the Italian Senate, and making frequent visits to the Vatican. Several conflicting descriptions of her date from this period, but the most credible one—credible because he was in other respects an accurate reporter and had no reason to lie—is contained in a dispatch from Antonio Suriano, the Venetian ambassador: "The *duchessina*," he wrote, "is in her thirteenth year; she is very lively, shows an affable character and has distinguished manners. . . . She is short and thin; her features are not delicate and she has protruding eyes, like most of the Medici."

In April, 1532, now as the formally announced Duchess

of Orléans-to-be, Catherine returned in state to Florence in order to make final preparations for her wedding. In addition to its secret clauses, the marriage contract had also made provision for a conventional dowry. As her guardian, Clement undertook, "on account of the singular love and affection he bears her, and in consideration of the splendor and high station of the house into which she is being admitted" to settle on his niece the sum of 100,000 ducats, with an additional consideration of 30,000 ducats to compensate her husband for her claims on the stolen Duchy of Urbino which she was relinquishing. Whether because he was embarrassed for ready cash or, more likely, out of ingrained habit, Clement borrowed the money from a wealthy Florentine banker, Filippo Strozzi, putting up as collateral a magnificently carved gold and diamond brooch by Benvenuto Cellini which formed part of one of his ceremonial vestments.* To provide for the finery also required by the marriage contract ("The Holy Father shall furnish to his kinswoman suitable raiments, jewels and accoutrements. . . .") a simple personal loan would not do. Alessandro, now firmly established as sole ruler of the city, obliged by imposing a special tax on his subjects, declaring that it was necessary to help rebuild the city's fortifications.

This still did not solve the problem of the bride's trousseau. Three years after the ravages of its siege, the glorious city on the Arno which had so enriched the world with beauty still could not produce seamstresses deemed skilled enough for the task. There is in the municipal archives of Mantua a letter to the Most Illustrious and Excellent Duchess Isabella d'Este from her dear friend the Duchess of Camerino, writing from Florence on August 6, 1533, to ask whether it would be possible to have two dresses and two petticoats em-

---

* Strozzi, who was related to the Medicis, should have known better. Clement made no effort to repay the loan. After his death, his successor confiscated the brooch as belonging to the Vatican, and therefore never Clement's to pawn.

broidered. "I send three pounds of gold, two pounds of silver and two pounds of silk," the Duchess wrote. "If by any chance there is also in Mantua some good piece of work of black silk or of crimson and gold, I beg that your Excellency will do me the kindness to cause it to be given to the bearer of this letter, who has money to pay for everything. They are to be used for bedcoverings and curtains." And, the Duchess added, "as Madame d'Orléans is obliged to leave here shortly, it will be necessary that the work be accomplished as soon as possible in order that she may carry them with her."

Presumably the order was ready in time because late on the afternoon of September 1, 1533, the small wedding party consisting of the bride, a few of her distant male cousins, and her ladies-in-waiting, some of them still so young that they were accompanied by their governesses, left Florence. Moving by slow stages, Catherine retraced the road toward France which her mother had traveled fifteen years earlier. She was to live another fifty-six years, during which the epithet "the Florentine" would become attached to her as a malediction. But she herself would never set foot in her native city again.

IV

Immediately after Catherine's wedding, if the testimony of one of the guests, the Milanese Don Antonio Sacco, is to be believed, when the dancing was done and the last of the revelers had returned to their lodgings, King Francis and the Queen accompanied the newlyweds to the bridal chamber that had been prepared for them. Francis, moreover, "insisted on himself putting the young couple to bed, wishing to see them jousting, and indeed each of them did joust valiantly."

More circumspect, Clement waited until early morning, before they had risen, to pay the two a visit and assure himself that the wedding had been celebrated in the eyes of man as well as those of God. He and his predecessors had been bedeviled by disenchanted royal bridegrooms demanding divorces on grounds of nonconsummation; in this instance he had particular interest in avoiding such a complication. Clearly, what he saw satisfied him, because he returned from his social call "as happy of countenance as anyone ever re-called seeing him." His optimism was premature, for it would be another ten years before Catherine could produce an heir.

Meanwhile, as her uncle sailed off for Rome after a final round of benedictions, she became an insignificant addition to the most brilliant, complicated establishment in Europe—the French Court. And within that establishment the most important person to her, she realized immediately, was not her new husband who shunned her in private and barely spoke to her in public, but her new father-in-law, Francis of Valois-Angoulême, the Very Christian sovereign monarch of France.

Of his birth, which in the tradition of his native region of Cognac had taken place outdoors under a broad, shady tree, his mother wrote in her *Journal:* "François, by the grace of God King of France and my peaceful Caesar, saw the light of day at approximately two o'clock on the afternoon of the twelfth day of September, 1494." It was an extra-ordinary concept, for France's reigning King, Charles VIII, was still a young man, newly married to a healthy young wife who had already presented him with an heir. More were likely to follow, and there were other families with a clearer claim to the throne. But Francis's mother, Louise of Savoy, was herself an extraordinary woman. As a scrawny, orphaned girl whose entire being seemed concentrated in her deep, unsmiling grey eyes, she had lived by sufferance in the great house of Mme de Beaujeu, Charles's older sister and Regent of France. Her standing can be summed up in an annual entry of the household expense books: on each New Year's Day, eighty *livres* for a satin dress for Louise, so that she may look presentable before company.

When she became twelve, Louise was married off to a distant cousin. Land-poor, in political disgrace, the thirty-four-year-old Count of Angoulême ran a peculiar household in his dilapidated castle of Cognac. The chatelaine was his long-time mistress, Jeanne de Polignac; other favorites came and went. Louise uncomplainingly joined in and fulfilled her role. Twice, both wife and mistress found themselves pregnant at the same time. The Count preened himself, suffered a chill while carousing with out-at-the-elbow neighboring squires, and died suddenly. Louise, who was then nineteen and had nursed him dutifully, recorded the fact in her *Journal:* "On the first day of January in the year 1496, I lost my husband." A favorite little dog that died two years later received notice more affectionate to the extent of two adjectives.

Louise's firstborn had been a girl—Marguerite, the future author of the *Heptameron.* On her second, her "peaceful Caesar," she heaped all of her repressed affection and ambition. At four, Francis had learned how to sit a spirited horse; at eight, he could recite tales of chivalry and make attempts at composing polite verse. Meanwhile, childhood disease, sudden death, and lingering illness were methodically, miraculously clearing his path to the crown. Louise's *Journal* notes: "On the day of Sainte-Agnès, January 21, Anne, Queen of France, had a son, but he could not impede the exaltation of my Caesar, for he lacked the breath of life." The young Dauphin was swept away by a fever; then Charles VIII himself died, at the age of twenty-five and as the idiotic result of smashing his forehead against the lintel of a passageway at the castle of Amboise. The new King, Louis XII, promptly divorced his own barren wife and married Charles's widow, but in sixteen years she could do no better than beget two sickly daughters before she, too, died. A grieving Louis ordered her tomb made large enough for two and vowed that he would soon join her.*

But before doing so, he persuaded himself that he owed his country one last try and agreed to take as bride the eighteen-year-old Mary Tudor, a gay, strapping, and exceedingly pretty girl with all the lively appetites of her royal brother, Henry. Even though he was fifty-two and in uncertain health, Louis insisted on behaving like an impetuous bridegroom, riding out to Abbeville to meet his bride and escorting her back to a whirl of nuptial festivities. Court wits watched the goings-on, listened to the bleary-eyed King daily confiding to friends how nobly he had acquitted himself the night before, and noted that the good King Henry sent Louis a sprightly filly to speed his way to heaven.

Louise had duly recorded each calamity that brought her son one step closer to the throne, and which had, in fact, by 1514 placed him next in line. With her usual lack of emotion, she entered this latest disaster: "On October 9, 1514, was celebrated the loving marriage between Louis XII, King of France and Mary of England. They were married at ten o'clock, and that evening slept together."

But Mary Tudor knew better. Sensing that, despite her husband's brave words, she was not about to become a mother and would therefore be sent back home, she hit upon the idea of tapping a surer source. And who was more likely to provide assistance, to say nothing of consolation, than the dashing young Francis of Angoulême? He was a resplendent young giant forever at the center of attention, excelling equally at jousting, hunting, dancing, and other activities of the court. Early on he had developed a taste of luxury and

---

* The tomb is still there, at Saint-Denis, and the visitor looking at the two likenesses of the Queen—the one showing a youthful girl! in solemn prayer, the other a spent, exhausted woman, drawn so faithfully from life, or rather death, that the naked body bears the embalmer's incision—can only wonder at what could have happened in the intervening years.

the good life which far eclipsed that of King Louis XII himself. His spurs were made of gold, as were the buttons on his clothes. His fingers were covered with rings. The household objects around him—candlestands, toilet brushes, and flagons, the *rebec* he sometimes strummed—were silver. Whatever touched his body—sheets, handkerchiefs, shirts—was made of the finest Holland linen and impregnated with delicate scents. A single tailor's bill, for "tournament livery," humbly requested the payment of 15,600 *livres*.

By all accounts, he was not at all reluctant to cheer up the pining young Queen. His private visits to her apartments became so frequent, and their object so obvious, that it was her own chief chamberlain, Jean de Grignols, who took Francis aside and tried to explain the facts of life to him: "The King is old, but you are young and warm and so, by God, is she. . . . It will take like glue, and then what?" Apparently Francis remained unconcerned, because Grignols also reported the goings-on to Louise, who for once gave her precious son a lecture that left him speechless. Then, still not wholly trusting him, she arranged to have relays of her own ladies remain at Mary's side night and day. To Louis, who was puzzled by this arrangement, she explained with total truthfulness that it would stifle certain scurrilous rumors which had reached her ears.*

The vigil was not lengthy, for on January 1, 1515, less than three months after his marriage, Louis XII died of a head cold complicated by severe physical exhaustion. The next entry in Louise's *Journal* spills out over the page, as if a dam had at last been permitted to let go: ". . . [M]y son was anointed and consecrated at the church in Rheims. For this divine grace I am thankful, for it fully rewards me for all the adversities which were visited upon my early years and

* Despite this handicap, Mary tried her best. After Louis's death, she took to wrapping towels around her slim waist, suffering fainting spells in public, and in general carrying on like a prospective mother. This plan, intended to gain time, was also foiled by Louise who demanded a thorough medical examination.

the flower of my youth. Humility has kept me company, and patience has never abandoned me."

Almost immediately after these words were written, Louise parted company with humility forever, and thus established the pattern that was to last for the rest of the century. Because of Francis's dependence on her, and her own fierce possessiveness, Louise would in any case have assumed an important role in the background of his reign, but even this mild dissimulation proved unnecessary. Not quite twenty-one years old when he ascended—leapt upon is a more accurate description—the throne, Francis viewed kingship primarily as license to play his favorite games on a far grander scale than had been previously possible. His first royal act, therefore, was to gather an army of 30,000 men and 370 pieces of artillery—an enormous force for its time. His second act was to proclaim his mother Regent of France, formally empowered in his absence to handle all matters of state.

There was no secret about the army's objective. At his coronation, Francis had ordered that "Duke of Milan" be included in his list of titles and honors, even though Milan was ruled by the Sforzas and had resisted ten separate attempts by Francis's two predecessors to capture it. Surrounded by his boyhood playmates now elevated to the dignity of marshals, constables, grand masters, and admirals, Francis led his troops over the Col d'Argentière, a thought-to-be impassable Alpine route, and swept down into the plains of Lombardy. The battle which took place at Marignano stretched over two days—the afternoon of September 13, 1515, and the following morning—but its issue was never in doubt. Francis, who had spent part of the night impatiently resting against a cannon carriage after smoke and dust had so obscured the moonlight as to render fighting impossible, wrote to his mother: "There has not been seen so fierce and cruel a battle these last two thousand years. . . ."

Francis returned home and settled down into a routine which the Venetian diplomat Marcantonio Contarini described succinctly: "The King's way of life is as follows. He rises at eleven o'clock, hears Mass, dines, spends two or three hours with his mother, then goes whoring or hunting, and finally wanders here and there throughout the night, so one can never have an audience with him by day."

One of the topics which increasingly came up in the discussions with his mother was a new campaign, a peaceful one this time. Soon there was to be an election for a new Holy Roman Emperor, a position which conferred nominal sovereignty over the mosaic of principalities, duchies, free cities, margravates, baronies, and kingdoms which compose much of what is now Germany, as well as the Low Countries, Savoy, and much of northern Italy. By tradition, the Emperor was chosen by seven German princelings—the Duke of Saxony, the Margrave of Brandenburg, the Elector Palatine, the King of Bohemia, the Archbishops of Mainz, Trèves, and Cologne—whose titles were more impressive than their probity. Joachim of Brandenburg, for instance, was affectionately known as "the father of all greediness." The crown itself was largely honorific, but Francis vowed he would have it even if it cost him three million écus in gold.

There were two other contenders, but one of them, Henry VIII, could be dismissed as a meddler; he did not have the means even to tempt the electors, although the Archbishop of Trèves, in an effort to raise the stakes, did let it be known that he considered the English king an "excellent choice." The other contender was more serious. Younger than Francis by five years, Charles of Spain was in almost every quality and circumstance his opposite. The Venetian Giustiniani, who had served at both their courts, prophesied: "They will hate each other until one of them dies." Small and sickly as a child, marked with the unmistakable Hapsburg chin and the perennially half-opened mouth of the chronic adenoidal sufferer, Charles slipped imperceptibly into cold, phlegmatic youth and premature adulthood. Greys, blacks, dull browns, and a yellowish cast are the colors that predominate in the

many likenesses of him that exist. Calm, short-spoken, averse
to ostentation, he was—to use just one measure—probably
the only ruler of his time who detested hunting.

His personal qualities almost exactly matched the glaring
gaps in Francis's own character: tenacity of purpose, a firmness in judging other men's intentions, total self-control and
patience. But his greatest asset by far was fortune's choice
of grandparents for him: on his mother's side, Ferdinand
of Aragon and Isabella of Castille; on his father's side,
Maximilian of Austria and Marie of Burgundy, daughter of
Charles the Bold. In addition to being King of Spain, he was
by virtue of this heritage also the ruler of "Sicily, Jerusalem,
the Balearic and Canary Islands, the Indies and the Mainland
on the Far Side of the Atlantic; Archduke of Austria; Duke
of Burgundy, Brabant, Styria, Carinthia, Carniola, Luxembourg, Limburg, Athens and Patras; Count of Habsburg,
Flanders and Tyrol; Count Palatine of Burgundy, Hainault,
Pfiart, Roussillon; Landgrave of Alsace; Count of Swabia;
Lord of Asia and Afric." No Christian monarch, not even
Charlemagne, had held such vast possessions. Indeed, at the
age of nineteen, Charles of Spain was, in the words of one
historian, "a coalition in his own person."

And he won election, as Charles V, to the Imperial crown.
Louise undertook most of the vote buying for her son, but
could not overcome Charles's greater resources. Every *écu*
which she raised he matched with a gold florin borrowed
from the inexhaustible supply amassed by the Fuggers of
Augsburg. When the Margrave of Brandenburg hinted that
he might be swayed by more delicate compensation, Charles
offered him the hand of the Queen Dowager of Spain. Louise
countered with Louis XII's daughter, Renée. Charles outbid
her again with his own sister.

Disappointed, mother and son now sought an alliance
across the Channel. England was hardly important in the
affairs of Europe—certainly less so than its assertive monarch
pretended. But with Charles now camped on three sides of

France, there were few places left to turn. For his part, Henry was ever ready to stir up trouble.

Looking today at any of the several paintings depicting the meeting between the two sovereigns, one could conclude that the artist had reached into fantasy in order to create the setting: a small, sheltered valley dominated by two fairy castles and almost entirely covered by a sea of golden tents, of pavilions and galleries bedecked with streaming pennants, of jousting lists and artificial gardens. But every detail is confirmed by contemporary chroniclers. Francis had brought along a retinue of 5,172 and established himself in a gold- and silver-embroidered tent that was sixty feet high and crowned with a full-sized wooden statue of St. Michael bearing the arms of France on his shield as he plunged his lance into the dragon. Nevertheless, Henry surpassed him with his own accommodations. He had ordered a large three-story palace to be prefabricated of wood and canvas painted to resemble stone. Shipped to France in sections, it was assembled and fitted out with large, diamond-paned windows. Four great crenelated towers, also of canvas, guarded the corners. The entrance was flanked by two fountains, representing Cupid and Bacchus, which poured forth a constant stream of claret wine, "for all who wished to partake."

No ceremony or opportunity for display was overlooked. As Shakespeare relates:

> . . . Each following day
> Became the next day's master, till the last
> Made former wonder its. To-day the French
> All clinquant, all in gold, like heathen gods,
> Shone down the English; and tomorrow they
> Made Britain India: every man that stood
> Show'd like a mine. . . .
> —*King Henry the Eighth,* Act I, sc. I

When they were not trying to outdo each other, the two kings fell back to playing like schoolboys. Early one morning, while Henry was still asleep, Francis appeared in the English camp escorted only by two gentlemen. To the startled guards, he announced that he had come to serve as Henry's valet, and insisted on being allowed to help him get dressed. Henry was delighted, and rewarded his new valet with a ruby collar worth 200,000 gold ducats. Francis reciprocated with an even more valuable bracelet. Another prank had a less happy ending. This time it was Henry who approached Francis and challenged "my good brother of France" to a wrestling match. Lighter but more agile than his slower-moving guest, Francis fought him fairly and threw him to the ground, whereupon Henry rose red-faced and stomped out. Icy politeness marked the rest of the ceremonies, after which Henry rode off to Gravelines, just across the border, where the Emperor Charles had patiently been waiting for him. Here, with hardly a drummer or trumpeter in attendance, the two men signed a treaty of friendship and alliance.

Whether Francis would have gained anything by diplomatically allowing himself to lose the wrestling match appears doubtful. During all the goings-on, which lasted the better part of June, 1520, Louise had made repeated and unsuccessful attempts to negotiate some sort of agreement with Thomas Wolsey, Archbishop of York and Henry's principal minister. But it is now known that before the English king and his party ever crossed to France, Charles himself, despite his own far greater importance, had quietly journeyed to Dover to see him. Everything was arranged then, including which French provinces Henry would receive when France was dismembered; a promise was also made to Wolsey that he would receive the Pope's triple tiara if he should prevent the French alliance. All the rest, the pageants, the wrestling, the glitter that gave the meeting at the Field of the Cloth of Gold its name, had been foolishness and show.

Francis shrugged off this setback, too, and set off on a leisurely tour of his kingdom. Worse yet was about to descend on him, precipitated by an unexpected but hardly ominous event. At the age of forty-six, after more than a quarter century of widowhood, and for the first time of her life, Louise of Savoy fell hopelessly, idiotically in love. To be sure, there had been men in her life, although probably fewer than her enemies credit her with. But in an age when noble ladies were assumed to have less than frosty relationships with their *valets de chambre*—and their husbands, in exchange, were permitted to select comely young ladies as their personal attendants—this was normal housekeeping practice. At least Louise had good taste: one of her long-time favorites was the poet Octavian de Saint-Gelais, who in her honor translated Ovid into French.

The Regent of France could not pick just anyone as the object of her affection. Louise chose—and Freudians would nod—Francis's splendid young friend, Charles of Bourbon-Montpensier. He was darkly handsome, imperious, overwhelmingly proud, and second only to the King in the wealth and magnificence of his estates. Francis had made him Constable of France—commander of all the nation's armies —and he bore this rank and his other distinctions with such arrogance that the shrewd Henry VIII, who had met him at the Field of the Cloth of Gold, said, "If that man were a lord of mine, his head should not remain two days on his shoulders."

No one knows how long Louise nurtured her passion in private, but the death of Bourbon's young wife in 1521 emboldened her to make overtures. Bourbon's reply, which he unfortunately made in public, was that he would sooner enter a monastery than accept an ugly, dried-up harridan.

It was a mistake, for in her fury Louise set out to destroy him. Using her enormous power, she suborned judges, fabricated evidence, and succeeded in stripping Bourbon first of his titles and then of most of his lands. Anticipating that Francis might moderate the punishment, she warned him, "My son, I will disown you and consider you a coward unless you avenge me."

This, too, proved to be a mistake because Bourbon, embittered and with no other place to turn, defected to the side of the Emperor, taking most of his troops with him.

Meanwhile, the Emperor Charles had been cultivating his diplomatic garden, adding the Pope, Ferdinand of Austria, as well as Venice, Savoy, Tuscany, and lesser Italian city-states such as Lucca and Monferrato to his anti-French alliance. The treachery of Bourbon permitted him to seal the ring of iron and begin closing it. Spanish troops moved up the Atlantic coast to nibble at Bayonne; Henry VIII, from Calais, made huffing noises toward fertile Picardy; Bourbon, understandably more vindictive than the others, laid siege to Marseilles, which Charles particularly wanted because its possession would turn the western Mediterranean into his private lake.

Several strategies were open to Francis, but he did not hesitate. Almost as if he were seeking to start everything all over again, he assembled his troops and, in October, 1524, led them again over the mountains toward Milan. Louise, who had vainly tried to dissuade him, accompanied her son as far as Lyons and settled down to wait for the news she dreaded.

It was not long in coming. Cruelly, the first reports were of great victory: Milan had been retaken without a fight. But the enemy had not retreated far; only to Pavia, whose ancient walls made it easier to defend—so easy that the battle that took place on February 24, 1525, Charles V's birthday, was again never in doubt. Within less than two hours, to Imperial shouts of *"Victoria! España!"* it was over, the blackest day for French arms and French honor since Agincourt 110 years earlier. Eight thousand French lay dead; nearly all the rest were taken prisoner, including Francis himself, who had fought first on horseback and then on foot until he could no longer swing his sword for the bodies piled around him.

What followed was captivity, first in Italy and then in

Charles's stoutest fortress, the Alcazar in Madrid. The Regent of France had been the first to hear of the disaster, directly from her son: "Madame, In order that news of me may be of some small comfort to you, I have begged to be permitted to write to you. . . . Of everything, there remains to me only honor and life itself." Heart-stricken, she rallied a stunned country, wrote encouraging letters to Francis who threatened to perish of grief like a caged nightingale, persuaded Henry VIII that by attacking a defenseless France he would only be playing into the Emperor's hands. Then, with immediate collapse averted, she began negotiations with Charles for her son's release.

Charles, who had not believed the first reports of his great good fortune, did not know what to ask for, so he demanded everything he could think of: the return of Burgundy, which he claimed as his inheritance even though it had for a century been as French as its own good red wine; Francis's promise to abandon all his claims on Italy; the restoration of the Constable of Bourbon's dignities and titles; the payment of a ransom of two million *écus*. And finally, to bind their respective houses in eternal friendship, he required Francis to marry his sister, Eleanor.*

Too ill to carry on the negotiations himself, Francis instructed the French delegates sent by his mother to accept all these terms. Charles sensibly did not trust his captive to honor his word and added a final condition: that Francis would have to turn over as hostages his own two eldest sons, then aged eight and seven. To this final, cruel demand Francis also consented.

The Treaty of Madrid, the most humiliating document a French chief of state would put his name to until 1940, was

---

* Francis's first wife, whom he had married before he became king and partly to assure his succession, was Claude of France, the elder daughter of Louis XII. He ignored her studiously, save for having seven children out of her in ten years. Then immediately upon her death at the age of twenty-six in 1524, she was elevated to martyrdom, and is today best remembered for the succulent green-yellow plum that bears her name.

signed on January 14, 1526. Two months later, the exchange of prisoners was made across the Bidassoa River, the Franco-Spanish frontier, three miles upstream from the sea at San Sebastian. Both sides of the river had been cleared of human beings—farmers and shepherds as well as men at arms—for a depth of ten leagues. At the appointed moment of seven o'clock in the morning, Francis, accompanied by a Spanish officer and ten gentlemen armed only with swords and daggers, appeared on the southern bank of the river while his two young sons, accompanied by a French officer and ten gentlemen similarly armed, stepped up to the opposite bank. They boarded two identical barges manned by the same number of oarsmen, which touched off and made for a raft moored in the center of the river. Here, all disembarked. The boys kissed their father's hand, and he in turn embraced them. "Sire," the Spaniard said, "Your Highness is now free; let him do as he promised." "All shall be done," Francis replied. The two parties then exchanged barges and completed their short voyage.

Of course, Francis reneged on every condition of the Treaty of Madrid; even the first installment of the ransom was discovered by the suspicious Spaniards to have been paid with underweighted gold coins. As for Eleanor, Francis let it be known that she could stay home in Madrid; he would as soon marry the Emperor's mule as his sister. Meanwhile, whatever time he did not devote to diversion was spent in planning elaborate new military combinations against Charles. If anyone at Court remembered that the young royal princes were also waiting in Madrid, they did not have the temerity to say so out loud in Francis's presence.

Louise did remember. She also knew that there was no likelihood that Francis and Charles could ever sit down together, much less conclude a truce. Their hostility was bound to destroy them both, along with their exhausted countries. With her son's permission, she therefore addressed herself directly to Margaret of Austria, Governor of the Netherlands and Charles's aunt. The two women, who had known each other since childhood, agreed to meet at Cambrai, in Flanders. The occasion was marked with no pomp, and no one save the citizens of that ancient cathedral town paid much attention as the ladies—Louise was fifty-three years old, Margaret seven years younger—arrived, prayed together, and settled down in adjoining houses. Nor was there a secret gallery this time; the common wall was simply pierced to permit free access. From July 7 to August 5, 1529, they talked daily, but since neither had brought along a retinue of advisers or secretaries there was no one to record what was said. It can be surmised, however, that compassion and mutual tolerance were touched upon as well as boundary adjustments and the payment of reparations, for the document which they drew up together was so eminently fair, reasonable, and just that neither son nor nephew could find a pretext for not accepting it.

The Peace of Cambrai, inevitably the Ladies' Peace, permitted the young princes to return to France—Eleanor herself escorted them home and was duly married to Francis. It also marked the last great service that Louise of Savoy was able to render her son. Never very strong, her health had been strained during the trying period of Francis's captivity and the anxious years that followed it. In 1531, she fell ill and expressed a desire to return to her own childhood home in Romorantin, but death caught up to her when she was still some distance away. Nor was her son at her bedside. He was hunting at Chantilly when the news reached him.

V

On July 24, 1534, after five years of peace, Francis announced his intentions by issuing an ordinance that demanded the creation of a new standing army of 42,000 men. Alerted by their ambassadors, the countries of Europe resigned themselves to play backdrop again to a resumption of the rivalry which had time and again touched the most innocent of its citizens. Catherine de' Medici was a conspicuous example of how deeply and personally the effects of this rivalry could reach. The marriage into which she was born was a direct result of Francis's attempt to secure his early gains in Italy. Her childhood had been tormented by his failure to do so, for it was the battle of Pavia which had let loose the Imperial armies that gutted Rome and strangled the Florentine Republic. Her own marriage, with its elaborate secret clauses, was the central part of a plan to establish a new alliance against Charles. Even the character and personality of her husband, Henry of Orléans, were the consequence of Francis's misfortune. Henry had been the younger of the two hostages demanded by Charles, and if he was silent and serious as a bridegroom, and later as a husband, it was because the four years of captivity to which his father had committed him had marked him forever. John Taylor, Henry VIII's ambassador to France, met the young princes at Amboise before their departure for Spain and reported, "Verily, they be goodly children. Your Majesty's godson [Henry, born before the Field of the Cloth of Gold, had been named in honor of the Tudor king] is the quicker spirit and the bolder, as seemeth by his behaviour."

Later, one of the few French visitors permitted into the glum castle where the two boys were kept under heavy guard reported seeing, "a dark chamber with neither tapestries nor hangings in which the two lords sat on little stone seats opposite the window, furnished both within and without with solid iron bars and so high that only with difficulty could they enjoy air or light." So cut off were they from all things familiar that Henry had nearly forgotten his native language by the time Louise of Savoy finally secured his release and that of his older brother. Years later, an ambassador marveled at his healthy, virile good looks, but added that "few people at the court could ever remember hearing him laugh."

Time and again Francis had been bested or beaten. His acceptance of Catherine as daughter-in-law was no exception. On Clement VII's past record of keeping his promises, it is unlikely that he would in any case have honored his part of the secret marriage contract. Poor health, however, spared him the necessity of this additional deceit. Within a year of his return to Rome, he died. His successor, Paul III, a Medici-hating Farnese, immediately repudiated the agreement and Francis, one of whose many redeeming qualities was his lack of self-delusion, could in full justice observe, *"J'ai pris la fille comme toute nue"*—("I took the girl naked as a babe").

The French Court, behind his back, was not disposed to be as philosophical. The papal repudiation confirmed their view that the marriage, from the start, had been a shameful mismatch, the squandering of a royal prince on a grocer's daughter—scornful recognition of the fortune which the early Medicis had amassed in the spice trade. Even Charles V, whose spies kept him informed throughout the protracted negotiations between Francis and Clement, did not take their reports seriously. To trade off an illegitimate daughter in exchange for a great city, as he had done to gain Florence, was sensible diplomacy, but no man would give a son—and a legitimate son at that—for so uncertain a prize as Clement's word.

There is evidence from letters she later wrote that Catherine herself at times did not fully believe the great honor which had been accorded her—and this impression is important in order to understand many of her subsequent actions. For the moment, however, she merely sought the shadows. The earliest description of her as a French princess comes from the same Venetian, Giustiniani, who had perceptively characterized the future relations between Francis and Charles. After reporting that the marriage had "displeased the entire nation," he noted that the *duchessina* was *"molto obbediente.*" But he also added that "the King appears to be very much attached to her."

There were two reasons why Francis should have grown to like his young daughter-in-law. The first is that, for all her quietness, docility, and self-effacement, she was extremely bright and precocious. Moreover, she was far better educated than any of the royal princesses or other highborn young ladies of the Court.

The second reason is that Catherine tried desperately hard to please him. One of the earliest of her letters, written in 1533 from Florence where she was making preparations for her wedding, is addressed to her maternal uncle, the Duke of Albany, and entreats him to secure for her the services of a dancing master, to complete a neglected portion of her education. Once in France, she pursued her studies of mathematics, astronomy, and even Greek, which, according to one chronicler, she learned to speak "as well as any man." She also showed a keen interest in hunting; someone looking for something nice to say to her had once complimented her on her well-turned ankles, so—a small vanity indeed—she rejected the customary ladies' chairlike *planchette* and introduced the fashion of riding sidesaddle.

The skeptical and hostile historians see in all this confirming evidence of her cunning nature and instinctive flair for the jugular of power—again the damned and devious Florentine. But the fact is that Catherine loved strenuous exercise and especially riding, a Medici family trait she practiced until she was well into her sixties and long past the need to ingratiate herself with anyone. As for her attraction to Francis, it is easier still to understand. She was at this time a girl in her middle teens, now married to a youth whom she loved—and would still love faithfully for thirty years after his death—but who had neither wanted her nor had the desire or capacity to understand her. As a younger son he had no duties or household of his own. The daily records of the French Court have been almost entirely reconstructed, but for the first years after his marriage there is scarcely a mention of Henry, Duke of Orléans, either in his official functions or in his private pursuits.

Francis, on the other hand, was an exhilarating, irresistible figure. Despite his total failure at statecraft, he was the *Roi-Chevalier,* the splendid, generous Renaissance prince, knowledgeable patron of the arts and letters, magnificent in manner, kind and lofty in spirit, gracious in personal courtesy.

All monarchs were expected to leave palpable traces of their passing. Francis chose to sow great castles as lesser men might plant trees. Blois, to which he added a great, open circular staircase and a daring three-story loggia laced with windows and thrust out beyond the steep rock on which the original building stood; Chambord, which he ordered built in the depths of an untouched forest and on which up to nine thousand workmen toiled for twenty-eight years at a cost which grew so high that Francis hid parts of it as "military expenditures";* Fontainebleau, which had been the crumbling, abandoned ruin of a twelfth-century royal keep when he came across it one day while hunting.

As characteristic as what Francis built was what he tore down. The Louvre, and the entire center of Paris, had for three centuries been dominated by an enormous tower whose stone walls, 22 feet thick and 144 feet in circumference at its base, rose to a height of 96 feet. The *Bourgeois de Paris,* the anonymous diarist whose *Journal* provides a rich daily thermometer of middle-class French opinion in the early sixteenth century—in some aspects it has not changed much

---

* Because the original plans have disappeared, it is not known whether the castle was ever completed. What does stand is a giant labyrinth of great halls, hidden passages, cozy private apartments measuring 510 feet by 380, and surmounted by a turreted terrace upon which a thousand guests at a time could stroll comfortably and observe the progress of the hunt in the surrounding woods. Francis was proud of Chambord and took pains to permit his most distinguished visitors to admire it as well, but apparently he himself was never happy with it, for despite the personal care he gave to its construction, he spent, in the course of his life, just thirty-nine days there.

in the intervening years—was scandalized when the tower, which he pronounced "very beautiful, lofty and strong," was destroyed on Francis's orders.

But not even the King of France could dismantle the University of Paris, a realm unto itself ruled by the inflexible, obscurantist theologians who, by self-perpetuating right, deemed themselves second only to the Vatican itself as arbiters and custodians of all knowledge. Francis therefore established a rival institution, the Royal Lectureships. It was at first no more than a few students who received a small stipend to sit at the feet of Guillaume Budé, the greatest Hellenist of his day, but when word spread that such forbidden pagan authors as Virgil could be read and discussed, applicants began arriving from all over Europe. They still come, and the most fortunate of them are accepted into the institution which has long since changed its name to the *Collège de France.*

Another of Francis's innovations was the introduction, on a level higher than simple utility, of women into the royal circle. "A court without ladies," he is quoted as saying, "is like a garden without flowers." In retrospection of the Mmes de Pompadour and du Barry, of Louis XV's Deer Park, of the acres of Fragonard's and Boucher's dimpled bathers, this may seem a redundant observation. But all that came later. Prior to Francis, the Court of France had been a preserve as exclusively male as a regimental reunion and correspondingly as dull. Some biographers suggest that the King's motive was to introduce, painlessly, a civilizing or at least a gentling influence. More skeptical, Gaspard de Tavannes, who had been a young page at the Court before becoming one of the great French soldiers of the century, wrote in his *Memoirs:* "Alexander the Great took up with women when there were no affairs of state to occupy him. Francis took up affairs of state. . . ."

From the corners of France the ladies came, and the more fortunate and gifted of them were further admitted into the tight group of Francis's own *Petite Bande*. These chosen few were his constant companions, to an extent not shared by his ministers or advisers. They hunted with him, dined on the same dishes, traded witticisms with him. Francis personally undertook to select their gowns and pay for them. Thus we learn from the royal household accounts that a sylphlike form was not a prerequisite for membership, because while most of the ladies could be fitted out with ten or eleven ells of silk or velvet, one Mme de Canaples regularly required sixteen.*

At the time of Catherine's arrival in France, the acknowledged leader of the *Petite Bande* was Francis's official mistress, the fair, spectacularly elegant and spirited Mlle Anne d'Heilly. One of thirty children of a Picardy squire, she had been discovered by Louise of Savoy and summoned to become one of her own ladies-in-waiting—a position in which she would be sure to come to the attention of her son. The scholar Paulin Paris, who traced the transaction, suggests that Louise's motive was probably to ease her son's distress over the necessity of marrying the stolid, dark-haired Eleanor. If so, she succeeded, for Anne became, in effect, a member of the royal family. She was, for instance, very much in evidence at the wedding of Henry of Orléans, where Catherine met her for the first time.

To be admitted into the *Petite Bande* became Catherine's supreme ambition. Though no documents bear it out, save a passing mention in one of Catherine's own letters written almost fifty years later, there is no doubt that she sought Anne d'Heilly's sponsorship. One can well imagine the scene: the young, awkward girl with the too-prominent eyes and the figure still blurred by baby fat speaking in the earnest,

---

* From these same accounts, we also learn that new practices did not completely supplant old customs. An entry reads: "François, by the Grace of God King of France to his friend and loyal treasurer, Jehan Duval: We wish and order you to pay from our funds to Cécile de Viefville, lady of the *filles de joie* following our Court, the sum of 45 *livres* for services during the month of May just passed."

Italianate French—a language she never fully conquered. There was nothing she could offer now or in the future to the poised, self-assured woman—nothing Anne did not already possess or could have for the asking. Yet, as she would time and again, Catherine succeeded. We know she joined in the hunts from some verses composed by Ronsard and describing, with poetic license, the young Duchess of Orléans in her fourteenth year:

> *Toujours dès l'aube du jour*
> *Alloit aux forêts en queste*
> *Ou de reths tout à l'entour*
> *Cernoit le trac d'une beste;*
> *Ou pressoit les cerfs au cours;*
> *Ou par le fendant des roches,*
> *Sans chiens assailloit les ours*
> *Et les sangliers aux dents croches.*

> At break of day she could be found
> Deep in the forest, where all around
> The nets were placed to drive the beast
> And set the stag upon its course.
> Or else alone and without hounds,
> Among the broken, tumbled rocks,
> She pressed to find the waiting bear,
> And the wild boar with frightful fangs.

We know it, too, from a few letters such as the following, occasioned by a minor military victory over the Spaniards: "To our Sovereign Lord the King: Sire, our unspeakable joy robs us of sense and control of the pen to write to you. Although the capture of Hesdin was confidently expected, nevertheless we have been since Monday so full of fear that we were half dead, and this morning the messenger revived us with such marvelous consolation that, after running one to another to announce the good news more by tears of joy than by words, we have come here to join in praising Him who in all your affairs has granted you His favor. . . ." The letter was signed: "Your very humble and obedient subjects,"

and bore among others the names of Catherine, Marguerite
(Francis's daughter), and Anne.

VI

Henry VIII had once described France as a "fair, abundant
kingdom." So it was. At the time of Catherine's arrival, it
nourished amply some twenty-five million inhabitants, to
England's four million or so. Cities thrived; highways were
alive with travelers—merchants, students, soldiers, royal and
princely couriers, and the first trickle of ordinary tourists.
Fields of grain, vineyards, orchards, pastures imposed a pleasing mosaic on the land, much as they do today. From every
hillock, the view revealed a half-dozen church steeples, each
standing knee-deep in the midst of a cluster of houses—stone,
brick, or wood depending on the region, but all well warmed
in winter and amply provisioned the year round. What
feudal castles still remained were already picturesque ruins,
being replaced by great, comfortable manor houses. Rivers
teemed with sailboats and barges. The Seine ran so plenti-
fully with salmon that apprentices in Paris refused to accept
the fish as the staple of their daily diet. Factories, mines,
forges, quarries from one end of the kingdom to the other
worked to the rhythm of the sun, and employers grumbled
that there were too many feast days.

It took all this wealth and more to keep up with Francis.
One of the helpful Venetians estimated the running cost of
the royal household at one and one half million *écus* a year—
including 85,000 *écus* for expenses of the table, 60,000 for the
falconries, 20,000 for gardeners, 60,000 for Masses and other
matters *in spiritualibus,* and a round 500,000 for the King's
personal gifts and presents. Renaissance rulers made it a
habit to move frequently from one of their residences to
another, but for Francis, ever restless and curious, sheer move-

ment became an obsession. In his report, Giustiniani complains that "my mission as ambassador lasted forty-five months. Never during the whole time was the court in the same place for forty-five days." A patient scholar has calculated that during his entire reign of thirty-two years Francis stayed put for only 3,796 days. The other 7,982 were spent on the move—hunting, warring, visiting.

If Catherine could consider any single place home during her first years in France, it was Fontainebleau. Francis had transformed the ruined keep into such a splendid stage that Vasari, after his first visit, could only describe it as "a new Rome." The palace was much smaller than it is now, two wings connected by the perfectly proportioned gallery which still bears Francis's name. The main entrance was the Porte Dorée, which gave onto an arrow-straight alley that led directly into the forest and the principal daytime diversion, hunting. The interior decorations had been entrusted to Primaticcio and Rosso, some of whose best work was unfortunately improved upon by Napoleon III. In Francis's own apartments, a modest four rooms, he kept part of his private collection of paintings, including the *Mona Lisa,* for which he had paid a very shrewd 4,000 gold ducats.

The inspiration for Fontainebleau had come from a book entitled *Il Libro del Corteggiano* (*The Book of the Courtier*) written by a minor Italian nobleman and diplomat named Baldassare Castiglione. It so impressed Francis that he commissioned its translation into French for the edification of his own courtiers. But Castiglione's precepts were too elusive; one of the qualities that he deemed essential, for instance, was the ability to "conceal art and create the impression that what is done and said is accomplished without effort and even without its being thought about." If a literary model for Francis's Fontainebleau is to be sought, a more accurate one would be Rabelais's Abbey of Thélême, where men and women lived together and observed the benign, uncomplicated injunction to "Do as Thou Wishest."

François Rabelais was born at approximately the same time as King Francis and was reared in the same lush Loire Valley. There is more than coincidence in the manner of Gargantua's birth outdoors, in full daylight, and screaming lustily for wine. The image of Pantagruel unconcernedly combing cannon balls out of his hair as if they were so many grape seeds recalls the spirit of Marignano, if not of Pavia. The enormous physical appetites—whole oxen spitted and roasted, herds of sheep, netfuls of salmon, barrels of wine consumed at a sitting—had their exact counterparts in the daily records of the royal accounts.

There was, of course, much more to Rabelais's world than gluttony and lechery. The full freedom urged upon the inhabitants of Thélême had a deeper purpose. Rabelais wrote: "Free people, well-born and gently nurtured . . . have a natural instinct, a spur which urges them on to virtuous deeds, and withdraws them from vice. . . . These same people, when deformed and enslaved by vile subjugation and constraint, divert from its true course the noble affection by which they are willingly impelled unto goodness. . . . For we always set forth on forbidden enterprises and covet that which is denied us."

Rabelais's prescription was too advanced for his time—perhaps for ours as well. Nevertheless, there was something to show for all Francis's expense and exertion: the grandest, gaudiest, peripatetic house party Europe had ever seen. If true wit flourished and intellect shone, only fragmentary evidence of it has survived. Rather, to judge by the memoirs of some of the participants, the jokes tended to be broad and the humor frequently physical. Yet the French Court was by common consent the most scintillating gathering on earth, the envy of all visitors.

And among the guests—still very obedient but now also fully aware that she had achieved her great ambition—was the grocer's daughter, the most illustrious student of the good Sisters of the *Santissima Annunziata delle Murate.*

Part Two

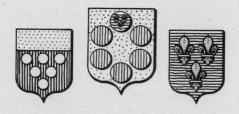

Patience

I

In 1536, two events occurred which completely changed the course of Catherine's life, and with it the history of France and of all Europe. The first was the sudden, untimely death, on May 15, of the Dauphin, Francis. Only a year older than Henry, he was an entirely different sort of youth who had managed to overcome much more successfully the effects of Spanish captivity. He moved freely among the ladies, having selected for his own one of his stepmother's young, lusty, and complaisant maids of honor. Under the tutelage of his father, who called him "my son so full of promise," he had begun to participate in deliberations of state. He held a command in the army. And, of course, he took part in the games that filled so many of the days' hours. It was this last, most harmless occupation that led to his death. As Brantôme, the chief chronicler-gossip of the century, reports: "The Prince, having played at ball in a field all day, bade a page of his chamber go and bring him cold water in the little vase which Donna Agnese Pachecho had given him." Donna Agnese was one of the ladies in waiting whom Eleanor had brought with her from Spain; the vase was a small, tawny, earthenware pitcher, "so subtle and fine that it has the virtue that whatever cold water you put into it you see it boil and make little bubbles as though it were on the fire, nevertheless it does not lose its coldness. . . ."

Far better had it not possessed such wondrous quality. Overheated from his day's exertions, the Dauphin drained the cold liquid. "At once," the account continues, "he felt sick and ill, from which afterward he died." To be precise, four days later.

Such was the temper of the time that the death of any

notable person, and especially death connected with eating or
drinking something seemingly harmless, was immediately
suspect. In this instance, suspicion verged on certainty because of the name of the unfortunate groom who had filled
and brought the pitcher. It was Sebastiano de Montecucculli.
Later on, when calumnies of every sort were being piled on
Catherine de' Medici, it was she who was accused of having
secretly hired Montecucculli—after all he was her compatriot—in order to advance herself by one essential step
closer to the throne of France. For the moment, however, a
more acceptable villain was Francis's old enemy, Charles V.
Hadn't Montecucculli been sent into service of the royal house
by the Duke of Ferrara? And wasn't the Duke a loyal vassal
of the Emperor? At the order of a distraught King Francis,
Montecucculli was questioned closely and in the time-honored
manner about his principals. Before the interrogators were
fully satisfied, he had named not only his patron, but also
Federigo de Gonzaga, a cousin of the Duke of Mantua, and
Antonio de Levya, the imperial general who had taken
Francis prisoner at Pavia. All of them, he admitted, were
acting in concert, and under Charles's orders, to remove first
all of Francis's heirs, and then the King himself, thus leaving
France in the grip of anarchy. After this confession, the trial
was merely a formality to impose appropriate sentence, which
was that the miserable man "be drawn by four horses, and
afterward the four parts of his body be hung at the four gates
of the town of Lyons and his head put on the end of a lance
which shall be placed on the bridge over the Rhone."

The Dauphin's death did in fact bring Catherine one
important step closer to the throne by making her husband
heir apparent. At the same time and of far greater concern
to her, it also tore away the veil behind which she had tried
to mask an ominous failure. In three years of marriage she
had not yet satisfied even once her principal duty as a royal
princess.

The second event of that year, in retrospect not unconnected with the first, was that Catherine's husband took a mistress. There was nothing unusual, at Francis's court, about such an accommodation. What was unusual was the woman he chose, or as is more likely, who chose him. She was a familiar figure around the court, her cold remoteness accentuated by the widow's weeds she perpetually wore in honor of her husband, the late Grand Sénéschal of Normandy. Black, it also happened, was especially flattering to her fair complexion. She had been born at the close of the previous century—December 31, 1499, is the date assigned her by most historians—the daughter of Jean de Poitiers, Seigneur de Saint-Vallier, a nobleman of good but not distinguished family, and in due course was married off to Louis de Brézé, the Grand Sénéschal of Normandy. It was quite a coup for Saint-Vallier, for the bridegroom was the King's first lieutenant in one of his most prosperous provinces, and moreover was himself of royal blood—the natural grandson of Charles VII through his alliance with the already legendary Agnes Sorel. Quite irrelevant was the additional fact that he was notoriously short-tempered, stern, ugly, humpbacked, and fifty-six years of age. Or that the bride, Diane de Poitiers, had just turned fifteen.

Soon after the wedding, both her father and new husband went off to war, leaving Diane to preside as chatelaine over the chill, square-towered, and moated castle of Anet. As befitted her new station, she also began appearing at important affairs of state. Contemporary chronicles mention, for instance, that in 1518 she and her husband were among the guests gathered in Amboise to celebrate the wedding of Lorenzo, Duke of Urbino, and Madeleine de La Tour d'Auvergne. Approximately a year later, as that marriage ended in double tragedy and the birth of a frail girl baby in Florence, Diane sat for the earliest of her portraits to be preserved. A pencil sketch in the three-color style then in vogue, it shows a face of classic symmetry and calm, far more striking for its strength than its beauty.

In 1523, Diane's father, Saint-Vallier, was implicated in the treason of the Constable of Bourbon. In prompt order, he was arrested, tried, found guilty, and sentenced to death. Under ordinary circumstances, and especially because of the nature of the crime and the abundant evidence of guilt, such a train of events would have continued swiftly to its conclusion: public beheading in the Place de Grève, behind Notre Dame in Paris. In this instance, however, a last-minute royal reprieve arrived just as the condemned man, too frightened to stand, was being hoisted onto the scaffold. At the time, it was accepted that the pardon had been secured through the intercession of the Grand Sénéschal, who invoked his own loyalty and long service to his country, and indeed this is the reason given in the official decree which halted the execution. A later explanation, however, gives full credit to Diane herself, who appealed not to the King's sense of loyalty but to a baser instinct, and who sealed the bargain with the gift of her person. This account first appears in the writings of Protestant historians who, as will be seen, had no great reason to appreciate Diane de Poitiers. It was variously repeated and embroidered upon. Brantôme, who could not pass up the story in his *Memoirs,* even invents a suitable line of dialogue for the reprieved prisoner. "God preserve," he has Saint-Vallier say as he steps down from the scaffold, "the fair c – – of my daughter, which has served me so well." More recent and impartial scholarship, however, appears to have laid the story finally to rest on both historic and psychological grounds—a pity, because it robs Diane of the distinction of having been mistress to father and son, both kings of France.

Whatever the reason for his magnanimity, Francis remained on excellent terms with both the Grand Sénéschal and his wife and was a frequent visitor to his estates. Indeed, it is one of history's small ironies that he happened to be staying there when the negotiations with Clement VII over the marriage contract which brought Catherine de' Medici to France were concluded. The original of that document bears the line: "Done at Anet, the 24th of April 1531."

Later that same year, Louis de Brézé died, at the ripe age of seventy-two. Diane supervised with care all details of his funeral. The widow settled upon a suitable memorial—an alabaster and black marble reclining figure of almost shocking realism. Its creator, testament to her fine eye, was an unknown apprentice named Jean Goujon, then just sixteen years old. Part of his commission was to inscribe, in a discreet corner of the monument, these words: "O! Louis de Brézé, Diane de Poitiers, stricken by the death of her hubsand, has raised this sepulchre to thee. She was thy inseparable and very faithful wife in the marriage bed; she will be the same in the tomb."

Then she packed her black dresses, closed up the fortress-like Anet, and left to join the Court.

II

Diane de Poitiers was thirty-seven years old when she captured the affection of the seventeen-year-old Henry, and she kept it unchallenged and undimmed until he died and she was entering her sixties. Biographers, hers and his, have considered it necessary to invent scenes which would explain this extraordinary hold. According to one such story, Diane was among the Court ladies who accompanied the two young princes on the melancholy journey which would lead to their captivity as hostages. In Bayonne, their last stop on French soil, she was so moved by the sad, abandoned, and spiritless little boy, then barely seven years old, that she ran to him just as he was being taken away by the military escort, hugged him to her bosom and kissed his forehead. According to another story, it was on his return home, when he was utterly lost in the commotion surrounding him, that this scene or another very much like it took place. This version provides an additional fillip. There were, of course, tournaments to celebrate their return. As they took the field, each of the combatants stopped to beg a lady's permission to carry her colors into the arena. The young Henry, Duke of Orléans, saw Diane sitting in the tribune and shyly indicated with a tilt of his lance his wish to be her champion—a desire which was graciously granted. He would at the time have been eleven years old.

There is no evidence that any of these events took place, or that Henry was more than casually aware of Diane's existence for several years after his return from Spain. He had little taste and less aptitude for the Italianate aspects of Court life—a disposition which unfortunately included the young wife whom he had not even seen before the day of their wedding. Much more to his preference were strenuous games, at which he excelled, and occasionally heavy-handed practical jokes. He was aware that his father did not especially care for him—Francis often said that he had no use for slow-witted children—and far favored his older brother. A more prosaic but defensible explanation for Diane's success is that Henry never really had a mother; his own died before he was five. Whatever other roles she filled, the older woman certainly would be able to satisfy, at least in the beginning, this gaping void. Even the foreign ambassadors—the well-informed Venetians included—reported that, close as the attachment appeared to be between the new Dauphin and Madame La Grande Sénéschale, it was more of a spiritual union than they had been accustomed to see at the French Court.

Regardless of the nature of the relationship, its effect was the same as far as Catherine was concerned. Henry, who had paid her only slight attention during the three years of their marriage, now lost all interest and virtually stopped seeing her altogether. The pain affected more than her pride, for there is ample evidence from her own correspondence, that Catherine was genuinely in love with her husband—a love which admittedly may have been born of gratitude, but which grew far beyond it. One of Catherine's most moving letters was addressed to her daughter, then married to Philip II of Spain. It was written after Henry's shocking sudden death, and only the most hopeless cynic can imagine the author giving a thought to anyone's reading or assessing it other than its intended recipient. "For this reason, my daughter, recommend yourself well to God, because you have seen me as contented as you are, without a thought of ever having any other trouble than not to be loved as much as I wanted to be by the King, your father, who honored me more than I merited. But I love him so much that I had always fear, as you know, in many ways, and God has taken him away from me. For this, my dear daughter, remember me and let me serve as an example, so that you do not trust so much in the love which you bear your husband and in the honor and the ease which you have at this present moment, as to forget to recommend yourself to Him, who can continue your happiness, and also when it pleases Him put you into the state in which I am; for I would sooner die than see you there."

Only once did Catherine yield to the jealousy which must have been consuming her. When staying in a bedroom directly above that of her rival, she ordered a small hole drilled in the floor, and looked. What she saw, according to Brantôme who relates the story was: "A very beautiful, fair woman, fresh and half undressed, was caressing in a hundred ways her lover, who was doing the same to her. The better to enjoy themselves, for it was a warm day, they slipped down from the bed and on to the carpet, without interupting their play."

As to Catherine's public attitude toward Diane, historians

agree that it was at all times polite and even deferential, that of a young woman for an older one of at least equal rank. Critics of Catherine, both contemporary and latter-day, point to this as further evidence of the Florentine's duplicity. Catherine herself only made one comment of her own about her husband's relationship with Diane. This, too, was in a letter, sent to one of her oldest friends and counselors. Its date is 1583, when the forces tearing France apart were long past the point of being affected to the favor of either side by the intimate revelations of an adulterous affair by then a generation old: "If I made good cheer for Madame de Valentinois, [one of the many titles which Diane de Poitiers accumulated], it wes the King that I was really pleasing; for never did woman who loved her husband succeed in loving his whore. One must call a spade a spade, though the term is an ugly one on the lips."

Still, the price of pleasing her husband came high. As Diane became more certain of her ascendancy over Henry, she required his constant attendance and attention. In a dispatch which dates sometime after the liaison began, the Venetian Contarini notes that "she knows everything that goes on . . . because everyday [Henry] goes to pay her a visit after dinner, remaining an hour and one half, discussing matters with her and making her aware of all that is happening." Contarini also lays to rest the vestiges of any purely platonic friendship between them: "He has always loved her much and still takes pleasure from her, despite her age." And he adds an observation which, whatever its source and authenticity, is unusual information to be included in a diplomatic report. "Often," he says, to underline Diane's influence over Henry, "it is she who exhorts him to go to sleep with his wife." It is just possible that the Grande Sénéschale was moved by pity for the poor, neglected little wife. Far more likely, however, she appreciated that a barren marriage might lead to divorce and the appearance on the scene of a new, more challenging rival.

III

Catherine's barrenness has, to this day, remained a medical mystery. It lasted ten years then apparently cured itself. Certainly credit cannot be given to any of the remedies she assiduously tried. Gynecology, and especially the aspect of it that dealt with the all-important question of fertility, was, in the sixteenth century, a developed if entirely empirical art. A common test for fecundity, for instance, consisted of inserting a clove of garlic into the vagina. If, after twelve hours, its presence could be detected on the patient's breath, all was well. If not, then the womb was suffering from four possible classes of disorders: excess of heat, cold, dryness, or moisture. Elaborate regimens had been worked out to overcome all these difficulties, and described in such treatises as Jean Liebault's *Thrésor des Remèdes Secrets pour les Maladies des Femmes,* which first appeared in 1536.

If diagnosis indicated that the womb was excessively warm, Liebault recommended that "it should first be purged of bilious or sanguine humor with cassia, rhubarb or similar medication. Then a moderate bleeding should be administered, both from the arm and the foot. But above all, it is by proper diet and regimen that the offending parts may be refreshed. Let the woman eat moderate meats, such as kid, chicken, suckling pigs and young lamb, seasoned with lettuce, spinach, *courgette* and the like. Let her drink light, delicate wines, well watered. Let her especially drink the juice of sour fruit, and bathe in fresh, tepid water, after which it will be useful to anoint her parts liberally with a paste made of goose, duck and rooster fat mixed together and liquified."

The cure for a womb suspected of being too cold sounded less like a medical treatment than a recipe for *pot-au-feu.*

The patient was first thoroughly purged with a syrup made of absinthe, oregano, hyssop, citronella, and valerian. The offending womb was then encouraged to reach proper temperature with a regimen of ten-days' marinade in hot baths perfumed with juniper, laurel, basil, rosemary, thyme, and bay leaf. It was further noted that "during this period the husband and wife must remain chaste, with the result that afterward they will be more avid and stimulated to caress each other and frolic together." In preparation for this, the husband was further encouraged to utilize one of the many concoctions which, as was well-known, stimulated the production of semen and enhanced its potency.

Having covered the ailments of the womb, the author conceded that on occasion it could be the male who was responsible. Appropriate steps were described to cope with this condition as well: "If may be that it is the virile member which is too short. If so, it can be lengthened by frequent use, followed by extended friction, and by the application of an unguent compounded of castor oil, spikehard seeds, earthworms and fermented goat's milk, which has the faculty of heating and exciting the expulsive urge. Those members which are too long cannot be as easily shortened; the most efficacious method is to prevent nourishment from descending to the site, an objective which can be achieved by the application of green hemlock leaves all around it. . . . For those members which are curved or crooked, because of a shortened ligament, it is most useful to employ compresses containing an ointment of fresh butter, linseed oil and sweet almonds. For those which are soft or flaccid, it is useful to employ meats which generate heat; to apply leeches to the buttocks and groin; and to anoint the *os sacrum,* the hips, kidneys, groin, lower belly and genital member with an oil of chervil to which has been added a powder reduced from the procreative parts of a bull or stag, as well as fine grains of onions and dandelions."

Henry avoided these ministrations by the irrefutable argument, while traveling in the Piedmont, of producing a child by a young girl named Philippa Duci, the attractive daughter of a local gentleman who had extended him the courtesy of his house.* With the burden of failure squarely on her, Catherine turned to the philtres and recipes of the ancient alchemists. She swallowed elixirs of mare's milk, rabbit's blood, and sheep's urine. She wore next to her skin a belt woven of goat's hair and around her neck a small sack containing the ashes of a large frog—the one because it would stop menstrual flow, the other because it assured a male child. She foreswore riding a mule, for it was well known that this animal, itself sterile, could communicate its affliction to women. She amassed amulets and charms by the boxful. Retained out of sentiment, they were duly inventoried, after her death, in her estate.

When none of these worked, Catherine anticipated the worst and threw herself at Francis's feet. She had heard, she said, that he planned to give another woman as wife to her husband, and had come to beg not to be sent away. If it were necessary for the good of the state that she cede her position, could she at least be permitted to remain in order to serve the new Dauphine in whatever capacity could be found for her? This appeal, calculated to touch Francis's sense of chivalry and generosity, succeeded. Although there were no eyewitnesses to this domestic scene, tradition holds that the King bent down to help the prostrate girl to her feet and told her, "My daughter, have no fear. Since God has willed that you should be my daughter-in-law and wife of the Dauphin, I do not wish to make any change, and perhaps it will please Almighty God to grant to you and to me the gift we so much long for."

It was granted. On January 19, 1543, the long ordeal ended

* Born in 1538, the child was named Diane and brought to France where she was reared at Court with love and attention. This has led to the speculation that she was in reality the daughter of Diane de Poitiers, and that the entire Piedmontese episode was invented as a cover for her chastity.

with the birth of a child, and a boy at that. A physician named Jean Fernel received both the credit and a lifetime pension for finding the long-sought remedy to Catherine's barrenness. He never revealed it publicly, but knowing gossips reported that he had instructed the Dauphin in "a new manner of caressing the Dauphine." Whatever it was, the method was repeatable, for Catherine produced another nine children during the next thirteen years, of whom all but three survived to maturity. It was Henry who finally closed the floodgates, fearful that he would not be able to provide adequate estates and dowries for a larger brood.

IV

Meanwhile, a deadly earnest struggle had developed which at first titillated but then divided the Court. It was not between wife and mistress—that was no match at all—but between mistress and mistress; the lover of the King, Anne d'Heilly, and the lady of his son. In 1536, when Henry had become Dauphin and subsequently acquired Diane, a bonus in the form of a ducal coronet had come to the durable Mlle d'Heilly, who after a decade at Francis's side was as beautiful and as blonde as ever, and if anything more sharp-tongued and certain of her position. Two years earlier, following established procedure, Francis had married her off to a suitable husband: someone of high enough birth to confer unimpeachable standing on her, of adequate intelligence to comprehend the situation, and of low enough fortune to accept it. The candidate who satisfied all three conditions was Jean de Brosse, a Breton count whose family had fallen out of royal favor for some unremembered offense a century earlier. After a hasty honeymoon which Francis was too magnanimous to deny him, he retired to his ruined estates in

Brittany, now about to undergo extensive restoration, and scrupulously kept his part of the bargain. When informed of the royal decree which, purely as a side effect, had created him Duke of Étampes, he even made a point of sending his thanks to his sovereign by messenger.

As for the new Duchess of Étampes, she flounced around with renewed assurance and took cognizance of Diane's rise to prominence by observing to anyone who would listen how odd a coincidence it was that she happened to be born almost on the exact day of the Grande Sénéschale's marriage. Actually the Duchess was cheating just a little, because there was only nine years' difference between their ages. Henry took great umbrage at this and similar slanders, to the extent of prohibiting Catherine from having anything to do with the Duchess of Étampes. For her part, Diane could afford to be patient because she knew she was backing the younger of the two horses, and because Francis's health, moreover, was beginning to deteriorate. But being female and also farseeing, she could not resist planting little seeds of calumny of her own, to be harvested at the proper moment. It is, for instance, to her inspiration that we probably owe the tale of the Emperor's diamond.

According to this story, Charles V was paying a formal state visit to Francis and was washing his hands prior to going in to dinner when the Duchess of Étampes, who had been accorded the honor of passing him the imperial towel, felt something dropping into her own hands. Looking down and seeing that it was a large diamond ring, she started to return it, but was prevented from doing so by the Emperor. "No, Madame, it is now in too beautiful hands for me ever to consider removing it." The denouement of this little scene, of course, is that the diamond was down payment for services to be rendered. By accepting it, the Duchess became a paid spy for the Emperor, placed in such a high position that she was able to overhear and pass on to his agents much valuable military and diplomatic information. The story is completely baseless, but it served its intended purpose of blackening the Duchess's name, if not with her royal friend, then with generations of patriotic French scholars.

The two ladies clashed in innumerable ways, fighting over every royal appointment and favor that might be turned to their own advantage. So disruptive did their conflict become that a simple, grizzled soldier like Blaise de Monluc grumbled in his diary: "The misfortune of France is that the women are permitted to meddle into too many things. The King ought to shut their mouths. . . ."

But the King was only a helpless male, and the further misfortune of France was that of all the grounds they could have selected on which to pitch their fight, the two ladies chose religion.

The name of Martin Luther had first been heard in France in 1518, a few months after his posting of the ninety-five theses in Wittenberg. Within a year his ideas were being widely discussed, but the supreme authority in matters of this kind, the Faculty of Theology of the University of Paris, did not take formal notice of them until 1521, when they pronounced them heretical and excommunicated their author. To underline their concern, they also ordered the burning of the first heretic in France—a printer named Jean Vallière. Francis did not share the theologians' alarm. Out of innate humanism more than dogmatic conviction, he saw little virtue in the notion pressed upon him by the good doctors of the Sorbonne that being tied to a stake and then set on fire was good for a man's soul. In fact, when the scholar Louis Berquin was arrested and locked up in the Conciergerie in 1523, for the deadly sin of having translated the writings of Erasmus and Luther, the King sent his own archers to transfer him to the Louvre, where he would be safer from salvation. But Francis could not be everywhere to intercede. Nor were the dissenters satisfied to adopt the passive tactics of the early Christians. Even though the Church had the heavier artillery, each act of barbarism on its part brought new defiance. During the night of October 17, 1534, for instance, a poster appeared on doors and walls around Paris and in the provinces attacking the Church in language that spilled over into the scurrilous. It referred to the Mass as an "idolatrous rite," and to the established hierarchy, from the Pope down to monks and priests, as "vermin, false prophets, damnable deceivers, apostates, wolves, false shepherds, seducers, liars and execrable blasphemers, murderers of souls, renouncers of Jesus Christ, of his death and passion, false witnesses, traitors, thieves and robbers of the honor of God and more detestable than devils." And it went on to make this suggestion: "Light then your fires to burn yourselves; not us, who refuse to believe in your idols, your new God and your new Christs."

There is no evidence that, in taking their respective stands, either the Duchess or Diane de Poitiers was influenced by this rhetoric or, for that matter, by the faintest moral or theological principle. Because Francis had determined to protect, or at least tolerate, the reformers, the Duchess became their most vocal champion at Court. For the same reason, Diane imposed on herself the Christian duty of preserving orthodoxy against its enemies. The alliances could have worked out as satisfactorily the other way around.

No one was more aware of the situation than Catherine de' Medici. Whatever gaps may have been left in her education, at least she had been given the opportunity to observe at first hand the workings of papal diplomacy and the extremely elastic uses to which religion could be put. What she could not yet foresee was the extent to which her own life and survival would become a test of just how well she had learned these lessons. For the present, however, there was no need to worry. So long as Francis was King, she would always be on his side.

But slowly, Francis was fading. He still looked the part; in fact, one of the most striking descriptions we have of him, composed by Marino Cavalli, dates from this period: "The

King is now fifty-four years old. His appearance is utterly regal, of such manner that without ever having seen his face or a portrait, a stranger would say on first beholding him 'This is the King.' All of his movements are so noble and majestic that no prince is capable of equaling them. . . . [H]e is of very sound judgement, of very wide erudition; listening to him, one recognizes that there is scarcely a subject, study or art upon which he is unable to discourse as pertinently as those who have devoted themselves to it." And the perceptive Venetian continued with an assessment which the hindsight of four centuries has left valid: "Truly, when one reflects that despite these skills, so many exploits have escaped him, one is disposed to conclude that his wisdom is rather on the lips than in his spirit. Frankly, I believe that the adversities of this King derive from the lack of men capable of realizing his designs. As for himself, he has never wished to take part in their execution or even to supervise them. To him, it appeared sufficient to propound plans for subordinates to carry out. . . . [W]hat one might wish from him is a little more attention and patience, and not quite so much brilliance and knowledge."

In 1546, when this was written, the Court still moved at Francis's whim. If anything, his pace quickened to that of a man who wishes to have a last taste of every place he had ever enjoyed. When he could no longer hunt on horseback, Francis had himself carried after the hounds on a stretcher, and promised that "after I'm dead, I shall continue in my coffin." He had been seriously ill during the previous year— ill enough to cause Henry to make some premature remarks that reached Francis's ear and all but completed the alienation of father and son. The rift had started several years earlier, and it resulted in Henry's being excluded from the inner councils of state. It was further widened by the sudden death of Francis's third and youngest son, which plunged the King into a state of melancholy he had not known since the black days of captivity in Madrid. In addition to his sense of personal loss, there had been intricate plans to marry the young prince to one of Charles V's nieces, and thus to regain Milan and possibly much else besides. All this was now gone, and as despondency turned into bitterness, Francis directed it toward Henry, as if to reproach him for having been the only one of his sons to survive. On Diane's advice, the Dauphin quietly slipped away from the Court. It could not take much longer now.

During the winter, Francis fell ill again, rallied, and then began sinking. Just as poison was suspected in any sudden, unexplained death during the sixteenth century, so any lingering painful demise was ascribed to syphilis. In Francis's case, an inordinate amount of questionable scholarship has been lavished on disproving—or, depending on the bias of the writer, proving—this diagnosis. The famous story of the *Belle Ferronière*—an early, attractive conquest of Francis's whose vengeful husband intentionally contracted the disease himself so that she could relay it to the King—has been shown to be a latter-day invention. A more telling indication is an entry in a diary of Louise of Savoy noting that in the year 1512 her son had been taken ill "in the secret part of his nature." Since no cure for syphilis existed, the timing for the tertiary phase of the disease to flare up appears to fit. But the firmest clue to the nature of the disease comes from the royal accounts themselves; in 1543, Francis paid to send a ship to the island of Hispaniola in order to bring back a supply of gayac, a tropical wood now known as lignum vitae and prized for its unusual hardness and heaviness. The far greater value of gayac in the sixteenth century derived from an altogether different and unique property: its alleged ability to cure venereal disease.

The news of another death—that of Henry VIII on January 26, 1547—particularly affected Francis. Martin du Bellay, who was at his bedside, writes in his memoirs: "[It] occasioned the king much sorrow . . . because they were almost of an age, and of the same constitution; and he feared that he must soon follow him." Inevitably it reminded Francis of the meeting of the Field of the Cloth of Gold, and perhaps also of a subsequent quarter century of lost opportunities and of enormous effort which could have been better spent, for as du Bellay also notes, "Those, moreover, who were about his person perceived that from that time he became more pensive than before."

On March 29, at the castle of Rambouillet, the final vigil began, initiated by Francis's own request for extreme unction. Afterward, he asked for the Duchess of Étampes and gently ordered her, for her own safety, to leave the castle. "Earth," she cried, crumpling to the floor outside his chamber, "swallow me!"

It was, as matters turned out, not an unwise request. As one of his first acts, the new King stripped her of her titles and properties, and ordered her indicted for treasonable correspondence with the enemy. Her servants were thrown into prison; she herself went to live as a tolerated relation with one of the many brothers who had benefited handsomely from her long association with Francis. But most humiliating of all was the attitude of her husband who, after all these years, reappeared to take notice of her in his will: "As regards my wife, since she has chosen to live away from me, she is to inherit nothing."

Last to be summoned to Francis's bedside was Henry. Between bouts of pain, the old King expressed regret for many of his own actions, such as having "on some occasions made war on light pretexts." He admonished his son to behave in such fashion that he would not have any remorse over having caused any person intentional harm. He commended the Duchess to his son's courtesy, remembering that she was a woman and therefore deserving of consideration. And he pressed Henry—another piece of advice that went unheeded—to retain his ministers and be guided by their counsel. Above all, he urged that Henry not submit himself to the will of others—"as I have myself done," he added.

Henry in turn asked for his father's blessing and then "fell in a swoon upon the King's bed; and the King held him in a half embrace and was unable to release him." Then, between two and three o'clock on the afternoon of March 31, 1547, Francis I died, in the fifty-fourth year of his life and the thirty-third of his reign.

Queen Eleanor had not been at Rambouillet during her husband's final illness. In the intensity of conflicting emotions, no one remembered to send for her, so it was only two days after her husband's death that she learned that she had become a widow.

V

Francis had been an exceedingly popular king and his death was mourned widely, both by Catholics and those who, though growing in number, still had no collective name other than "those of the Religion." But not one of his subjects felt grief more sincere or anguish more acute at his passing than his daughter-in-law. His death made her, at the age of twenty-eight, Queen of France—an estate so high that neither Pope Clement VII nor any of the far greater Medicis who had preceded him had envisaged it as ever gracing their family.

Catherine de' Medici was the Queen, but if there was any lingering doubt about who was the first lady of France, King Henry II dispelled it at once. It was traditional that, upon the death of a king, all public office holders, from lowly clerks to the superintendent of finance, resign their positions. For a consideration, the *paulette,* a sum that varied according to their stations, they were then reappointed and their privileges restored. By custom, the amount thus raised—some 300,000 *écus*—should have gone to Francis's sister. Henry decreed that it be given to Diane instead, and that all additional income from future appointments would also be hers. He created a new title for her, Duchess of Valentinois, without bothering with the charade of marrying her off. He gave her the royal jewels. He levied a special tax on all the churches in France and turned its proceeds over to her personal use, a fiscal innovation that prompted François Rabelais, who detested her, to observe that "the King had hung all the bells in the kingdom around the neck of his new mare." There was no gesture too insignificant for Henry to demonstrate his special regard for her. Wheat grown on Diane's estates was exempted from export duty; her builders received special permission to cut down trees in the royal forests of Dreux to facilitate the elaborate reconstruction of her late husband's family seat at Anet. A manuscript in the Bibliothèque Nationale laconically lists other items of income which found their way into her coffers, including the proceeds of the sale, to the highest bidder, of six hundred Turks and Moors captured by a French royal warship in the Mediterranean. Her wine steward received the worldly goods of an unnamed counterfeiter caught and burned alive for his crime. This last was just the tip of an iceberg: through the years of Henry's reign, as heretics and other criminals were brought to justice, a substantial portion of their former holdings, frequently including large and valuable estates, were given by royal order to the Duchess of Valentinois. In all, one historian estimates that during the first years of Henry's reign nearly one quarter of all the revenues which would have flowed into the national treasury of France went instead to her private account.

Still, this was not enough. In order to honor her and affirm their relationship, Henry requested that the ritual of his own coronation be amended to permit her participation. This, it was pointed out to him, could not be done. The elaborate ceremony had followed a prescribed course for centuries, and not even a queen had ever been permitted to share it with her husband. Henry then complained that the ceremonial vestments he was expected to wear had become old and faded, and demanded that new ones be prepared for him. They were a faithful copy of the originals, but with one exception. The sky-blue satin tunic sewn with golden *fleurs-de-lys* and trimmed with crimson bore an added decoration: a border of pearl embroidery fashioned to spell out the initials D and H, in the familar form ⬭, which soon began appearing on palaces and monuments, on churches, on the covers of richly bound books, on interior decorations, and eventually even on the southern inner façade of the Louvre, where it is flanked by the interlaced monograms of other kings of France and their more legitimate if less esteemed consorts.

Rewards descended also on those of Diane's supporters who had been prescient enough to take her side against the Duchess of Étampes. Two days after becoming King, and while the lengthy funeral ceremonies for Francis were just beginning, Henry pointedly ignored his deathbed advice. In a single sweep he dismissed all of his father's close advisers and ministers, and replaced them with men of his own and Diane's choosing. Nothing of this sort had ever happened in France before. As the historian François Decrue noted, "France presents in her government some resemblance to Turkey. One assists there at the disgrace of Sultans, and the replacing of Grand Viziers, at veritable revolutions of the palace. In 1547, it is not a King who dies; it is an entire Court that disappears."

Francis had specifically warned Henry about one family of courtiers, the Guises. Beware of them, he had said, for "their aim is to strip you and your children to their doublets, and your people to their shirts." But the Guises had taken particular care to become friends of Diane—a friendship built on a solid base of mutual distrust and coinciding interests. Catherine, of course, was beneath their serious notice. That she had become Queen was only an aberration due to one of Francis's many miscalculations and of no political consequence. In Henry's newly constituted *Conseil Privé* there were not one, but three Guises—brothers who along with their numerous progeny were to blight the remainder of the century and contribute to the rivers of blood that flooded it.

One would like to say something favorable about the Guises, if only because history has dealt so harshly with them. But it is difficult. They were, to begin with, not French at all, but of German extraction—from Lorraine. In time, they would claim with spurious genealogies direct descent from Charlemagne and behave like an imperial house temporarily without a crown; but the beginning was more humble. There was little enough to share in Lorraine, so a cadet son of the family, Claude, had come to France just before the end of the previous century to seek his fortune. The most direct course was on the battlefield, and Claude distinguished himself well enough, first for the old King, Louis XII, and then for Francis, to earn the title of Duke of Guise in 1527. Meanwhile, he had also found a slower but surer path upward by way of the nuptial bed. His own union with Antoinette de Bourbon, a true French Princess of the Blood, spawned twelve children who did not need to be told where their duty lay. One of them, Francis, became the most celebrated soldier of his generation, and married the beautiful Anne d'Este, a granddaughter of Louis XII. Another took as bride one of Diane de Poitiers' two daughters. Women, too, were expected to carry their weight, so a sister, Marie, was married off to James V of Scotland—the same potential bridegroom whom Clement VII had spurned as of too little importance for Catherine many years earlier. To collect a fortune adequate to their number and suitable to their rank, the family embraced the most likely source, the Church. In one generation, they squeezed out of it two cardinal's hats, and so many bishoprics, abbacies, and grand priories that their combined income exceeded that of the King. Those were the Guises at the time of Henry's accession, and more, much more, was to be heard from them.

Diane's position in the new scheme of things was described in a long dispatch to his master by Jean de Saint-Mauris, Charles V's ambassador to France. It is dated April 20, 1547— less than a month after Francis's death: "The King continues to yield more and more to the yoke of Silvius [the code name for Diane] and has become her subject and slave entirely.... After dinner he visits the said Silvius. When he has given her an account of all the business he has transacted in the morning and up to that moment, whether with the ambassadors or other persons of importance, he seats himself upon her lap, a guitar in his hand, upon which he plays, and inquires often if the said Silvius has not preserved her beauty, touching from time to time her breasts and regarding her attentively, like a man who is ensnared by his love.... The King has many natural good qualities, and one might hope much from him, if he were not so stupid as to allow himself to be led as he does. As for Silvius, since she has come into authority, she has changed her humor and her behavior, and people find her, in short, very haughty and insolent; while, apart from that, she is endeavoring with her wiles and her attractions to remain in the good graces of the King, and to extract from him everything that she possibly can."

Despite all her responsibilities, the Duchess of Valentinois did not neglect her domestic duties. Having taken care of her other daughter by marrying her off to Robert de la Marck, Duke of Bouillon—and assuring the couple's future by having her new son-in-law named Marshal of France— she undertook to supervise the proper raising of the royal children. As rapidly as Catherine produced them, they were whisked away and put under the care of Monsieur de Humières, a kindly and dedicated governor whose principal qualification for the job was that he was Diane's cousin.

It was a genial if cruel stroke, for it permitted her at

once to cement her hold on Henry, for whom the long-awaited children were the embodiment of his dynastic hopes, and to put Catherine forever in her place by usurping the only function left to her. As in everything else she did, Diane did not permit the slightest detail to escape her attention. Of the 106 of her letters which have been collected, 28 are addressed to Humières, whom she pointedly called "My Ally." One of them reads: "I have heard that Madame [Elizabeth, Catherine's eldest daughter] is suffering from the measles, and wish to let you know that the King was upset not to have been notified. I explained to him that your letter was in all likelihood lost, and suggest that you report this to him, and also that you summon whatever physician you may require from Paris. Meanwhile, I am sending you some *licorne* as he will undoubtedly prescribe it in any case." Another letter reassures Humières over the indisposition of one of the children: "I have read your report that Madame Claude [Catherine's second daughter, who was then four years old] found herself indisposed the other night because of coughing. We are distressed to hear this, but nevertheless do not consider it dangerous in view of the fact that Madame her sister suffered from the same condition at her age." Or, "I have received your letter regarding the good state of health of Messieurs and Mesdames which I communicated to the King and the Queen, and which relieved them greatly. Nevertheless, I have heard reports that there may be danger of plague in the neighborhood of Blois, and urge you to be ready to leave without delay. . . ."*

The rest of Diane's correspondence is concerned mainly with business matters, the dispensation or rejection of favors,

---

* Because it clearly served Diane's purpose to have her self-assumed maternal duties be recognized as widely as possible, it is probably at her own suggestion that Guillaume Chrestien, one of the royal physicians, dedicated one of his textbooks to her, noting that "not only did she take care of the conception and birth of the children, but she also undertook to have them properly raised by prudent governesses and instructed by wise teachers in the knowledge of virtue and in the love and fear of God."

instructions on the management of her estates, reminders of promises made and not kept, and the solicitation of favor for herself, her daughters, her sons-in-law, her friends, and her protégés. At times, the tone of voice becomes that of an executive addressing a slow-witted and not wholly trustworthy clerk. She complains to her cousin, the Count of Bouchaige: "I send you this to remind you that I had authorized you to permit the cutting of wood amounting to the sum of 900 *livres* from my property at Rouveray. I am now told that the sale of the said wood has exceeded 1,200 *livres*. I have no wish to quarrel with you, but . . ."

Occasionally, however, there is a letter which suggests that Diane's dominance over the King was not lost upon even the highest-placed nobles in France. Thus she replies to the Marshal of Brissac, then campaigning against the Spaniards: ". . . [A]s regards sending you additional forces, I can assure you that the King has no wish to leave you deprived of them, and I hope that he will remedy the situation as soon as possible. Indeed, I am confident he will be notifying you himself shortly, thus avoiding my having to write again. For the present, my esteemed Marshal, I wish to thank you for the excellent care you have taken of my son, d'Aumale [the husband of Diane's elder daughter]."

Oddly enough, there is not among Diane's correspondence, or in any other document which bears her bold, unmistakable signature, a single word addressed to Henry. All the heavy breathing was on his part. He writes to her from Fontainebleau in 1547: "I beg you to send me news of your health, because of the distress with which I have heard of your illness, and so that I may govern my movements in accordance with your condition. For, if your illness continues, I should not wish to fail and come and see you . . . since I did not fear in time past, to lose the good graces of the late King, in order to remain near you. I should scarcely complain of the trouble that I might have in rendering you any service, and I assure you that I shall not be at my ease until the bearer of this returns. . . . Being far from her upon whom all my welfare depends, it is very hard for me to be happy."

Or, this time writing from Flanders where he was leading his army into war: "I intend setting off the day after tomorrow [and] I hope to put myself into such condition that I shall prove myself worthy to wear the scarf which you have sent me. I shall not write you anything . . . save to entreat you always to keep in remembrance him who has never loved, nor will love, anyone but you."

As for the object of his passion, one small incident, having to do with her acquisition of Chenonceaux, sheds as much light as appears necessary. The gemlike castle had been built on the ruins of an old mill on the bank of the river Cher by Thomas Bohier in 1513. Because Bohier, neither of noble birth nor of conspicuous wealth, had been a royal superintendent of finances, it is reasonable to assume that the costs of construction had been borne largely and informally by public funds. This was not a unique case; several of the great Renaissance châteaux of the Loire, including Azay-le-Rideau and the now-destroyed Bury and Gallion, had all been built by paymasters, treasurers, and other watchdogs of the national purse. Francis had taken a liking to Chenonceaux and unilaterally acquired it from Bohier's heirs for a purely nominal sum; Henry, who inherited it, gave it to Diane in recognition of "services performed on behalf of the crown by Louis de Brézé," her long-deceased husband. Even as she settled in, however, Diane was nagged by the remote possibility that the Bohiers or their heirs might some day challenge the validity of the forced sale to Francis. She therefore undertook a lengthy, complex legal process which dragged on for eight years and resulted in the royal confiscation's being annulled and the castle put up for public auction on June 8, 1555. There was only one bidder, and her offer of 50,000 livres—not quite enough to furnish one of the smaller upstairs bedrooms—was accepted. And even that very reasonable sum was paid out of the royal treasury.

That this—a grasping, vindictive, but above all eminently practical middle-class, middle-aged woman—was Diane's true character appears to have been known to everyone of importance in France, as was the fact that she ruled the King as totally as he ruled his country. Saint-Mauris's report to Charles V is echoed in other diplomatic correspondence. Alvarotto, the ambassador of the Duke of Ferrara, reported: "As far as His Majesty is concerned, it does not appear that he is preoccupied with other matters than playing games, hunting, and paying court to the Sénéschale, with whom he spends at least eight hours a day. . . . The impression appears to be that the King is not aware of what is happening, and that in any case he is being, as they say here, led by the tip of the nose." Sir John Masone, the emissary of Edward VI of England noted simply that "The Duchess of Valentinois ruleth the roast," and further passed judgment on how little regarded Catherine was at Court by barely mentioning her name in any of his lengthy, detailed dispatches.

VI

Everyone, then, knew it and snickered about it except one person—the only one who counted. But no practical-minded woman approaching her fifties would repose her entire future on her continued ability to hold the fascination, to say nothing of the unrestrained love, of a man twenty years younger, virile, and, now that his interest in sex had been aroused, able by his position to satisfy his slightest whim. Diane de Poitiers owes her success, and her place in history, to the fact that she found a way to do it.

She had one enormous advantage that any performer will

readily appreciate. She knew her audience of one intimately
—his grim childhood, his rejection by his father coupled
with the preference shown for his brothers. Like Henry, and
totally unlike the sad little wife who had been thrust upon
him, Diane was not especially gifted intellectually nor given
to any pastime which called for the slightest exertion of
the mind. Paradoxically, she had the advantage of not even
being, by any standards, beautiful. The many celebrated
representations of her—on canvas, in bronze or marble—are
the creative inventions of Cellini, Primaticcio, the Clouets,
Jean Goujon, and others who may never even have seen her
and were, in any case, more concerned with perpetuating a
legend than in portraying its living embodiment. Those few
portraits, mostly pen and ink sketches, which by reason of
date, authorship, or external evidence can be accepted as
being faithful, show a stern-faced woman with an ungen-
erous mouth, a nose a trifle too long, and eyes that do not
appear accustomed to smiling. Even her lover, in the full
tide of his love, is not blinded. He writes: "It is not beauty
which a light breeze can ruffle, as much as you that pleases
me." And it is not hard to imagine that he is thinking not
only about his beloved but also about the unlamented
Duchess of Étampes and all the clouds of pretty butterflies
that fluttered around the figure of his father.

The contemporary explanation for Diane's extraordinary
hold on Henry was that she had bewitched or enchanted him.
That she did, but not with drugs—any more than she owed
her eternal youth, as Brantôme relates, to drinking a daily
potion concocted of powdered gold. Her conquest was
achieved with his willing cooperation and with the attributes
she had: a fondness for the outdoors and a healthy, robust
constitution which she guarded by simple living, ample exercise and, anomalous for her time, daily baths in clear, cold
water. These, and above all the happy coincidence of her
name.

PATIENCE

Diane de Poitiers became, by the sheer force of her will, Diana the huntress. As in every other project she undertook, there was nothing haphazard about planning the transformation. A recent study* succeeds in tracing how Diane herself created the myth and encouraged every step of its development, a "stunning conjunction" whereby a living person appropriated for herself a ready-made, divine personality. The part was perfect. Not only was Diana the goddess of the hunt, still the supreme pastime of royalty, but she had also acquired, during the Christian moralization and adaptation of classical mythology, attributes of chastity and purity. What better way to set the proper stamp on the royal liaison —to distinguish it from the profane adulteries of past monarchs—than to have the King worship at such an altar? And what satisfaction it must have brought to the Duchess of Valentinois who, in common with her lowly sisters of the bourgeoisie, shared an abiding preoccupation with maintaining all the appearances of respectability.†

During Francis's time, Diane could not launch her campaign without risking ridicule. Although the King was unfailingly courteous to everyone, and particularly to so high a personage as the Grande Sénéschale of Normandy, his chivalry was not shared by all his subjects. Clément Marot, the King's informal poet laureate, annually amused the ladies of the Court by addressing to them New Year's Day greetings —his *Étrennes*. He could turn a graceful compliment, but he could also throw a well-aimed, cruel barb, such as this stanza directed to Diane:

* *Diane de Poitiers et le Mythe de Diane* by Françoise Bardon (Paris, Presses Unversitaires de France, 1963).
† Once, while the King was staying at Les Tournelles, one of the royal residences in Paris, and Diane was lodged at a nearby house which had once belonged to the Duchess of Étampes, she chanced upon an underground passage that connected the two establishments. She indicated her desire that the fact of its existence should be discreetly made known at Court, but ordered the passage sealed.

Que voulez-vous, Diane bonne,
Que vous donne?
Vous n'eûtes, comme j'entends,
Jamais tant d'heur au printemps
Qu'en automne.

What do you wish, Diana fair,
What can I bring you?
You did not have, so I am told,
As much good fortune in the spring
As you are having in the fall.

The Duchess of Étampes also seldom failed to take the opportunity of reminding one and all about Diane's advanced age, referring to her habitually as "La Vieille" (the old lady) and commissioning lesser poets to compose lengthy, heavy-handed "odes" to her grey hair, false teeth, and pomaded, wrinkled cheeks.

Shortly after Francis's death, however, a long, anonymous poem appeared, ostensibly addressed to Henry and asking him, in his new quality as King, to redress an ancient wrong. This faux pas had been committed by a young Trojan shepherd boy named Paris, who in the callowness of youth, had awarded a golden apple to Venus, thereby spurning and offending her rival goddesses, Juno and Athena. In this new version, the cast of contestants was altered to the extent of substituting Artemis—Diana—for Athena and having her emerge victorious from the contest. The theme of the new mythology had been sounded, and every poet in France who valued his patronage was quick to devise his own variations upon it. Jacques Pelatier du Mans wrote:

Ne vante plus, o Rome, ta Lucrèce,
Cessez, Thébains, pour Corinne, combattre:
Taire te faut de Pénélope, o Grèce,
Encore moins pour Hélène débattre,
Et toi, Égypte, oste ta Cléopatre:
La France seule a tout cela et mieux,

PATIENCE

En quoy Diane a l'un des plus beaux lieux,
Soit en vertu, beauté, faveur et race!
Car si cela elle n'avoit des Cieux
D'un si grand Roy n'eust mérité la grace.

Praise no longer, O Rome, thy Lucrecia!
Stop, Thebans, to boast of Corinne!
Sing not of Penelope, Greece!
Nor will Helen our contest now win.
Cleopatra, O Egypt, forget!
For France can surpass them in fame;
Diane outstrips them all
In her virtue, her beauty, her line and her name;
These gifts to her only Heaven could bring
To earn the favor of so great a king.

Even Pierre de Ronsard, the most illustrious poet of the age, could not escape wholly from participating in the chorus, although the verses he contributed were not among his most inspired:

Seray-je seul vivant en France de vostre age,
Sans chanter vostre nom, si craint et si
puissant,
Diray-je point d'honneur de vostre beau
croissant,
Feray-je point pour vous quelque immortel
ouvrage?

Shall I alone in the France of your time
Not sing your name, so feared and sublime?
Shall I not honor the fair moon's rise
By offering you an immortal prize?

That Pierre de Ronsard was capable of better effort mattered neither to Henry, who would not have discerned the difference, nor to Diane. She accepted graciously the lines dedicated to her, but her own tastes ran to more substantial expressions of artistic enterprise: sculpture, gold medallions, and, above all, architecture. A proper goddess required a proper temple, and Diane determined to erect hers at Anet.

81

The house had remained as she had left it after her husband's death, a frowning stone fortress with vast, echoing chambers and all the functioning paraphernalia of an earlier era—moats, watchtowers, and battlements. In 1545, Diane began quietly acquiring the properties adjoining the dense woods which surrounded the house. Two years later, when Henry's elevation had put her beyond the reach of criticism, she ordered the ancient building to be razed and commissioned Philibert Delorme, the most gifted architect of the time, to begin construction of a new establishment. Unfortunately, all but a few tantalizing fragments were pulled down by the vengeful mobs of the Revolution, but a complete description as well as minute drawings of the new château, which was not completed until 1554, are included in Androuet de Cerceau's great work, *Les Plus Excellens Bastiments de France*.

The new Anet formed an immense rectangle, three sides of which consisted of a graceful *corps de logis* (detached building) the like of which had never before been seen in France, or anywhere in Europe since antiquity. Searching for a unifying theme that would embody stateliness, grace, elegance, and timeless purity, Delorme rejected the models of the Italian Renaissance which had been so freely adapted by French architecture. Instead, he reached back to the glory of classical Rome. The entire ground floor of the palace consisted of a continuous Doric colonnade so contrived that its repeated pattern of capitals, entablatures, and friezes formed both a decorative unity and a balcony supporting the windows of the upper story. The colonnade enclosed a court of honor laid out in the formal fashion of a French garden. Beyond the principal structures lay the heronries, the aviaries, the stables, and, in a corner of the old fortress which has been left standing, the kennels. At Henry's suggestion, the basic building material was to be white Normandy stone to which small deposits of black silex had been added, so that the entire edifice would literally carry Diane's chosen colors. Everywhere—on the capitals of the columns, the pavements, the inlaid floors, the doors and windows, the ceilings, the carpets and paneling, even the plates and crockery—the interlaced initials H and D confronted the eye. But Anet was intended by Diane to be more than a sumptuous trysting place for lovers. The wonder of the palace, the unmistakable statement of its central theme, confronted the visitor as he approached the principal façade. Surmounting the three-tiered gate with its frieze of interlaced crescent moons stood a great clock and what appeared to be a hunting scene frozen in bronze. Upon the hour, however, the pack of hounds leapt forward and the stag turned to run, striking off the hour with a delicate paw.

Inside, Diane crammed the spacious rooms with the product of two decades of assiduous acquisitiveness: chimney pieces that Cellini had made during the years he spent in France under Francis's patronage, a collection of Limousin's enamels, paintings of Primaticcio and Rosso, a series of tapestries recording episodes in the life of the other Diana, gifts of furniture, silver, statuary, and other thoughtful re-membrances from dignitaries French and foreign who knew the surest way to please the King of France. To stock her library shelves, Diane devised a simple scheme. When Francis had determined that there should be a comprehensive national library, he had decreed that a copy of every book published in the country should be sent to the Dépôt Royal. At Diane's suggestion, Henry amended the rule to increase that number to two copies.

Inside and out, Anet was an establishment of such studied perfection that only a goddess could preside over it, which was precisely the point. And should Henry ever be tempted to doubt this fact, he had only to look out into the garden in order to behold the goddess's actual image in marble. Jean Goujon's *Diane Chasseresse,* now one of the showpieces of the Louvre, represents the goddess as somewhat larger than life and perfectly nude. She is shown in a semirecumbent position, with her two dogs and a stag around whose neck one arm is gently thrown. The proportions of the impossibly long legs, the small, girlish breasts, the full shoulders and mature, ripe body are all wrong, but the total effect is of perfectly achieved, unearthly grace. Small wonder that Diane was pleased with the statue; the artist could not have succeeded more completely if he had read her mind.

VII

If dignitaries were quick to perceive how to please the new King of France, his humbler subjects were even quicker. For many centuries, the principal cities of France had vied for the honor of offering their sovereign an *entrée,* a triumphal welcome for which elaborate, appropriate pageants and tableaux were prepared and enacted. On Sunday, September 23, 1548, less than eighteen months after Henry's accession, this honor fell to Lyons. Because the city was then enormously wealthy as a banking center and the meeting place of great trade routes to Italy, Spain, and the Rhine, the ceremonies were especially lavish and splendid.

Just inside the gate through which Henry was to enter, fully grown live trees, shrubs, and bushes had been transplanted to create an artificial forest. Tamed deer and their young grazed peacefully while a stag stood guard over them. Then trumpets announced the arrival of the King, with the Duchess of Valentinois at his side, and the scene came to life. Out of the forest appeared a band of maidens led by a strikingly beautiful girl dressed in a brief black tunic covered with silver stars, and carrying a bow in her hand and a quiver over a bare shoulder. She paused as an enormous lion strode into view and tamely halted at her booted feet. With a graceful gesture, she looped a halter made of silver and black silk around its great mane and led the beast over to where the

'INA DE MEDICI OLHE
HENRICO II RE DI FRACIA

Catherine de' Medici, as she was portrayed in an Italian woodcut
published to celebrate the occasion of her *entreé* into Lyons in 1548.

King stood, begging him in appropriate verses to accept it as a modest gift from the grateful city. There was more—a combat of twelve gladiators, dressed in the fashion of Roman antiquity; a naval battle between galleys on the Rhone—but the point had been made. And underlined, for everywhere, decorating buildings and triumphal arches, hanging across the streets, even on the chairs reserved for the honored guests, were the interlaced initials H and D, embroidered in silver on black.

By tradition, the King and the Queen made their *entrées* separately, so that each could be suitably greeted without impinging on the honor accorded to the other. As Diane arrived with Henry, Catherine had therefore waited outside the gates. The Spanish ambassador later wrote home: "I am sending Your Highness a printed account of the King's entry into Lyons. I was present myself and I can assure you that it is accurate. It is indeed true that little could be seen when the Queen made her entry, because night came on . . . and the people say that, as she is not good looking, the King gave orders that her pageant should be kept back until a late hour, so that Her Highness should pass unnoticed."

Indeed, she was not good looking—not by conventional standards. One of the Venetians, Matteo Dandolo, writes that "She has the big eyes and thick lips of the Medici. Many say she strikingly resembles her great uncle, Pope Leo. But nevertheless, she loves the King above every other thing, so much so that the object of all her thoughts seems to be nothing else but how to please him and to be with him. For this reason, without having any regard either to the labor or to any sort of fatigue, she follows him always wherever she can."

The same account contains a description of the object of her affection: "His Majesty is in his twenty-ninth year, and notwithstanding that I have previously represented him to your excellencies as a prince of pale countenance and disposition so melancholy that many of his familiars had never seen him laugh, I can assure you that he has now become gay,

that his disposition is cheerful and that the state of his health
is excellent. . . . He is extremely well-proportioned of body,
rather more tall than short, and in his person both pre-
possessing and courageous. He favors the game of tennis to
the point of never failing to play every day, and sometimes
even after such exertions passes two or three hours at games
of arms, which having witnessed them myself, I can say
are not always without danger. . . . He is temperate in his
personal habits, and as for carnal pleasures, if one were to
compare him to the King his father or to certain other de-
ceased kings, one may well call him chaste. Moreover, the
Court which was then among the most licentious, is now
quite proper."

This last observation is testament to Diane's success in
achieving the appearance of respectability. But the Senate
of Venice was less interested in Henry's domestic arrangements than in his probable behavior as King of France, and
in this respect the ambassador could give his superiors only
scant assurance. His Majesty, he reported, was disposed to
enlarge his state and was not disinclined from war as a means
of achieving his end. Furthermore, the Venetian noted,
"though the King speaks French, Italian, and Spanish, he is
not well educated." And, most alarming of all, ". . . the King
his father was not fond of him and, during his own lifetime,
did nothing to train him for the management of the state,
to the extent that when he came to the throne he was, one
may say, barren of all notions of how to govern so powerful
a kingdom."

There is no indication that Henry tried to remedy this
lapse. Nor, given the character of the men with whom he
surrounded himself, was he likely to have received sound or
impartial counsel. Almost from the start they had chosen up
sides—everyone else against the Guises, with Diane skillfully
and profitably playing the game of balance of power—and
appealed to Henry's sense of loyalty to advance their private
causes. A far more intelligent man would have found it

difficult to govern under these circumstances; Henry hardly attempted it. With time, his mind hardened along with his body. Unable to comprehend the subtle forces that pulled at him—both inside his kingdom and around its frontiers, where Spain, England, Rome, and the new Lutheran princes of Germany were waiting for their chance to pounce—he retreated into a more congenial age.

In the middle of the sixteenth century, when Montaigne and Cervantes were writing and the Elizabethan Age was about to dawn, Henry II tried to will France into a new, romanticized Middle Ages. Castiglione was forgotten, Rabelais proscribed, and Machiavelli unread except by Catherine de' Medici. Instead, the Court avidly followed the adventures of Amadis de Gaule, a long series of chivalric potboilers which had been written in the fourteenth century by an obscure Portuguese hack named Vasco da Labeira. They had first been translated into Spanish around 1500 and then into French in time for Francis to enjoy the first installments as a pastime during his last, painful years. Amadis, as given in French, is written in the simple, naïve style of a children's story as it follows the complicated, improbable adventures of the title character. He is a road-company Lancelot or Tristan who wanders through magic forests, single-handedly challenges giants and sorcerers, and attacks impregnable castles, all in honor of the proud Orianne, his fair lady. There were in all twelve volumes in the cycle, which appeared in France between 1540 and 1556. Midway, the translator apologizes for taking certain liberties with the original text "in order better to reflect the customs and the fashions of today." Indeed, the original author would have had to be clairvoyant to have known that Amadis would quarrel with his aging father and be obliged to leave the Court. Or that, in exile, he would take for himself the name of *Le Beau Ténébreux,* which both in appearance and temperament is an apt if flattering description of Orianne's real-life champion. But lest there were any lingering doubts in anyone's mind, the last two volumes were dedicated to the Duchess of Valentinois.

The first family of France—or more precisely, two thirds of it—read Amadis to each other during their long, leisurely afternoons and evenings together. Others followed suit, to the extent that the story became "less the mirror in which a generation is reflected than the model it chose to emulate."* How much of the narrative Diane took seriously is a matter of conjecture. What mattered was Amadis's unshakable constancy and, of course, the purity of his passion. Henry, however, entered zestfully into the make-believe world. The custom of jousting, which had almost completely fallen out of favor with France's maturity, was revived. At every pretext, gentlemen led by the King caused themselves to be encased in full-dress armor and rode out behind trumpeters and heralds to belabor one another with sharp and heavy instruments while the ladies whose colors they carried sat in tribunes and marveled at their skill.

In contrast to this violent, occasionally cruel side of his nature, Henry was a patient, gentle, and devoted father. By 1556, the royal family was complete. Catherine's last confinement, on June 24 of that year, had produced twin girls who died almost immediately and whose birth came close to costing her own life. One son had died in 1550, at the age of two, but still living were four boys, three of whom were in turn to become Kings of France, and three girls. Raised together with them, as was the custom, were the two natural children Henry had produced. One was the girl, Diane, whose birth had confirmed the suspicion of Catherine's sterility. The other was a boy, named the Bastard of Angoulême, who was the product of an extremely transitory affair with a Scottish girl named Mary Flemming. The weight of evidence seems to hold that she was assisted in seducing the King by one of Diane's political rivals, who

* Edouard Bourciez in Les Moeurs Polies et la Littérature de Cour sous Henri II, published in 1886, but still the key work on the subject.

wished thereby to undermine her hold on him. The plan was only partially successful because, having blossomed into motherhood, the very attractive young lady was so proud of her achievement that she could not stop talking about it as if it had been accomplished by special divine favor. Diane and Catherine, who knew better, for once joined forces to demand her dismissal from the Court.

Henry's eldest son, the Dauphin, was named Francis after his grandfather, but unhappily heredity played a cruel trick on him. He was an awkward, waxy-cheeked child whose early years were a chain of accidents, misfortunes, and diseases. One senses that Henry empathized with the boy and took pains to make his childhood happier than his own had been. There is, for instance, in the royal correspondence, a letter written to the children's guardian when young Francis was approaching his fourth birthday: "He does not want to be dressed as a girl any longer," wrote the father, "and I quite agree with him. It is quite reasonable that he should have breeches, since he asks for them."

But Henry's favorite in the royal nursery—"the most perfect child that I have ever seen," he once called her—was a little girl who was not even his own. She had arrived in 1548 with all the retinue appropriate to her rank, for although not quite six years old she was, by the sad occasion of the death of her father and the absence of other children, Queen of Scotland. Her inclusion in the royal household of France, however, was not due to her rank alone, nor to the unsettled state of affairs in her own kingdom. This situation had simply advanced her arrival by a few years because she was already formally betrothed to the Dauphin. The alliance had been eagerly pressed by members of the Guise family, whose sister was the prospective bride's mother, and who therefore stood to add one half of the throne of France to their other holdings. No one, of course, could foretell then that what appeared to be a stunning coup would soon enough become the cause of tragic consequences. For the moment, a single ray of happiness had entered young Francis's life. Quick, lively, pretty—everything that he was not—Mary Stuart became the center of the boy's existence. He followed her everywhere, and she returned his affection. The Italian Giovanni Capello, who visited the Court in 1555, noticed that the two children were fond of "going off together hand in hand to the corner of a room, where no one could overhear their little secrets."

VIII

Elsewhere in France, uglier scenes were being enacted. Brutality and cruelty had never lain very deep beneath the veneer of manners upon which the century prided itself. Hunting, violent games, and above all war, the supreme gentleman's sport, served as outlets for their expression. That captured cities were looted, their defenders butchered after they had surrendered, and their women abused or raped, were all accepted standards of behavior. Nor did looting end with inanimate objects; frequently, young girls and children were taken as victors' spoils, to be held for ransom or sold under one guise or another. Civilians, too, were offered an opportunity to participate, at second hand at least, in these grisly pleasures. For Parisians, a favorite occupation was to stroll to the Place de Grève, the great cleared space which sloped from the rear of Notre Dame to the edge of the river. Here, crowds including gentlemen and ladies as well as artisans, students, and clerks on their day off, gathered early to secure a good vantage point of the stage, a raised wooden platform on which the scenery varied with the nature of the program. For common thieves and cutpurses, it consisted of a horizontal cross so constructed that arms and legs could be stretched taut and then broken sharply at the joints with a round-tipped iron bar. The victim was then bent back on himself so that he could be attached to the circumference of a wooden wheel and left to the contemplation of his sins. Prostitutes were brought naked, riding backward on a donkey, then tied to posts and whipped. But the best show—for it seemed to bring forth the most agonizing screams and desperate convulsions—was the slow burning of blasphemers and heretics. There was, after Henry had come to the throne, no shortage of this sort of performance.

In fairness, his father had bequeathed him an unresolved problem. Francis had never brought himself to support the measures urged on him to eradicate the movement toward heresy—or, depending on the point of view, religious reform. Rather, he had chosen to pretend the issue no longer existed. By virtue of divine clemency and the punishment already meted out, he pronounced in his edict of Coucy on July 16, 1535, that heresy had formally ceased in France, and that those few who persisted in their wrongheadedness had only to abjure it in order to receive full pardon. The period of amnesty was twice extended to give the last of the laggards a chance for painless absolution. But far from flocking back, the heretics attracted new converts. Moreover, now stirred by a new voice, they began to organize themselves in earnest.

The voice belonged to the son of a minor ecclesiastic lay official named Gérard Chauvin. Born in 1509 in Noyon in the province of Picardy, the boy, Jean, was just completing his studies as a lawyer when he saw first his father and then his older brother excommunicated, hounded, and finally refused Christian burial for having allegedly flirted with forbidden ideas. He abandoned his new profession and gave himself over to the study of the same ideas. Obliged to move constantly, once arrested and released, he finally left France and settled in Switzerland, where in 1536 he Latinized his name and as John Calvin published a book entitled *Institutes of the Christian Religion*.

Martin Luther had cast a cataclysmic blow against the established Church. He had challenged its infallibility and therefore encouraged others to tinker with its teachings, accepting some and rejecting others in favor of interpretations of their own. But he did not, in France at any rate, lay the foundation for a new religion. That remained for the *Institutes,* which its twenty-seven-year-old author dedicated to Francis I, to accomplish. In clear, lucid Latin, which Calvin himself translated into French in 1541, the *Institutes* set down doctrine, discipline, and the basis for organization. Nevertheless, it had been impossible in a single volume, even one whose first edition ran to 520 pages, to anticipate every problem and detail of dogma, ritual, or procedure. From Geneva, where he established himself, Calvin maintained a steady, voluminous correspondence with his followers in France, tirelessly answering their questions and adjudicating their disputes.*

Calvin's influence, coupled with royal clemency, caused reform to flourish, particularly in southern and central France. When new royal decrees of escalating severity did appear, their effect was blunted by the far more effective organization of the reformers. Calvin had taught them to band together—the term "Huguenot" which was soon to come into use is most probably a Gallicization of *Eidgenossen,* the German for "confederates" or "comrades." Sporadic attempts to disperse local groups of reformers ended up as pitched battles or butcheries, depending on the odds. To deal with them all, as the Church urged, would have given great parts of France over to civil war.

* But he could not escape the ultimate irony. Having dedicated himself to destroy intolerance, Calvin found it necessary to resort to it himself, to the extent of condemning to be burned at the stake a critic named Michael Servetus whose ideas he deemed dangerous. A sense of humor not being among his gifts, he tried to still the clamor which this act occasioned with a pamphlet entitled *Declaration Wherein It Is Demonstrated That It Is Proper To Punish Heretics.*

93

Henry was reluctant to take this step, not so much out of compassion or tolerance, for he possessed little of either, as because he had other plans for his troops than to order them to slaughter fellow citizens. But there were other methods. Among the first of his royal acts was the creation of a special court in Paris charged with the specific duty of prosecuting heretics. For self-evident reasons, this tribunal rapidly became known as the *Chambre Ardente*.

The edifice of Renaissance justice still rested on its medieval foundations of "preparatory questions" and "extraordinary questions" posed to suspects with the aid of ropes, red-hot metal, boiling liquids, sharp objects. One common procedure consisted of seating the suspect on a stool, placing two stout boards on either side of each foot, securing them tightly at the ankle and just below the knee, and tying the entire apparatus together. Wedges of metal or wood were then hammered in between the two inner boards until a satisfactory answer was received, or until the bones gave way and cracked open through the flesh and skin. Under normal circumstances, such methods could not be used before presumption of guilt had been established. To ease the juridical duties of the *Chambre Ardente,* Henry ordered this nicety suspended; it was sufficient for a witness to swear that the accused was a heretic and for the presiding magistrates to believe him. In 1551, another edict was issued to provide additional motivation for both parties: henceforth, informers would receive one third of the goods of those on whom they had informed, and every three months special sessions of the court would be held to test the continued, unshaken faith of the magistrates themselves. Their record of convictions was, of course, the most eloquent evidence of that faith.

Despite Henry's efforts, and possibly in part as a result of them, the reformers increased in both number and fervor. By the hundreds, they journeyed to Geneva to listen to Calvin and then returned home to start new congregations—consistories, as they were called in the new evangelical system.

IX

Little has been recorded of Catherine's activities during the early years of her husband's reign, and none of it suggests that his attitude toward her changed in the least. On the contrary, he appeared to take every opportunity to humiliate her publicly, as he had in Lyons. By ancient tradition, the King alone was anointed and crowned upon his accession. The Queen could, at his desire, be subsequently honored with a coronation of her own. It therefore may have puzzled some people familiar with the domestic climate of the Court when Henry accorded this recognition to Catherine on July 10, 1549. If so, both they and the great crowd that had gathered for the occasion were enlightened quickly enough. They saw, in the cortege entering the abbey church of Saint-Denis just outside of Paris, the Duchess of Valentinois walking among the Princes of the Blood, and noticed that she had for this one occasion eschewed her black robes and instead was wearing an ermine *surcot* over an opulent jewel-encrusted gown— an exact duplicate of Catherine's ceremonial costume. Further, and this had never happened before or would again even under the imperious Louis XIV, they saw the royal mistress solemnly take her place near the altar directly at the side of His Very Christian Majesty. Because of the length of the elaborate ceremony, provision had been made for the heavy gold and jeweled crown to be removed for a time from the Queen's head. At the appointed moment, one of the Duchess's daughters, both of whom had been given roles of the highest honor in the ritual, carefully lifted the crown and placed it on the cushion set directly at her mother's feet.

Three years later, as Henry was preparing to march off to war in Germany, it became necessary for him to appoint a regent to serve during his absence. Again, tradition dictated that this honor go to a close member of the royal family—the eldest son, a mother, a wife. Since the Dauphin was only eight years old, Henry had little choice. But still, when the formal document was drawn up at his orders it specified that Catherine would be obliged to share the regency with the Guardian of the Seals, a relatively obscure and unimportant Court functionary named Bertand who owed his position to the Duchess of Valentinois's influence. Again Catherine swallowed her pride, but her shame was such that she took the unprecedented step of refusing to permit the publication of the document.

Whatever her husband thought or was induced to think of her, more impartial witnesses who knew her held a higher opinion of her abilities. The Venetian Lorenzo Contarini, for instance, who had then known her for three years, wrote in 1552: "She is not beautiful, but she possesses extraordinary wisdom and prudence; there is no doubt that she would be adept at governing, even though she is neither consulted nor considered to the extent that she deserves to be." Catherine was thirty-three years old when Contarini ventured this opinion. Soon enough his judgment would be tested.

Meanwhile, since she was blocked from exercising more serious functions, her vast energies turned toward the creation of a world around herself. Contarini had also noted that her natural disposition was *liberalissima.* Her annual personal allowance was 200,000 *écus,* but because she maintained a "fine court of lords and ladies," this amount was not adequate and was supplemented with frequent extraordinary donations from royal funds. From the testimony of others, it appears that the money was well spent. The many personal memoirs of the period vie with each other in describing the sumptuousness and sophistication of the *Cercle de la Reine*—not failing to mention their authors' own participation in it. Brantôme, who served at the Court as a gentleman of the chamber, asserts that Catherine's circle was "a true terrestrial paradise, the ornament of France . . . where the fairest of ladies, dressed like goddesses but as accommodating as mortals, shone like stars in a clear night sky." Even a serious modern scholar such as Frantz Funck-Brentano yields to the spell of evocation.* "The seats were of unequal height," he writes in describing a typical soirée, "which enhanced the charm of the assemblage. Some of the ladies sat on low cushions, in such fashion that their voluminous silken robes, in the brightest colors, formed great glistening peonies with which the entire room appeared to be sown. . . . Let us imagine the apartments of the time, entirely painted in lively colors with accents of gold from the wainscotting to the ceilings, which were divided into deep caissons by decorated beams. Or else the walls were covered with great cordovan leather hangings, tinted and rubbed to shine dully like old copper or bronze. The floors were covered with oriental rugs which the Queen ordered in Venice. All the furniture was equally painted in bright shades, set off with gold. . . . Men and women dressed sumptuously: silk, brocade, cut velvet, lace, fine nets of spun gold encrusted with jewelry. Their faces were touched up with color of provocative shades. Servants, too, pageboys, lackeys and ushers, were dressed in uniforms of striking hue and combination—yellow and red, green and white." In truth, as Brantôme had said, "the world had never seen its like."

Catherine brought to the French Court its first touch of true cosmopolitanism. Among the two hundred or so young ladies who comprised her personal following—Brantôme lists 174 of them by name and breeding, and courteously apologizes for his oversights—were many Italian damsels whose parents had moved to France in order to escape the political uncertainties that chronically plagued their native peninsula. They had been joined by Spanish and Portuguese cousins, by some favored visitors from across the Rhine, by the Scots

* In *La Renaissance* (Paris, Librairie Arthème Fayard, 1935).

ladies of Mary Stuart's retinue. Some were merely decorative, but even they had at least to pretend and make an effort in order not to be ashamed, for artists and poets were as welcome in this Court as titled young gentlemen. Flirtation and gossip had their place, but a favorite pastime consisted of a form of impromptu theatricals in which elaborate charades, inspired by bits of mythology or classical verse, were enacted.

Spirituality, however, stopped short of the dining room doors. By the middle of the sixteenth century the French had become as convinced as they are now that they ate better, more knowledgeably, than any other nation on earth. Meals were taken four or five times a day. Dinner, which was served late in the afternoon, properly consisted of at least ten courses. In the case of one particular banquet which the city of Paris offered to Catherine, and for which the receipts have been preserved, one of these courses alone included thirty peacocks, thirty-three pheasants, twenty-one swans, forty pies of Guinea hens, and an equal number made with quail, as well as unnumbered quantities of capons, partridges, and pigeons. To wash down the contents of this aviary, there were six hogsheads each containing fifty-nine gallons of *vin clairet* and two hogsheads of white. Some delicacies of the period, such as herons, have now lost their places on most menus, but so esteemed were these birds, roasted whole and served surrounded with artichokes, chestnuts, asparagus, and tiny cabbages, that Francis had ordered two heronries built at Fontainebleau just to provide for the needs of the royal table. Chefs, rather than mere cooks, made their appearance in the sixteenth century and competed for acclaim with new concoctions. A novelty in Catherine's time was *pâté de foie;* another, which became a particular favorite of her future son-in-law, was mayonnaise. So firm was the belief that French cooking was superior, if indeed not the only one fit to be eaten, that when Henry sent two diplomatic emissaries on a short mission across the Channel to Edward VI, he forbade them or anyone in their retinue to touch any local food. Instead, they brought along twelve horses laden with every kind of game and fruit so succulent that, as Vielleville, one of the ambassadors, reports, "All the *milords* cursed the intemperance of their climate which forbade the existence of these dainties."

In the face of such temptation, the riding and hunting that still occupied so much of their days helped to prevent the young ladies from spilling out of their tight-bodiced gowns. But in addition, a new, more congenial form of exercise came into vogue. Dancing of one sort or another had long had a place in polite circles, but during Catherine's time it reached heights of popularity that can perhaps best be measured by the number of ecclesiastic tracts fulminating against it as a devil's creation leading to mortal sin—an objective that, in the minds of some participants at least, it certainly was intended to help achieve.

But for the most part the preachers' admonitions were unnecessary, or at least premature. No longer were royal funds expended for the upkeep of *filles publiques;* nor were seductions, real or feigned, a topic for morning conversations. The fiction of Henry's relationship with Diane dictated the moral mood of the Court; if a gentleman's gallantry gained him any reward, it had to be enjoyed under the deepest cloak of dissimulation. Catherine, if anything, was even more severe than her rival. Even a minor breach of decorum, such as that committed by an unfortunate gentleman who, in the heat of repartee, was heard to refer to Mlle de Meray, one of the more senior members of the Court, as *une grande courçière bardable* ("an easily mountable warhorse"), was punishable by exile, at the Queen's pleasure. When one of her maids-of-honor, the well-born Mlle de Rohan, had the poor fortune of being caught *in delicto* with the very dashing Duke of Nemours, she was given a royal tongue-lashing and sent home in disgrace to her parents. Summing it up, as knowledgeable an observer as Contarini could report that "the Court which under the late King was the most licentious, is now rather regular."

Henry was only an occasional participant at Catherine's circle. By preference he spent his time at Anet with Diane or else pursuing his royal duties. These, at the urging of the Guises, turned out after 1552 to consist of waging almost continuous war. The campaign that had begun in the spring of that year against Germany did little to add to the territory of France or to the luster of Henry's name as a warrior-king. What laurels there were to be had descended instead upon the brow of Francis, Duke of Guise, who captured the fortified town of Metz and held it through a winter's half-hearted siege by imperial troops.

Francis de Guise returned to Paris where he paraded in triumph at the side and modestly a half-pace behind his sovereign—a simple soldier expecting no reward other than the privilege of having been able to serve his country. But no such modesty restrained other members of his family, and notably his brother Charles who had succeeded their uncle as Cardinal of Lorraine. As adept at accumulation as his dear friend the Duchess of Valentinois, the Cardinal accepted whatever gratitude France, through her King, saw fit to show his family. An impartial observer—the Italian Michieli—noted: "The Cardinal, who is the principal man of the House . . . is by common agreement the greatest political power in the realm; no one is comparable to him. He has not yet reached the age of thirty-seven; he is endowed with a marvelous intellect which grasps the gist of what is being said to him before one has finished speaking; he has a remarkable memory, a fine and noble face, rare eloquence which ranges over every subject. He is very learned; he knows Greek, Latin, Italian; he speaks the last-named language with a facility that amazes us Italians ourselves. . . . But his great fault is avarice, which goes even beyond that which usually distinguishes the French nation."

In pursuit of another Metz, Henry sent his armies marching across one after another of France's frontiers, north into
the Lowlands, southward into the Italian quagmire, back
into Germany. Everywhere, the enemy was the same Charles
V who had successfully contained France for nearly forty
years and had frustrated the ambitions of two of her
sovereigns.

Francis, in the closing years of his life, had been able to
come to terms with the Emperor. Henry, who blamed him
personally for his own darkened childhood, never did. He
had started his reign by invoking an ancient feudal prerogative and commanding Charles, who by possession of certain
provinces was nominally his vassal, to attend his coronation.
The Emperor's reply was that he would be glad to comply, at
the head of 50,000 troops. Now, unable to beat Charles in
the field, Henry tried his hand at diplomacy, concluding two
alliances within two months which not only canceled but
contradicted each other. Finally, it was the Emperor who
broke off the rivalry. A strange, complicated man to the
end, he voluntarily stepped down from his several thrones
in 1556 and retired to the remoteness of a monastery at Yuste
in the Spanish Estremadura, having given the imperial
crown of Austria to his brother, Ferdinand, and the rest of
his vast holdings, including Spain, Naples, and the Netherlands to his son, Philip II.

His departure did nothing to advance France's fortunes.
On the contrary, Philip's marriage to Mary Tudor restored
the old alliance between Spain and England and placed a
dangerous enemy only a short sea passage from France. The
threat became urgent with the landing of a force of English
troops in Flanders, where they joined an army led by Philip's
ally, Philibert, Duke of Savoy. Deprived of his own best
forces, which Guise had taken into Italy where there was
hope of reaping some glory, Henry assembled his available
regiments to intercept the invaders. The two armies met on
August 10, 1557, at Saint-Quentin on the River Somme,

which was to cost France so dearly of her young manhood in centuries to come.

In this instance, the technical details of the encounter are of interest solely to military historians, and then only as a classical example of bungling. Within five hours, the French army was in full flight, having left behind 3,000 dead and 7,000 prisoners, including their commander in chief and most of his principal officers. Paris, which lay undefended three days' march away, reacted predictably to the news of the disaster. Those citizens who had the means fled the city; those who did not took advantage of their departure to begin looting; the Dauphin was whisked away to the safety of the Loire. The Duchess of Valentinois discovered urgent business which required her presence, not in Anet, which lay dangerously close to the battle lines, but in Chenonceaux.

Catherine stayed behind. From Compiègne, where he had established his field headquarters, Henry sent her a message by the hand of one of the royal secretaries, requesting that she obtain from the municipal administration new funds adequate to raise a fresh army to continue the war. It was, after nearly a quarter century in France, the first great public occasion of her life. How she discharged it is described in a dispatch from the Venetian Giacomo Soranzo, dated August 14, 1557: "Yesterday the Most Christian Queen went in person to the Parlement . . . and in a very grave form of speech represented the present need. Her Majesty spoke with such earnestness and eloquence that everyone was moved; and she said in conclusion that the Most Christian King required a vote of 300,000 francs, adding that she would then retire, to leave them free as usual to deliberate, which she did by withdrawing into a room. It was immediately voted to comply with Her Majesty's demands. . . . The Queen thanked them in so sweet a form of speech that she made well-nigh the whole assembly shed tears from emotion. Thereupon [they] adjourned, greatly applauding Her Majesty, and with such marks of extreme satisfaction as to defy exaggeration; and all over Paris nothing is talked of but the prudent and gracious manner adopted by Her Majesty in this business, everybody declaring that, had it been managed by any other person, there would neither have been so much liberality nor so much brilliance to give. The determination of this city to give His Majesty 300,000 francs will yield about a million and a half in gold; it being customary that when Paris forms a resolve of this sort she does so for herself and for all the other towns of the kingdom, each of them thus knowing her proportional quota. In a month the King will have about 60,000 men."*

X

By design or insensitivity, Henry had handled the matter of persuading the tightest-fisted citizens in Christendom to tax themselves as if it were the most commonplace domestic detail—a busy husband requesting his wife to fill in for him at a civic function. But even he must have been aware that something of moment had happened, because the very next commemorative medal that he ordered struck bore, for the first time in his reign, the profiles of both the King of France and its Queen. This could not have but pleased Catherine, but no doubt more gratifying to her was another novelty, noted by the diplomats at Court. They reported that it was now the King's habit to spend a few hours every evening in the company of the Queen.

In other respects, the order of things did not change. The

---

* The troops were indeed raised, but hardly in time to have defended the city had Philip determined to capture it. Instead, however, he forbade the Duke of Savoy from advancing. According to Monluc's memoirs, it was Providence that had lent a hand; "God," he writes, "was pleased miraculously to deprive the King of Spain of his right judgment." A more likely explanation is that the King of Spain did not wish a subordinate to reap the honor of capturing so great a prize.

Duchess of Valentinois, back from her estates, still held her position as if nothing had happened, and the Guises managed to improve theirs by one giant step. Immediately upon receiving news of Saint-Quentin, Francis de Guise had disengaged his troops and brought them by forced march across the Alps back into France. There, the sensible course would have been to dislodge the remnants of the Duke of Savoy's army which, in the accepted fashion, had settled down to live off the country. But such an enterprise, however much it would have been welcomed by the population, was not likely to add luster to a soldier's name. Guise chose instead to launch a surprise attack on Calais.

The port city and its outlying forts had been in English hands for more than two centuries, long enough for the French to have come to believe the inscription carved over one of its gates: "Then shall the Frenchmen Calais win when iron and lead like cork shall swim." Guise made elaborate preparations to invest the city, writing all his orders with his own hand so that there would be no possibility of misunderstanding or treachery. On New Year's Day, 1558, he threw all 20,000 of his troops against the outer ring of fortifications. The fighting was surprisingly light, for once again Guise's good luck held. The English, too, had believed their own inscription, and left the city guarded only by a midwinter garrison of some five hundred men.

The capture of Calais marked the final expulsion of the English from French soil, erased the humiliation of Saint-Quentin and completed the task of making Francis of Guise into a national hero. Nothing, no honor could be denied him. But there was still nothing he wanted for himself. Nor, this time, did his brother, the Cardinal of Lorraine. There, however, was one thing the King could do, something which had been planned and would sooner or later take place in any event: the matter of the marriage between the Dauphin and Mary Stuart, their niece.

Catherine was opposed to the idea. Nearly every mother

of a young son feels, sometimes irrationally and perhaps selfishly, that he is not ready yet to take a wife. In this case, however, there was little question about it. The prospective groom had just turned fourteen years old, but he had remained a feeble child who had now grown into sullen adolescence. There is, moreover, good evidence that, in physiological terms, he had not yet attained puberty. By contrast the bride was an extraordinary young creature, not only physically but, apparently, in intellectual achievement as well. A letter from the Cardinal of Lorraine to her mother —his own sister—written shortly after Mary had turned thirteen, reports: "Your daughter is so fully grown in grandeur, style, goodness, beauty and wisdom that she is as perfectly accomplished in all these virtues as one can be, and it is impossible in this entire kingdom to find her match. I am further delighted to report to you, Madame, that the King has become so fond of her that he passes many an hour in her company, and that she for her part is able to entertain him with good and wise counsel, as if she were a woman of twenty-five years of age."

The Duchess of Valentinois was equally opposed to the wedding, but for reasons which had nothing to do with the Dauphin's well-being. She had watched with concern the star of the Guises ascend, and their own deference to her wane in proportion. The game of power balance that she had played with success for so many years required at least two players of nearly equal strength. Marriage into the royal family—to the very step of the throne—would put the Guises beyond any equilibrium she could devise. But despite the urgings of both wife and mistress, Henry was determined to proceed with the marriage without delay. If his resolve appeared firmer than that of a man merely wishing to reward a deserving friend, it may well be because, in the intrigues which swirled about their scheme, the Guises themselves had not sat idly by. In addition to the formal nuptial contract, the prospective bride had, at the urging of her uncles, also signed another, secret treaty by which she agreed to transfer to the King of France, in the event of her death without children, the kingdom of Scotland and all of her rights to the crown of England, until an indemnity of a million gold crowns had been paid him. In pressing for the marriage, Henry was persuaded that he was not losing a son, but gaining one and possibly two additional crowns for France.

The wedding of Francis of Valois and Mary Queen of Scots took place on Sunday, April 24, 1558 at the Cathedral of Notre-Dame in Paris, and it was, even by the standards of the French Court, an event of rare splendor.

Huge crowds had already gathered before the church when the bride's maternal uncle, Francis de Guise, in his new capacity as Grand Master of the King's Household, appeared on the scene. According to the official account of the ceremony, he immediately "showed himself a kind prince" by asking a number of gentlemen and nobles who had taken choice places on the scaffolding to step down so that the humbler spectators might enjoy a better view of the pageant. Thereupon, the festivities started with a parade of "trumpets, clarions, hautboys, flageolets, viols, violins, citherns, and an infinitude of other instruments, playing so melodiously that it was delightful to listen to them." Then came the bridal procession; the royal Princes "so richly clothed and adorned that it was marvelous to see them"; the cardinals, bishops and abbots; the Dauphin, escorted by his brothers; the bride's mother, with Henry holding her right hand and her brother of Lorraine her left hand. Then Catherine, the princesses, and the ladies of the Court, "so nobly accoutred that it would be impossible to write of it without too much prolixity."

The bride wore "a robe white as the lily, fashioned so sumptuously and richly that it could not in justice be described. Its train, which was of marvelous length, was borne by two young demoiselles. Around the bride's neck there hung a circlet of untold value, formed of jewels of great price, and on her head she wore a golden crown studded with pearls, diamonds, rubies, sapphires, emeralds and other gems of priceless value, the most remarkable of all being a carbuncle set in the middle, which was valued at 500,000 *écus* or more."

The Bishop of Paris received the King and the bridal pair on the porch of the Cathedral, and delivered "a learned and elegant oration," the words or theme of which were not included in the account. Then, as the principals made their way down the nave, heralds thrice shouted "Largesse!" and threw gold and silver coins toward the crowd. People scrambled "with such tumult, cries and clamor that thunder could have not been heard above the din; some fainted, others lost their cloaks, others their hats and divers garments. . . ."

After the ceremony came the nuptial supper, for which the forbidding great hall of the Palace of Justice had been "so magnificently decorated that one might have compared it to the Elysian fields." As course followed course, introduced by strains of music, the guests were so transported with delight that "the dames and demoiselles leaped in the air for joy." Then came the ball, with "masques, mummeries, fantasies, melodies, recreations, ballads and other games and pastimes." For a finale, a "fleet of ships with silver sails appeared, sometimes rocking as in harbor, sometimes gliding forward as on the open sea. Each of the princes embarked on one of these vessels which sailed away to the table at which the ladies of the Court sat, where he selected a shipmate."

XI

Although the royal marriage, coming on the heels of the capture of Calais, had rekindled the nation's spirit and raised the stature of the Guises, it had done little to change the military or political state of affairs. Hostilities between France and Spain resumed almost as soon as the last of the wedding guests had returned home and changed from silk doublet to armor. By mid-June, Francis of Guise was on the Moselle, attacking Thionville; another army had moved northward into Flanders along the North Sea coast. Through the summer and fall the fighting continued, with no decisive victories or disastrous defeats for either side. If there had ever been any purpose to the war, it had long since been forgotten, and any hope of gain was dissipated by its ruinous cost. Even the two principals had had enough. At one point during October, Henry and Philip found themselves at the head of their respective armies, separated only by a narrow river. One final battle could have settled matters. By tacit agreement it did not take place. Only the Guises wanted to continue, and in the end it was their insistence that helped bring the insanity to an end. Diane de Poitiers had watched their progress with concern and the axiomatic certainty that what was good for them was bad for her. As usual, she acted with great discretion, but there exists a letter, dated November 15, 1558, sent by Cardinal Trivulzio, the Papal Legate in France to his colleague, Cardinal Caraffa in Rome: "I wrote yesterday to your Illustrious Excellency informing you that there was no hope of peace. Today I hear from a most excellent source that His Majesty, returned from hunting, had a long conversation with Madame de Valentinois. . . . He went from there into the council of affairs, where he said that he had come to announce his decision in favor of peace. When one of the counselors wished to continue an argument against his decision, he bade him be silent."

Obviously it took more than one conversation to turn the tide, but Henry did achieve his peace, with the signing of the Treaty of Cateau-Cambrésis on April 3, 1559. It was a long, complicated document, for it had to redraw long stretches of frontier obliterated by seven years of war, and reach farther back to settle grievances caused by Francis I's forays into Italy, and even the effects of the original French expedition into Italy which had been led by the dwarfish Charles VIII in 1494. At Le Cateau-Cambrésis, France agreed to renounce all her claims on Italy, thus closing sixty-five years of costly futility; in exchange, she was allowed to keep Calais and Metz. Recent conquests in the Netherlands and Picardy were reciprocally restored. The full provisions of the treaty were so intricate that the question of whether it benefitted France or damaged it is still a subject of lively debate among historians.* Contemporary opinion was more one-sided, and was summed up by Francis de Guise with more bluntness than any other subject of Henry II would have dared allow himself. "Sire," he said upon being shown the signed document, "you have given away more in one day than we could have lost for you in thirty years."

Among the less controversial clauses of the treaty were the inevitable marriages intended to bind the parties in eternal amity. Philip II of Spain had been rendered a widower at thirty-one years of age by the death of Mary Tudor on November 16, 1558, a sad event which had the immeasurably more important side effect of placing her younger half-sister, Elizabeth, on the throne of England. Philip was now to receive as his bride Henry and Catherine's oldest daughter, Elizabeth.† Philibert, Duke of Savoy and the victor of Saint-

---

* Whatever else it accomplished the Treaty of Cateau-Cambrésis proved that Henry II was no better at negotiating than at the other arts of statecraft. It now appears that he could have held out for a much more favorable bargain, for there exists a communication, recently brought to light, from Philip of Spain to his principal negotiator. It reads in part: "I find myself under an absolute impossibility of continuing the war. . . . I have already spent 12 hundred thousand ducats which I raised two or three months ago, and I have need of another million in the coming month of March. . . . The situation seems to me so grave, that, under pain of losing everything, I must come to some sort of arrrangement. I am waiting with a very active impatience for news, but on no account whatever must these negotiations be broken off."
† The fact that she was barely sixteen years old and furthermore pledged since infancy to his own son, Don Carlos, apparently disturbed Philip far less than it did Schiller and Verdi, who used the unusual triangle as subjects of a tragedy and an opera.

Quentin, had already been given back his family's former estates which Francis had annexed in 1536; he was to be further rewarded—and tied to the royal house of Valois—with the person of Henry's own sister, Marguerite, a spinster lady of excellent breeding, lively intellect, and thirty-six years of age.

The marriages had been set for June 22 and July 1, 1559, but preparations for them, down to the minutest detail, had begun late in April. Catherine sat down to write her good friend, the Governor-General of Piedmont, asking him please to look after the bolts of cloth she had ordered and "to send them quickly to France and not allow any export duty to be charged on them for fear of delaying their delivery." Henry meanwhile supervised the removal of the pavement from Rue Saint-Antoine, then the widest in Paris, where the jousting lists and spectators' galleries for the inevitable tournaments were to be erected. Observing all the activities, the English ambassador, Nicholas Throckmorton, could report to his new sovereign that "'the King has borrowed 1,100,000 crowns to defray the setting-out of all those triumphs, and for the entertaining of all the princes which come hither."

The princes themselves began arriving on June 16, and with them opened the program of endless banquets and feasts, balls and parties. On the 18th, a thanksgiving service for the ratification of the Peace of Cateau-Cambrésis was held; on the 21st, the betrothal of Philip II and Elizabeth took place in the great hall of the Louvre, and on the following day the nuptial ceremony was performed at Notre-Dame. That same day, the Duke of Savoy who had courteously waited his turn, arrived, accompanied by "one hundred and fifty gentlemen dressed in doublets of red satin, crimson shoes and cloaks of black velvet embroidered with gold lace." The contract for his marriage to Madame Marguerite was signed on the 27th, and on the next day began the tournament—the last ever to be held at the Court of France.

The first two days' events passed uneventfully, and the morning of June 30 was warm and already turning hot when heralds marched out onto the field to announce that four gentlemen were prepared to take on all challengers. Three of them were Francis of Guise, Alphonse d'Este, Duke of Ferrara, and Jacques, Duke of Nemours. The fourth needed no identification, for it had been many years since anyone else in France had worn the colors of black and white. All the seats, row on row, were packed with a glittering audience, and the galleries themselves were garlanded and hung with tapestries and great squares of vivid, brocaded velvet. In the center, under an azure canopy, sat the four Queens—Catherine, her daughter-in-law of Scotland, her own daughter newly of Spain, and, a few places apart, the other, uncrowned Queen of France. Banners and standards rustled lightly with the breeze; the sun glinted brightly off the heralds' trumpets and the champions' armor. It was a setting appropriate to an episode out of Amadis of Gaul, but an episode which, with stunning suddenness, went terrifyingly wrong.

The ritual of jousting called for each rider to run three courses during each of which he tried, with a long wooden lance, to unseat his opponent while himself remaining in the saddle. Despite the clanging of armor, the pounding of hooves and the kicking up of great clouds of dust, it was in fact considerably safer than other forms of combat—the worst injury usually being to the loser's dignity when he was sent sprawling. Nevertheless, it was to the enormous relief of his wife that Henry accomplished his three runs. Far more rational and intelligent than most, Catherine was nevertheless as superstitious as almost anyone of her era, and she had never forgotten the enigmatic prophecy which Nostradamus had made four years earlier:

> The young lion will conquer the old
> On the field of battle in single combat;
> In a golden cage he will pierce his eyes,

This the first of two smashings, then comes
a cruel death.

It had not happened. Then on impulse—and possibly because he had lost a stirrup and been visibly shaken during his
final course against the young Count of Montgomery, captain
of his own Scottish guard—the King indicated that he wished
to break another lance with him. What followed, according
to the account of the Bishop of Troyes who was present, is
that "several princes begged him to joust no more that day.
But the more they entreated him the more obstinate he
became, and opposed their wishes, swearing on the faith of
a gentleman that he would break this one lance more. . . .
The valiant young captain of the Scottish guard excused
himself, and begged the King not to command him. His
Majesty became angry and to such a degree that [Mont-
gomery], turned his bridle, took a lance, and tilted against
the King."

Then, the impossible accident happened. Montgomery's
lance struck the King's helmet precisely underneath the
visor, tipped it up, and plunged into the socket of the right
eye. "So heavy and furious was the blow," continues the
Bishop, "that the King inclined his head toward the lists,
striving to recover his seat; turned toward the other side
and would have fallen, if the princes and gentlemen who
were near him, afoot and on horseback, had not come to his
aid. They relieved him of his armor and found him fainting,
the splinter in his eye and his face covered with blood. They
strove to revive him with fresh water, rose water and vinegar,
but, though he recovered consciousness, before ever he got
to his chambers he fainted twice."

Henry died hard. For ten days he drifted in and out of
consciousness—once to order that no harm come to Montgomery, another time to command that the marriage of his
sister take place as scheduled. It did, but not as planned;
rather than in Notre-Dame, the ceremony was held at midnight in the small church of Saint-Paul near the Tournelles

Palace where the King lay. For the few guests, including Catherine who sat alone, bathed in tears, it could as well have been a rehearsal for a funeral. The King's own physician was Ambroise Paré, whose reputation as a surgeon and anatomist was second only to the illustrious Vesalius. He, too, was soon at the bedside. Sent for by Philip II, whose subject he was, he arrived from Brussels on July 3. Neither of the learned doctors, unfortunately, was quite certain how to proceed. The splinter that had been taken from the wound was, in fact, a jagged shard almost four inches long. Three other smaller pieces had also been found and removed, and the wound was rinsed and dressed according to normal practice with a paste of coagulated egg whites. During the night, the King had become feverish, so he was purged with a potion of rhubarb and camomile, bled of twelve ounces of blood, purged again, and given refrigerants and barley gruel—all standard treatment in the management of fever. Nevertheless, there appeared to be no improvement in his condition. Vesalius, who later wrote a long report on the case, was of the opinion that the blow had torn the membrane that envelops the brain. Four condemned prisoners were hastily executed and their severed heads brought to the surgeons who attempted to simulate on them the blow struck by Montgomery's lance. Dissection of the heads did not, however, offer any useful suggestions. Meanwhile, to cause the King as little pain as possible, the dressing was changed daily, but no attempt was made to cleanse the wound thoroughly.

Throughout, the sickroom was crowded with people— Catherine who scarcely left the bedside, the Duke of Guise and his brother the Cardinal of Lorraine, the Princes of the Blood, state secretaries, and noble visitors. Twice, the Dauphin was brought to see his father and twice he fainted at the sight and had to be carried out. Diane, who had last seen her Amadis as he was being carried off the field, sensed the temper of the moment and did not even ask permission to see him. On July 4 and 5, the patient rallied, summoned his musicians, dictated some letters, and vowed that upon his recovery he would make a solemn pilgrimage to Notre-Dame de Cléry.* But the fever continued to rise. By the 8th, the King complained of pains in his neck and the back of his head. As confirmed later by autopsy, a massive abscess had formed deep inside the infected wound. Gradually, Henry slipped into final unconsciousness. While Vesalius and Paré debated whether to hazard a trepanning of the skull, at best a risky procedure, extreme unction was administered. It is not likely that Henry was aware of it, and even less likely that, as later accounts relate, he had a final flash of lucidity during which he again sent for his son and told him: "You are going to be without your father, but not without his blessing. I pray God to make you more fortunate than I have been." At one o'clock on the afternoon of July 10, Henry II died. He had turned forty just three months earlier.

XII

Exhausted by her vigil, barely articulate with grief, Catherine left the body of her husband to begin the deep forty-day mourning period prescribed for Queens of France. The great, silent crowds that had gathered outside the Hôtel des Tournelles saw her move toward her waiting carriage and then, just as she was about to enter it, pause and permit the sixteen-year-old Mary Stuart, who as Queen now outranked her, to precede her. Francis II followed on unsteady legs, supported on one side by his uncle, the Duke of Guise, and on the other by his uncle, the Cardinal of Lorraine. At the

* That church, which still stands in the Loire Valley not far from Orléans, had special significance for the Valois. Louis XI had been buried there, although the silver gates to his tomb had long since vanished—melted down and minted on order of Francis I.

Catherine de' Medici at 30. Unsigned portrait at the Musée
de Versailles attributed to the school of the Clouets

The wedding of Catherine de' Medici and Henry of Orléans, as it was later recreated by Giorgio Vasari (see page 5 of the text)

At right, detail from *The Meeting at the Field of Cloth of Gold,* after Holbein. Principal figure in the procession is Henry VIII.

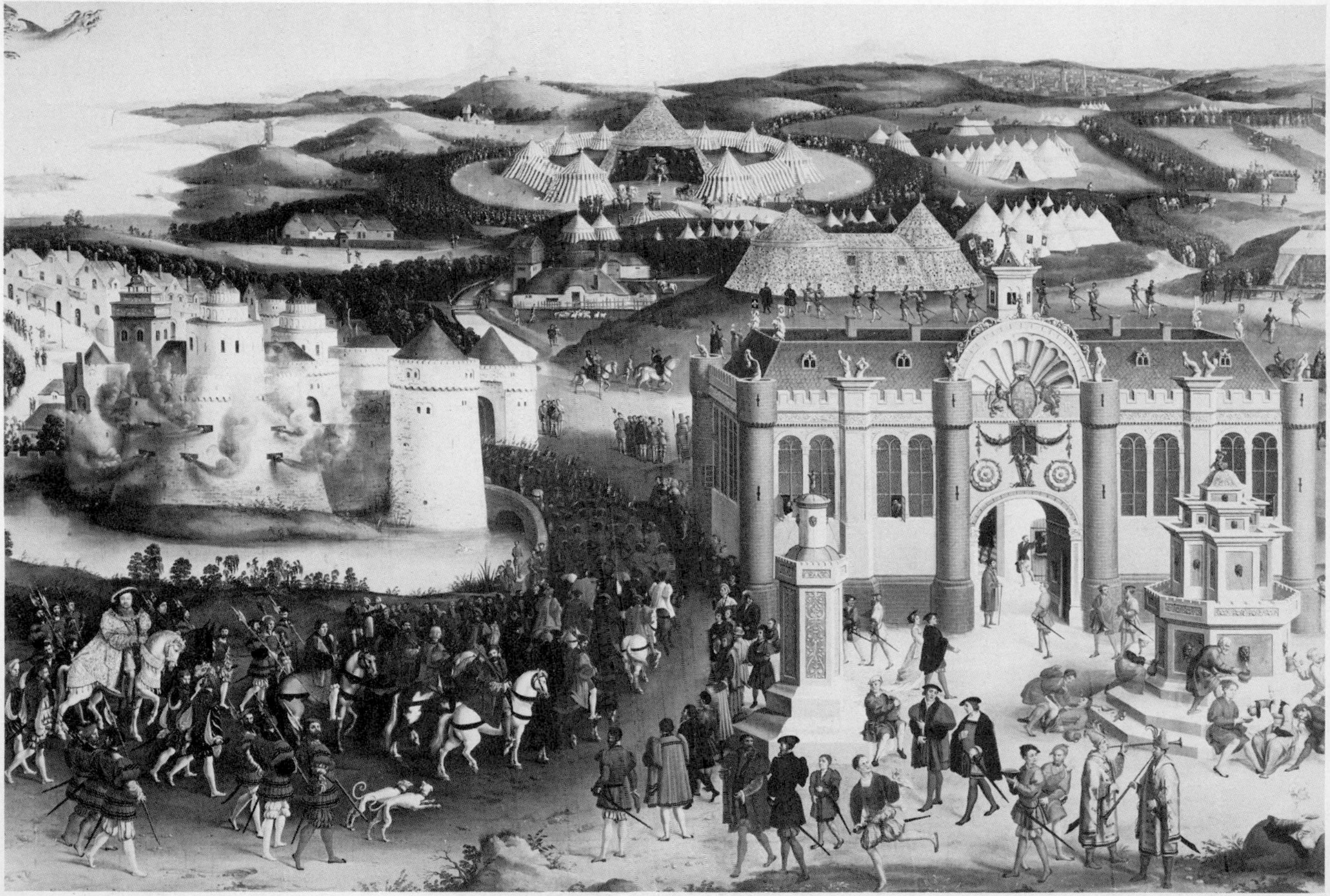

LAUROS—GIRAUDON

Henry II. Even in this formal portrait the interwoven initials
honor his mistress, Diane de Poitiers, rather than his wife.

Francis I, in an engraving after the Louvre's celebrated Titian portrait

Below, Charles V of Spain, with the long, characteristic Hapsburg chin; *at right,* one of the rare portraits, undoubtedly stylized, of Louise of Savoy, the mother of Francis I

MUSÉES NATIONAUX

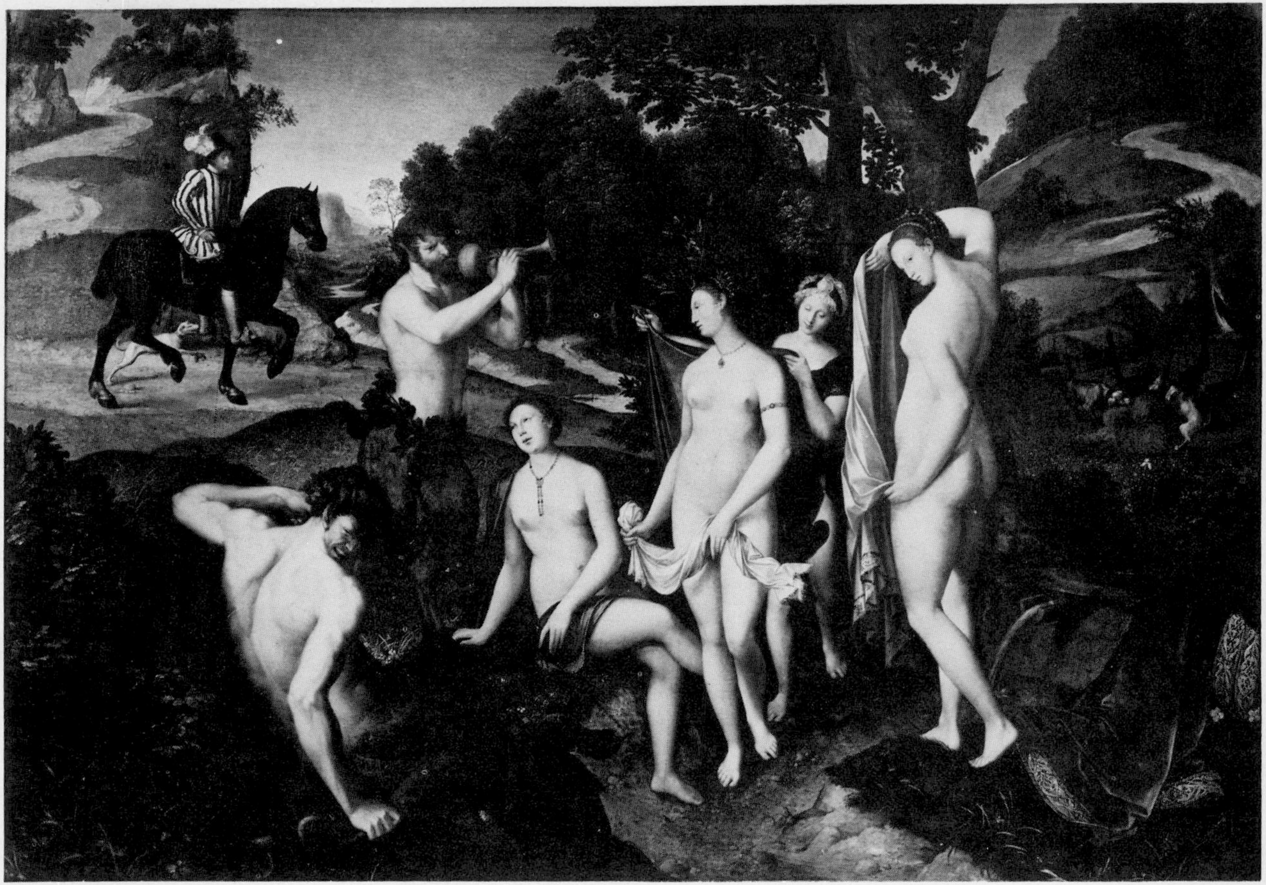

Three of the representations of herself inspired by Diane de Poitiers: *above*, as *Diana at the Bath*, the goddess surprised by a cavalier; *below*, eternally beautiful and feminine at her *toilette*, yet almost boyishly pure and sexless as, crescent in her hair, she sets out for the hunt

MUSÉES NATIONAUX

MUSÉES NATIONAUX

Madame de palentinoy

At left, Diane idealized in Jean Goujon's *Diane Chasseresse,* and in an unsigned 16th-century scene; *above,* authentic portrait of her at 51, at the height of her power over Henry II

Anne de Pisseleu, Duchess of Étampes and mistress of Francis I

Queen Eleanor, sister of Charles V and second wife of Francis I

Mary Stuart, in drawing done at time of her wedding, in 1559

Francis II as he looked shortly before his accession to throne

A family album from Catherine's own *Book of Hours*

The sons and son-in-law of Francis I

The wives and daughters of Francis I

Charles of Lorraine and Claude de Valois

Henry of Navarre and Marguerite

The Duke of Alençon

Francis II and Mary Stuart

Philip II of Spain and Elizabeth

Charles IX and Elizabeth of Austria

The death of Henry II. Catherine, flanked by the Constable and the Cardinal of Lorraine, clasps her hands at his bedside as surgeons prepare to operate. Artist has placed the bandage on the wrong eye of the patient.

Louvre Palace, where accommodations had been prepared for them, the Cardinal moved into the apartments which had been occupied by Anne de Montmorency, the Constable of France. The Duke took over the rooms, adjacent to the royal chambers, which had belonged to the Duchess of Valentinois.

Their former occupant had returned quietly to Anet, where she fared considerably better than her old rival, the Duchess of Étampes. The new King demanded the return of the crown jewels, which his father had given her. For her part, Catherine, who could have been forgiven a measure of vengeance, only required that Diane relinquish the Château of Chenonceaux, in exchange for which she received that of Chaumont, a far more impressive edifice overlooking one of the most spectacular views of the Loire.* All her other possessions and gifts from the crown Diane was allowed to keep. Nor did anyone disturb her. She traveled from one of her estates to the other, supervising their management. She dabbled a little in politics, and, like most ladies of her wealth and age, devoted part of her time to good works—especially the proper upbringing of young ladies of poor families. Finally, after seven years during which, according to one of her biographers, "It was impossible to place her in the ranks of inconsolable widows," she died on April 25, 1566, in her sixty-seventh year.

According to an ordinance dating to the fourteenth century, a King of France could be crowned and rule for himself if he had reached his fourteenth birthday. Francis II was in his sixteenth year, so there was no question of a regency. But he had not the intellect, training, or the slightest interest in being King. Furthermore, at the time of Henry's death he was, as usual, in poor health. This time it was an undiagnosed fever which caused his face, usually drawn and sallow, to puff out hugely and break out in such alarming

---

* Even on this transaction, Diane made a profit, because Catherine had purchased Chaumont from its owners for the sum of 120,000 *livres*.

red blotches that a rumor spread that he had contracted leprosy. Within days after his removal to the Louvre, a royal decree appeared announcing that the Duke of Guise and the Cardinal of Lorraine had been appointed to take charge of all fiscal matters, military affairs, and diplomatic relations. Then, having placed his wife's uncles in full command of France, Francis II shed both his grief and the cares of state. On July 17, a week after his father's death, he set off with a group of companions for an extended hunting trip. In his wake, Throckmorton, the English ambassador wrote home: "The House of Guise now ruleth, with whom I am in very small grace, and the Queen of Scotland who is a great doer here, and taketh all upon her, hath so small an opinion of me as I shall be able to do small service withal, therefore it may like you to use means for my revocation."

The decree appointing the Guises to run France, as well as all the other royal commands which followed included the phrase: "This being the good pleasure of my Lady-Mother, and I also approving of every opinion that she holds. . . ." It is extremely unlikely, however, that the words were anything more than ceremonial lip service. An old friend, the Venetian Lippomano, visited Catherine during her period of mourning and reported: "She was in a room entirely hung with black sheets so that not only the walls and windows but the floor as well was covered with them. There were no lights save two candles burning on a small altar which was also covered in black, as was the bed of the Queen Mother. She was dressed in the most austere of black gowns, with a long train and only a narrow collarband of ermine for decoration. The Queen of Scotland, now the Very Christian Queen, was entirely dressed in white, as were the other ladies present. On behalf of all of them, the Queen Mother responded to my condolences, but she did so in a voice so filled with emotion and so feeble that no one could have understood her words, however closely they listened. For, in addition to the weakness of her voice, she also wore a thick black veil which enveloped her head and even covered her face."

What token objection there was came from the Princes of the Blood, led by Antoine, who was also King of Navarre, and his younger brother Louis, Prince of Condé. By the laws of succession, their family stood to inherit the throne should the Valois line ever exhaust itself.* With three younger brothers to follow Francis, there seemed no likelihood of this happening, but the Princes felt that their station entitled them to a greater say in the management of the kingdom than the late King Henry had accorded them. He, just like Francis I, had ignored them, for the understandable reason that they were Bourbons, close kinsmen of the disgraced Constable. Though the Guises had no claim whatever of their own to the throne, they easily turned aside Antoine's pretensions, sensing accurately that the country was not yet ready to forgive the family its treachery.

For all their efforts to acquire it the France which the Guises took over was scarcely worth having. Henry II had died just in time to avoid the consequence of his foolishness. War, corruption, and his own personal prodigalities had all but completed the work begun by his father. In 1559, the national public debt stood at forty million *livres*. Salaries of officers, governors, judges, and clerks were in arrears; some had not been paid in four years. Income from all taxes amounted to some twelve million *livres* a year, of which more than half was needed to pay interest on the national debt, which averaged sixteen percent. Nor did this glum picture include the enormous dowries settled by Henry upon his newly married daughter and sister, neither of which had yet been paid. As superintendent of finances, the Cardinal of Lorraine instituted Draconian measures: royal pensions were

* All French kings since 1270 had descended directly from Louis IX— Saint Louis. In the absence of direct heirs, the ruling line simply passed, as it had from Charles VIII to Louis XII and then to Francis I, to the nearest cousin.

cut or eliminated; the army was reduced drastically in size; the annual subsidy which permitted the royal postal system to function was suspended. To cut expenses, the citizens of Rheims, who were in the midst of making the usual opulent preparations for Francis II's forthcoming coronation, were told that they would have to pay for the ceremony out of their own funds.

But France also suffered from other, more serious problems which belated fiscal responsibility could not solve. Not all of the nation had mourned the tragic death of its king. In towns and villages across the country where John Calvin's consistories had established themselves, thanks were offered up to God for having guided Montgomery's lance. Sincere as it unquestionably was, the sentiment was premature, because Henry's death only increased the severity of repressive measures. Edicts followed upon each other: houses suspected to have been the scene of heretics' meetings were to be razed and their owners put to death; people suspected of having had knowledge of meetings and failing to inform the authorities were to be treated as if they themselves were heretics; rewards for informers were raised to 500 *livres;* vicars and village priests were ordered to excommunicate those among their flocks who failed to denounce heretics; in order to force Calvinists to betray themselves, images of the Virgin were put up at street corners and all who failed to bow the head and bend the knee were arrested. During the first few months of Francis II's reign, more than twice as many victims were condemned and burned at the stake than during all of Henry's time.

But still the number of heretics grew, as plain, God-fearing people became revulsed by the viciousness and sadism of the ecclesiastic enforcers and switched allegiance to a creed that preached, if it did not always practice, brotherhood. In addition, as Monluc writes in his *Memoirs,* there were also converts of a different sort, called "Huguenots of the State." These included cashiered army officers with no pay in their pockets and no useful trade left to practice, great landowners who saw chronic inflation wipe out the value of the rents they collected, and lesser gentry who had lived off one royal bounty or another, now eliminated. In all, it was estimated by Claude Haton, himself a small-town Catholic priest and therefore not apt to exaggerate the number, that within a year of Henry II's death, fully a quarter of the population of France had embraced heresy.

Whatever else their motives, every one of the Huguenots had one bond in common: a burning hatred of the Guises. Because his brother, the Duke Francis, still enjoyed the reputation of a national military hero, most of it spilled out against the Cardinal of Lorraine. The pitch of virulence and intensity it reached is suggested by a pamphlet entitled *A Letter Sent to the Tiger of France* which appeared early in 1560. Borrowing freely from Cicero, the author rhetorically asked: "Mad tiger, venomous viper, sepulchre of abomination, receptacle of unhappiness, how long wilt thou abuse the youth of our King? Wilt thou never put a term to thy unmeasured ambition, to thy falsehoods, to thy stealings? Dost thou think that anyone is ignorant of thy detestable designs and fails to read in thy face the curse of our times, the ruin of this kingdom and the death of our King?"

The Guises did not attempt to suppress the pamphlet or others even more scurrilous. One of them, for instance, reported that, in view of the King's well-known physical incapacity, the Cardinal of Lorraine had entered into an incestuous alliance with the young Queen, his niece, in order to provide her with an heir. Such calumnies would not continue for much longer, for the Guises had evolved a solution —a happy solution which would at once find a scapegoat, distract popular discontent by creating a diversion, eliminate their potential rivals, and once and for all secure their position.

Through their own agents and those of foreign friends such as the arch-Catholic Philip II of Spain, they had for some time known that a gentleman-adventurer named Jean de Barry, Sieur de La Renaudie, was traveling through the provinces, recruiting former officers, unemployed functionaries, and others who had suffered as a result of the Cardinal of Lorraine's economy measures. His ostensible reason was to organize a delegation of loyal subjects who would call on King Francis II and present him with a petition begging for some sort of redress. But the real plan, once La Renaudie and his companions had gained access to the Court, was to arrest the Guise brothers and either hold them for trial before the Estates General or, better yet, dispose of them out at hand. Furthermore, and this nugget of information most especially interested the Cardinal, Louis, Prince of Condé, was reported to be deeply implicated in the scheme, with the obvious intent of assuming the Guises' place at the side of the throne after their removal.

Unknown to the Guises, for they would surely have used the fact to their advantage, was Elizabeth of England's entering into the plot. La Renaudie and other French Protestant leaders had sought her assistance, and Throckmorton, her own ambassador, had urged her that "there will never be a better time to spend some money." Religious consideration may have helped to make up Elizabeth's mind, but it is safe to assume that she was moved as well by another, earlier report from Throckmorton. In it, he had described a banquet offered by the new Queen of France, and pointedly mentioned that the food had been served on plates decorated with the quartered arms of France, Scotland and England.

It was almost certainly in order to facilitate the arrival and unloading of English ships, bearing arms as well as money, that the seaport of Nantes, at the mouth of the Loire, was chosen by the conspirators as their final meeting place before the coup. On February 1, 1560, when this meeting began, the Court had taken up residence at Blois, whose weather was deemed more suitable to the King's constitution

than the raw Parisian winter. On the 6th, after Francis II
had returned from his day's hunting, the Cardinal summoned the entire assembly to announce a matter of utmost
importance. Brandishing a fistful of papers and reports, he
spun out the story of La Renaudie's plan. In his version,
however, the plot's target was not himself and his brother,
but the King, who was to be kidnapped and held in ransom
of the malcontents' demands. There is no transcript of this
performance, but one of those present noted that "infinite
dangers were much increased by the vehemence and art of
the Cardinal of Lorraine." For his part, the Duke of Guise
then took the floor and urged that the entire Court move immediately to Amboise which, with its thick walls and
medieval towers, was safer than the unprotected, indefensible
Blois.

Catherine, who had sources of her own, did not believe
the Cardinal's dramatic revelation—certainly not the part
about its ultimate purpose. She knew that there was some
sort of plot afoot; everybody in France who was interested
in such things knew that much because La Renaudie had not
been very discreet in his recruiting efforts. But Catherine
also knew the names of some of those who had agreed to join
him. Many were loyal friends of her late husband, men who
would sooner lay down their own lives than do harm to the
person of his son, or of any king of France. There was, however, little she could do. Having seen the turn of events after
Henry's death, she had cut short her own period of mourning
in order to rejoin the Court. Perceiving the true designs of
the Guises, which they dissimulated behind excessive and
meaningless courtesy to her, she had begun to assemble a
countervailing force. It was still too early, however, to press
for a confrontation. As for her eldest son, it is probable that
many of the Cardinal's revelations were beyond him. As
Régnier de la Planche, his biographer, writes: "Unable to
resolve anything in matters of such difficulty, the King de-

clared the Duke of Guise Lieutenant General of the Kingdom," and gave him permission to "deal at will" with the
rebels.

The distance between Amboise and Blois, on opposite
banks of the Loire, is only twenty-two miles, but it was
enough to destroy the shaky structure of La Renaudie's plan
of action. No better a tactician than a conspirator, he had
ordered his men to break up into small groups—every man
wearing a white scarf to identify himself—and advance
toward Blois, where they were supposed to meet on March
10. When word was received of the Court's move to Amboise,
the rendezvous was put off until the 16th, but no clear orders
issued as to how the various parties were to get there. Some,
it appears, were not even told of the change in plans. As a
result, information began to reach the Duke of Guise that
small parties of gentlemen, wearing white scarves, were seen
wandering through the woods, which at the time stretched
almost continuously along the river to a depth of several miles
between the two castles. Taken prisoner and interrogated,
they revealed the names of other conspirators, who in turn
were arrested and put to torture. On the morning of the 16th,
a large number of men and some women—simple artisans,
farmers, and shopkeepers who had been led to believe that
they were participating in a peaceful appeal for religious
tolerance—appeared outside the walls of Amboise. With
some help from the royal guard, they were admitted into
the castle and thrown into its dungeons.

La Renaudie himself was killed on the 18th, in a manner
appropriate to the management of the entire conspiracy.
Accompanied only by his secretary and a servant, he was
riding through the dense forest of Châteaurenault when he
stumbled upon a large royal patrol. Rather than attempt to
escape, he chose to shoot it out and unhorsed one soldier but
then was himself shot through the head.

The death of its leader should have ended the abortive
conspiracy, but as far as the Guises were concerned all that

had happened had merely been prelude. By their own account, they had averted an act of regicide, for which the guilty must now be appropriately punished. Among the prisoners awaiting their fate were not only the rabble which had been collected outside the castle, but also a large number of gentlemen from some of the best and oldest families in France—by coincidence almost all recent converts to Huguenotry. And, of course, there was the Prince of Condé, who had dutifully stood by the King during the perilous days just ended. He had still to be dealt with. Under his powers as Lieutenant General of the kingdom, the Duke of Guise decreed that the executions begin.

Just after dinner on the afternoon of the 22nd—a time expressly chosen by the Duke so that the entire Court, including the ladies and the young royal children could watch —the first of the gentlemen was led out to a block set in the middle of the courtyard and beheaded. Two more followed that day, and others on the afternoons of the next nine days, until fifty-six of the leaders in all had been killed. Lesser fry, unnumbered, were hung, hacked to pieces, or simply beaten insensible and thrown to drown into the Loire.

First among the spectators to break was the Duke of Guise's own wife, Anne d'Este. Dragged day after day against her will to witness the butchery, she finally dissolved into hysterical sobbing. "My sweet God, so much blood," she managed to say, "surely some of it will fall upon our house." Even the King, still barely comprehending what was happening, was finally moved sufficiently to ask the Cardinal, "Why do my people detest me so?"

Neither the Cardinal nor his brother, the Duke, took the time to answer such insane questions. They had watched the executions—indeed staged them—with one hope in mind: that one of the condemned, hoping for a last-moment reprieve, would implicate Condé in the plot. It had not happened. As they had been led to the scaffold, some of the prisoners had walked in silence; others had sung, not the

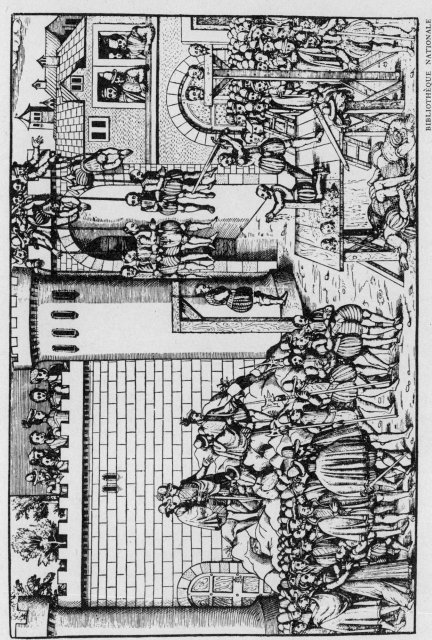

The Conjuration of Amboise. Fanciful scene shows La Renaudie, the plot's instigator, hanging from gibbet at center as the ladies of the Court watch the executions from behind the castle's walls.

ancient Latin chants, but the vibrant, new French versions of the Psalms which Clément Marot had bequeathed to the new religion. Some of them had acknowledged Condé's presence, to which he had responded with a barely perceptible nod of the head. But not one had said an incriminating word, and he still remained what generations of French historians have, with a sense of drama, styled their *chef muet*.

On March 31, Francis II signified his boredom with the monotony of the proceedings by riding off to Chenonceaux where his mother had prepared a surprise party for him and his young wife.* The more important participants of what was henceforth to be known as the Conjuration of Amboise went their separate ways, taking with them designs still frustrated and ambitions unresolved. "Never," said John Calvin, whose support La Renaudie had unsuccessfully tried to enlist, "was enterprise worse conceived or more stupidly executed." To the extent that the plot had cost hundreds, possibly thousands of lives, that it had served further to divide France along political as well as religious lines, that it had sown seeds of bitterness that were yet to produce a bountiful harvest, he was prophetically right. Condé had emerged with his life intact but with his adherents decimated. The Guises, far from solving their problems, had compounded them. From every part of France—Normandy, Poitou, the Dauphiné, Provence—their lieutenants reported that the Huguenots were gaining strength. From the Governor of the Languedoc came warning that he could no longer answer for the continued loyalty of his province. Worse, for Huguenots were not given to looting, robbery, or rape, marauding bands showing no discernible religious preference freely roamed wide stretches of the countryside and on occasion even hazarded to raid cities. To deal with

* This was the first of many such *fêtes* which Catherine was to produce, as much to relieve political tension as for the sheer fun of it. This one included not only the customary tableaux, allegories, and balls, but also such novelties as rocks that recited poetry, and trees that burst out into fireworks.

them required the reinforcement of military garrisons, and this in turn necessitated dipping into the treasury for funds.

On balance, the Guises still had the preponderant advantage because they still had the King. It was, in fact, this advantage that persuaded the Cardinal of Lorraine to agree when the new Chancellor of France, Michel de l'Hôpital, proposed to summon the Estates General. He had been Catherine's choice to fill the office, which corresponds roughly to that of senior advisor to the King, when it became vacant in March, 1560. As her first political act since the death of her husband, she made certain to select a man whom the Guises would find it awkward if not impossible to reject. L'Hôpital was then fifty-three years old and the possessor of an impeccable career virtually unique for its combination of probity, administrative skill, diplomacy, and resolute tolerance—a French equivalent of Sir Thomas More. He was, moreover, a poet of note and, in the words of the scholar Paul Van Dyke, "a wise man who, attacked by extremists of both sides, has nevertheless been praised by more historians of more varied types than any character of those troublous times."

L'Hôpital's purpose in calling the Estates, which had not met in seventy-six years, was to review the entire question of religious tolerance and to seek out an acceptable compromise. The Cardinal of Lorraine had, naturally, no interest in any such scheme. Rather, he saw a golden opportunity to put into effect his original plan to eliminate Condé. With the Cardinal's approval, letters went out at the end of August, 1560, under the signature of Francis II, commanding all seneschals and bailiffs to "assemble the three Estates within their jurisdiction in order that each of them may convene and draw up as many remonstrances, complaints, and charges as they wished to bring to the attention of the King."

As Princes of the Blood, both Condé and his older brother, Antoine King of Navarre, were, of course, invited to attend the meeting which was to be held in Orléans on December

10. Both firmly, and wisely, turned down their invitations. Personal letters from Catherine, who had now begun to formulate a plan of her own, failed to change their mind, as did a childishly petulant warning from Francis II: "You can be certain that if you refuse to obey me, I will know quite well how to teach you who is King." In the end, it was a solemn safe-conduct from the Cardinal of Lorraine that persuaded them to attend. With this in their pocket, the two brothers left Nérac, Antoine's capital in Navarre, and set off for Orléans. Shortly after they had crossed the border into France, a body of royal troops quietly slipped behind them and followed at a discreet distance. Though they did not know it yet, the two Bourbons were already prisoners.

Upon their arrival in Orléans on October 31, which they noticed was bursting with royal troops and mercenaries, they were granted a glacial audience by Francis. Waiving the commonest of courtesies, the King demanded to know what the two princes were doing to stamp out heresy in their provinces. As they prepared to answer, the door of the royal chamber flew open and a body of soldiers moved in and arrested both of them. Because of his rank as a reigning monarch, Antoine was merely placed under surveillance. Condé, however, was charged with treason, tried, and condemned to death—all in the space of less than four weeks. His request for a trial by his peers, a prerogative of his rank, was brushed aside.

While these events moved toward their planned conclusion, the Guises turned their attention to other matters. As delegates to the Estates arrived, each was instructed to take home with him declarations of Catholic faith which were to be signed not only by all judges and royal officials, but by every citizen, parish by parish, within their jurisdiction. The penalty for noncompliance, they were further told, would be their own arrest. Thus was heresy to be stamped out in France.

Whether this plan would have succeeded is unlikely—and

also academic, because it was never implemented. Ever since his departure from Amboise seven months earlier, Francis II had thrown himself into a frenzy of hunting so single-mindedly that it suggests not so much love of the sport as sublimation of his physical inability to consummate his marriage. On November 17, he fell sick. The most visible symptom of his distress was a continuous discharge from his left ear. Because he had suffered from this same infirmity since childhood, the doctors were disposed to ignore it and attribute his illness to a cold, contracted while he galloped across the frozen countryside. This time, however, Francis also complained of a violent headache which, despite purgings and medications, became so painful that he could not endure the slightest noise. By the 30th, he was running a high fever, and could not manage to retain the lightest nourishment.

His young wife and his mother sat at his bedside, attempting to comfort him, but their distress was nothing compared to that of the Guises. When the patient first failed to respond to treatment, they had threatened to hang the physicians attending him. Later, they tried to suppress news of the King's condition, particularly from the Estates General. They pressed Catherine, with no success, to advance the date of Condé's execution.

Meanwhile, Francis's condition grew worse. He was in constant pain now, moaning and begging for water "as if an entire river would not quench his thirst." Torn to pieces by her son's suffering, Catherine still found time to leave his chamber for hurried, earnest conversations with this and that dignitary—and particularly with Antoine of Navarre. On the evening of December 4, the physicians prepared a potent poultice and applied it to the King's ear. When they removed it seven hours later, the flow of discharge had stopped, and the patient's moaning had subsided. Uncertain whether this was a good sign or not, they called the Cardinal of Lorraine who foreswore the usual form and made Francis repeat these words: "Lord! Pardon my sins and impute not to me, thy servant, the sins committed by my Ministers under my name and authority." It was a strange prayer, and, as Edith Sichel writes, "the only suggestion we have that the Cardinal possessed a conscience."*

During the night of December 5, 1560, Francis II found merciful relief from his agony. On the following day, Catherine appeared before the *Conseil Privé*. Still red-eyed from weeping, she said: "Since it has pleased God to deprive ·me of my elder son, I mean to submit to the Divine will and to assist and serve the King, my second son, in the feeble measure of my experience." Her second son, now Charles IX of France, was not quite ten years old. "I have decided," she continued, "to keep him beside me, and to rule the State as a devoted mother must do."

Nor were these merely the brave words of a grieving woman. Well-trained ambassadors are never more alert than when power changes hands in the country to which they are posted. On December 8, 1560, three days after Francis's death, Giovanni Michieli reported to the Senate of Venice: "In the government, the Queen Mother is considered as the one whose will is supreme in all matters; it is she who will henceforth have her hand upon the most important negotiations, and within the Council there will be no chief other than herself. . . . The ambassadors have already received their instructions that when they wished an audience, they will request it of Her Majesty through the secretaries she has designated. . . . Henceforth, one will deal directly with the Queen, and if she senses the need of the Council, she will summon it at her pleasure."

Francis II had led a short, useless life, but he did perform a unique, incalculable service for his country. He gave his mother a second chance.

* In her *Catherine de Medici and the French Reformation* (London, Constable & Company, Ltd., 1905).

Part Three

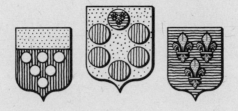

Power

I

Niccolò Machiavelli, after completing a diplomatic mission to France in 1510, noted that "The French people are submissive and hold their kings in great veneration." Catherine had been given personal opportunity not only to confirm her compatriot's observation, but also to draw its corollary—that this attitude did not extend to monarchs' consorts. As the widow of a king, she had been instantly turned aside and ignored.

Now, however, she was the mother of a king too young to rule. Tradition dictated that a council headed by the First Prince of the Blood—in this instance, Antoine of Navarre—should assume power. Indeed, Calvin, who had been following events in France closely, alerted his followers: "God, who struck the father in the eye, has struck the son in the ear. . . . The principal point upon which everything else now depends is to establish a council to govern. Unless the King of Navarre acts promptly, a mistake may be made which it will be difficult to rectify. For him to admit that a woman, and a foreign Italian woman at that, should be allowed to rule would cover him with dishonor."

But Calvin had miscalculated both the foreign Italian woman's political ability and Navarre's capacity for swallowing dishonor. As her son lay dying, Catherine had sent for Antoine. She recited all the accusations that hung over him as a result of the Amboise plot and pointed out that he was still under arrest. Furthermore, she reminded him that the entire Bourbon family, of which he was the head, was still in disgrace. Under the circumstances, whatever rights he might possibly have possessed to the regency had been forfeited. To the contrary, both he and his brother, Condé, were in serious jeopardy and needed a highly placed protector. She proposed to undertake that role and even, in order to show her high personal regard, to appoint him Lieutenant General of the kingdom. It was a bluff which a self-possessed man, aware that Catherine had neither power to wield nor protection to offer, would have called. Antoine, as weak as he was vain, hurried to accept.

This time, it was the Guises who had been outmaneuvered. The sight of a contented Antoine nodding acquiescence as Catherine told the *Conseil Privé* that "the King of Navarre will occupy first place in the Council as the nearest relative of the King, without whose knowledge nothing should be done," left them with no grounds for protest.

Writing to her daughter Elizabeth, Catherine described the arrangement in different terms: "Although I am compelled to have the King of Navarre next to me because the laws of this kingdom provide, when the King is a child, that the Prince of the Blood should be next to the mother, nevertheless I have so won him that he is obedient to me and has no commands to give except what I permit him to give."

Because anyone so easy to win could as easily be lost, Catherine took the sensible precaution of assigning someone she could trust to keep an eye on Antoine. And because his incorrigible chasing after young women was common knowledge—even Calvin had complained that he was "entirely given over to Venus"—she chose as her watchdog one of the most attractive of her own maids of honor, Louise de Rouet. For good measure, she also arranged for another of her ladies, Isabelle de Limeuil, to attach herself in the same capacity to Condé, whose freedom she had promised as part of her bargain with Antoine.

There was nothing new or extraordinary about using sex for political purposes, and Catherine of all people had excellent reason to be aware of the power that women could attain over men. She herself appears, after the death of her husband, to have no personal interest in any of them. No contemporary or later source even hints at sexual misconduct on her part—a rare achievement for the sixteenth century. Nevertheless, historians have professed to be scandalized by her choice of tactics. Possibly in recognition of their effectiveness—Louise so ensnared the willing Antoine that he offered to divorce his wife for her—Catherine's girls became collectively known as the *escadron volant* (flying squadron), and their unleashing on unsuspecting males was added to the catalogue of her evil dissimulations.

II

If Antoine personified one extreme of his century's code of behavior, the man who succeeded him as spokesman for the Huguenots represented the other. For the first thirty-eight years of his life, Gaspard de Coligny had followed the orderly career of a gentleman of good birth. Arriving as a young man at the Court of Francis I, he distinguished himself in the Italian campaigns and was rewarded with a knighthood and a promotion to colonel-general of infantry. Under Henry II, he fought at Boulogne and Metz, was promoted again to Admiral of France, and was taken prisoner at the ill-fated battle of Saint-Quentin in 1557. To pass away the long days of waiting for his ransom, he turned to reading, and discovered Calvin's *Institutes*. His interest aroused, he wrote to the author, and was urged in reply to seek conversion because "God hath given you the opportunity to profit in His school of adversity, as though He wished to speak to you privately in your ear." By the time of his release, in 1559, he had become a fervent Huguenot.

Catherine had known Coligny at Court and had even provided him with letters of introduction when he had once expressed an interest in visiting Florence, but he was then just one of her husband's military commanders. The man who returned from captivity was more complicated and deliberate. Furthermore, in the crisis-ridden atmosphere generated by the Guises he had remained an island of intellectual calm. When the time came for Catherine to appoint a new Council, she asked him to serve on it.

The Duke of Guise recognized the opportunity and moved quickly. If Huguenots were going to be admitted into the government, someone had better start looking out for the country's welfare. Neither Anne de Montmorency, who still clung to his title of Constable of France, nor the ambitious Marshal of Saint-André had done well in Catherine's distribution of offices. With no great difficulty, he persuaded them to join him in forming the Triumvirate to defend the Faith.

In intimating that the Faith needed protection, Guise had again chosen the safe, familiar ground of religion to issue his challenge. Catherine resolved, once and for all, to cut it out from under him. In her son's name, she sent a letter to the citizens of Geneva: "The King has found that the terrible troubles of his kingdom have their cause in the malice of some preachers, mostly sent by you or the chief ministers of your city, who have not only gone from house to house secretly impressing on the minds of the greater part of our subjects a pernicious and damnable disobedience, but by an infinite number of defamatory libels and by sermons in large assemblies have dared to incite our people to open rebellion. We beg them to recall these preachers and keep them from coming any more, or we will consider it a treacherous war on this kingdom and a just cause for a quarrel before God and the world."

Then she wrote to Philip of Spain, the most inflexibly Catholic of all Europe's monarchs: "We have during twenty or thirty years tried cautery with the idea of cutting out the contagion of this evil from among us and we have seen by experience that violence has not served except to increase and multiply it. . . . It has been said by many people of good judgment that the worst means for suppressing these new opinions is the public death of those who hold them, because it was to be seen that they were strengthened by such spectacles. I have been counseled to follow the way of gentleness in this matter, in order to try by honest remonstrances, exhortations, and preaching to lead back those who are wandering in the matter of faith and to punish severely those who shall be guilty of scandals or sedition. The evil is so deeply rooted that it is very difficult, not to say impossible, to drive it out except by the remedy of a general council."

In 1561, Catherine herself undertook to convene such a council, selecting as its site the secluded but amply comfortable Dominican monastery of Poissy, not far from Paris. Despite the Pope's expressed disquiet, fifty of the ranking prelates in France, including all five of its cardinals, accepted her invitation. Geneva sent a delegation of fourteen ministers and theologians led by Theodore Beza, who came as Calvin's personal representative.

It had been Catherine's hope that these distinguished men of the cloth could take a higher view and, in their collective wisdom, find some basis for accommodation. To her chagrin, she discovered that they had come only to preach at each other. Beza opened the debate with a lengthy statement of the Calvinist position, which he concluded by stating that "Christ's body is therefore as far distant from the bread and the wine as the highest Heaven is distant from earth." This absolute rejection of the core of Catholic belief, delivered with total assurance and a hint of derision, left little room for discussion. Indeed, the Cardinal of Tournon, forgetting the purpose of the meeting, started to walk out of the chamber before Beza had sat down. Catherine persuaded him to stay by pointing out that he had an obligation to bring those who had strayed back into the fold. But there was little chance of any conversions taking place at Poissy. Nor was the cause of harmony served when the General of the Jesuits, who was present as an observer, addressed the visitors from Geneva as "wolves, foxes, serpents, and assassins."

Catherine's ambitious ecumenical experiment closed with the Cardinal of Lorraine's pronouncing the anathema on the Calvinists. In order to save face, however, she claimed success in the report of the meeting, which went to the Courts of Europe. "There was no better nor more fruitful means," she wrote, "of causing these ministers to be abandoned and of withdrawing their adherents from them than by contriving to confound their doctrine and revealing and exposing the errors contained in it."

Unfortunately, the rank and file of French Huguenots did not receive copies of the letter and persisted in clamoring for the right to commit their mortal sins. In Guyenne, they sacked a village and besieged its governor in his own house. In Languedoc, an eminent lawyer was beaten and publicly hanged as "an enemy of the Religion." In Sens, a congregation was so moved by the eloquence of its preacher that it attacked and overran a monastery.

Taking alarm at the Calvinists' growing number and boldness, the Holy See proposed to the Triumvirate that it should openly ally itself with Spain and also urged Philip to take a personal hand: "Your Majesty would advance troops from Flanders and Spain on the frontiers of France. At the same time, the Queen Mother and the King of France would be made to understand the peril that threatens the kingdom, and it would be impressed on them that Your Majesty wishes with all his power to prevent the French King from being governed by heretics, and that you are determined to exterminate them and to drive them out of this country by arms. . . . Such an enterprise is, for Your Majesty, a duty, as well as a pious, just, honest, easy, and glorious Work."

Philip let it be known that he was prepared to accept the responsibility and paved the way by warning Catherine that he was scandalized by the meeting at Poissy, alarmed by the progress of heresy in France, and shocked by the favor she had shown its spokesmen. The Duke of Guise, acting for the Triumvirate, was not yet ready to throw in publicly with Spain, but he chose to signify his contempt for the goings-on at Poissy by leaving the Court and returning to his estates.

The move was, in retrospect, ill-advised because his departure, emulated by Catholic nobles of lesser stature, left a clear field for Coligny and the other Protestants. Beza in particular proved to be an effective advocate. When not engaged in theological dispute he was charming, quick-witted and eloquent—qualities which Catherine could all the more appreciate since they had so long been absent in the men around her. A measure of how well the two got along is contained in a letter from Beza to Calvin: "I affirm," he wrote, "that this Queen, our Queen, is better disposed toward us than ever she has been before."

The effect of Catherine's partiality was the publication of the Edict of January, signed on the 17th of that month in 1562. Its purpose, the preamble optimistically stated, was "to keep our subjects at peace until such time as God will do us the grace to be able to reunite them in one fold." The provisions were set down in carefully guarded language: "We forbid the ministers and leaders of the new religion to make any synod or consistory, except by leave. But if they consider it necessary to constitute among themselves certain regulations for the exercise of their religion, let them show these to our officers, who will authorize them." But the effect of the Edict was to give official sanction to the practice of Huguenotry. It was, in fact, the first formal pledge of toleration made in France since Luther's words had first been heard. Not even Francis I had ventured that far.

It can be safely assumed that Catherine was not moved by any sudden spiritual revelation. She could understand theological distinctions, but not the passion that drove simple, peaceable men to hack each other to pieces in their name. Humane considerations and the discovery that Huguenots were not necessarily hysterical zealots undoubtedly contributed to her championing of their cause, but her principal motive was purely political. The Catholics were by far the stronger of the two factions. By throwing her support to that side, she could probably have eliminated the Huguenots, or at least have rendered them impotent. But either of these circumstances would have left her dependent on the Guises, whose Catholic credentials were better than hers could ever be. On the other hand, the creation of a nicely balanced rival force—strong enough to pose a threat, yet not so strong that it could act independently of her—offered attractive possibilities for maneuvering.

She had also chosen her timing with care. Knowing that the Church was about to hold an important General Council, whose participants were even then gathering in Trent, she correctly anticipated that the Pope would wish to avoid an open rupture with her. In fact, Pius IV voiced only a weak protest over the publication of the Edict. Taking his cue from him, Philip of Spain huffed and puffed about heresy, but did not move his troops. London and Geneva were, of course, delighted. Everywhere that mattered, the end of Catherine's second year of rule saw her diplomacy accepted, if not approved.

She had, however, miscalculated the reaction of French Catholics. Paris was stunned and outraged. Placards appeared demanding the extermination of heretics. From the pulpits, she was denounced as a Jezebel and her advisers as the prophets of Baal. Copies of the Edict, printed for circulation in the provinces, were seized and burned. The Provost of the city's merchants called on her to demand a personal explanation. Attempting to minimize for him the effects of the Edict, she pointed out that the Huguenots had in any case been holding their prayer meetings, but in the relative discomfort of the open countryside. "Would you," she asked, "have the rain fall on their backs?" "Madame," he replied, "if it does not rain upon them, it will pour upon you and your children."

For their part, the Protestants began complaining that the

The Massacre of Vassy, which precipitated the first of the Wars of Religion. The pro-Huguenot artist has taken pains to illustrate the soldiers' brutality, even showing one of them robbing the poor box.

liberties granted them were already being violated. A demonstration called by Condé brought out 25,000 people, and suggested that perhaps Catherine had underestimated her new allies' true strength. The governor of Paris, frightened by rumors that other thousands were marching on the city, called for troops to maintain order. Only a spark was needed, and it was provided, appropriately, by the Duke of Guise.

Since leaving the Court, the Duke had divided his time between family matters and directing the affairs of the Triumvirate. He was returning home from a visit to his mother when, on March 1, 1562—a Sunday—he stopped to hear Mass in the small village of Vassy, near Châlons-sur-Marne. The local Huguenots were taking advantage of the new edict to hold their own services in a grange not far from the parish church, and the sound of their psalm-singing infringed upon the Duke's devotions. He sent a servant over to demand that they stop. Their refusal provoked a scuffle, during the course of which stones were thrown. One of them struck the Duke, who had come out to see what was happening, in the forehead. A man of quick reflexes, he ordered the soldiers of his escort to disperse the crowd. Thirty Protestants were killed and another 130 wounded. Before moving on, Guise ordered their preacher hung on an improvised gibbet for having incited his flock to riot.

In Paris, the crowds responded to the news of the massacre with great demonstrations of joy. Catherine tried to calm Beza and the other Huguenot leaders—"Good information will be taken and everything will be arranged, provided you contain yourselves," she assured them. An unrepentant Guise disobeyed her orders and led the Triumvirate into the city. Outmanned, Condé slipped out of Paris and made his way to Orléans, gathering frightened and indignant Huguenots as he went.

Sensing the likely outcome of events, Catherine followed and sought to talk to him. After twice agreeing and failing to keep his word, he met her on a plain outside the city where he appeared surrounded by a hundred horsemen wearing the loose, white surcoat which the Huguenots had adopted as a uniform.

"Why," she asked, "are your men dressed like a lot of millers?" "To show," he replied, gesturing toward the royal troops who had accompanied the Queen Mother, "that they are able to beat your donkeys, Madame."

The talks led nowhere, and as the two prepared to part, men from both sides dismounted to part as well. A Huguenot who was present recalled: "I had a dozen friends there, each of whom was as dear to me as a brother, and there were many others there in the same situation, so that, man after man asking permission from his officer, the two lines of white cloaks and crimson cloaks were soon mingled together in friendly talk, and when they separated it was with tears in their eyes."

The war began with a sense of high purpose on both sides. The royalists, led by the Triumvirate, now portrayed themselves as defenders of the royal family, and despite their own flouting of the Edict of January, of established order. The Huguenots, for their part, comported themselves as if they were on a holy mission. One of their captains recalled that "dice, cards, and women were banished from the quarters, plundering was strictly forbidden and arrangements were made for religious service every day."

Unimpressed, Catherine wrote to her daughter: "Everything that is done on one side and the other is nothing but a desire to rule and to take from me under cover and color of religion what power I have." To another correspondent, the Bishop of Limoges, she revealed her true fear: "I see all the great men and good captains and the leaders of the nobility armed against one another, and so embittered and inflamed that we can expect only the approaching ruin and loss of one or another party or perhaps both; the outcome

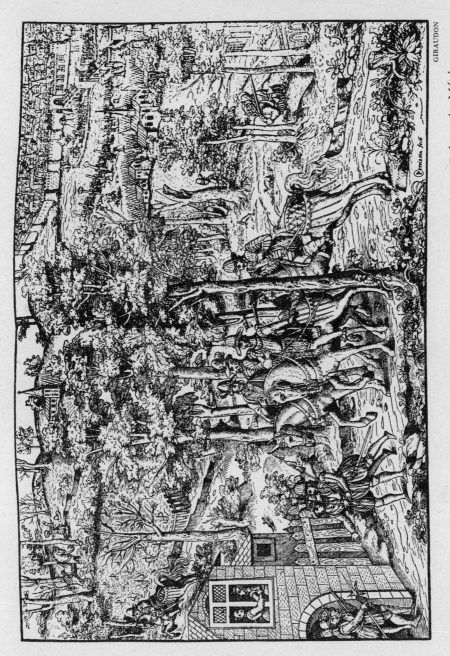

GIRAUDON

The Assassination of Francis, Duke of Guise. Dressed in royal uniform, Poltrot le Méré approaches the unwary Duke and brings him down. Artist has also shown the murderer fleeing away.

will be to open the door to all the foreigners who wish to invade this kingdom; it will be stripped and deprived of its defenders. . . . When I think of the appetites which such an opportunity may excite, you can appreciate my anxiety."

This eventuality had not deterred the belligerents, but fortunately their ineptitude prevented it. For all of their sword-rattling, few of the leaders on either side had any training in warfare. What they knew of it had come from their childhood reading of Caesar and Plutarch and their own experiences in the mock combat of jousts and tournaments. Because of this limited background, hostilities were short—ten months—and tinged with whimsy.

As Lieutenant General of France, Antoine of Bourbon spurned the undignified task of chasing the Huguenots across the countryside and elected instead to besiege the city of Rouen, one of their strongholds. When the defenders proved more stubborn than he had expected, he resolved to hearten his troops by marching alone through their ranks and relieving himself on the ramparts of the city. While so engaged, a heavy object thrown from the battlements felled him. The example served its purpose, for his troops stormed the city, but it also led to his downfall. Having insisted on riding in the triumphal procession despite his wound, he suffered a relapse and was carried back to his tent where he died in the arms of the beautiful Louise de Rouet, who had, quite naturally, accompanied him on the campaign. Taking no chances, he was attended during his last hours by both a Protestant preacher and a Dominican friar.

What turned out to be the decisive battle of the war took place near Dreux, on December 19, 1562. The two armies dazzled and belabored each other with a day-long ballet of feints, frontal attacks, and encirclements. When the dust settled, it was discovered that one of the Triumvirs, the Marshal of Saint-André, lay dead, and that both of the field commanders—Condé and the Constable—had been taken prisoner by the enemy.

Guise survived the carnage, but within weeks the summary justice he had so long and freely dispensed at last caught up with him. He was riding through the woods on his way back from inspecting an artillery position when a man wearing the royal colors approached him and, at point-blank range, shot him in the back. In the commotion, the killer escaped but lost his way and wandered back to the scene of his crime. Arrested, he was identified as Poltrot de Méré, a Huguenot who had joined the Catholic side as a pretended convert a few days earlier. The story immediately arose that Coligny had paid for the murder, and the Guises swore blood vengeance on him. Poltrot shed no light. During his interrogation he alternately confirmed and refuted the charge, possibly in an attempt to find the words that would satisfy his tormentors. Coligny, of course, denied complicity, conceding that he had never dissuaded anyone who claimed he could kill Guise, but insisting that "on his life and his honor he had never sought out or solicited anyone to do this, neither by word, nor by money, nor by promises, directly or indirectly." Given his character, historians have by and large tended to believe him.

Whatever her private feelings at the removal of her old, well-hated adversary, Catherine delivered a typical eulogy: "God has seen fit to strike me again and, with me, the poor country; for by the most miserable of deaths He has taken from me the one man who stood out alone and devoted himself to the King. M de Guise was the greatest captain in our realm and one of the greatest and worthiest ministers the King could ever be served by. . . . I do not know how things will go without M de Guise, because the Constable is a prisoner in Orléans and we have no man to command our army. . . . It is I who will have to take command and play the captain."

In that capacity, her first act was to call for an immediate armistice. The only serious difficulty in her way, under the circumstances, was to round up suitable signatories.

III

Among Catherine's clearest recollections of her early years in France were the great heartfelt outpourings of affection and loyalty that had greeted Francis I in whatever cities or villages he had chosen to visit. Her own son, Charles, was now thirteen years old, a tall, retiring boy who had inherited all of his father's slow taciturnity. Although Catherine had found an obscure precedent to have him proclaimed King in his own right, the unsettled state of affairs had prevented him from seeing his country. More important, it had prevented his country from seeing him. Profiting from the end of fighting and the providential disposal of her adversaries, Catherine undertook an ambitious project. In order to restore the public image of the crown and to gather its eroded authority, she would conduct Charles on a vast journey around his kingdom. The trip was to last twenty-six months, cover more than three thousand miles—nearly all of that distance on horseback—and touch the orchards of Normandy, the vineyards of Burgundy, the warm shores of the Mediterranean, the volcanic hills of the Auvergne, and the wheat-rich, endless flatness of the Beauce. It had another purpose as well, for its culmination was to be a meeting, at the French-Spanish border, with Catherine's beloved daughter, Elizabeth, and her husband, Philip II.

Travel was a well-organized activity in sixteenth-century France. The old Roman roads, long since torn up by peasants in search of stone for their houses, had been repaired or replaced by new highways radiating out of Paris; the one to Orléans measured fifty-two feet across. Published in 1553, Henri Estienne's *Guide des Chemins de France* described the country as being "twenty-two days wide and nineteen days long," and set down in great detail every one of its roads and byways, even to the inclusion of warnings about the likelihood of encountering brigands. Other guides provided information about inns and hostelries.* Travelers could hire a horse in one town and leave it in another, although they were enjoined under pain of an additional charge from galloping them to exhaustion.

But nothing had been seen like the royal cortège that wound its way out of Paris on January 24, 1564. Led by the Master of the Household and his one hundred gentlemen, it included the Swiss Guard, the Scottish Guard, the Grooms of the Stable, and the young ladies of the *escadron volant* as well as the platoons of valets, surgeons, falconers, musicians, barbers, secretaries, ambassadors, bakers, tailors, apothecaries, and ironsmiths whose services were equally essential to the Court. These were carts loaded with silver plate, furniture, tapestries, sets and costumes for theatricals, equipment for hunting and mock tournaments, a traveling menagerie, and a large coach drawn by six horses which Catherine could use when dictating letters or conducting affairs of state. As King, Charles was surrounded by his own household, which was duplicated on a smaller scale by those of two of the other royal children, the twelve-year-old Duke of Anjou, and Marguerite, who was not yet nine.

Catherine had planned out the itinerary with all the care and balance of a modern political campaign manager laying out his candidate's schedule. There was to be something for everyone. The first stop, a carefree, prolonged observance of Mardi gras at Fontainebleau, established the theme by evoking the happier days of Francis I. Next was Troyes, in Champagne, where a treaty of friendship with England waited to be signed. It was hardly a coincidence that almost one hundred and fifty years earlier in this same city an-

---

* Singled out as worth a detour were the Pewter Tankard in Caen, the Saracen's Head and the Square Tower in Rouen, the Red Hat in Chartres, and the Griffen in Blois.

other French queen—Isabeau de Bavière—had signed another treaty that infamously delivered all of France into the hands of England's Henry V. Because Catherine knew that this alliance with a heretic would not be well received in Madrid she instructed her ambassador to impart the news to Philip "as moderately and wisely" as possible. She also saw to it that her own next stop would be in Bar-le-Duc, where she presided over the baptism of her first grandson, the child of her second daughter, Claude, and the Duke of Lorraine, a good Catholic and a member of the Guise family.

Turning south into lush, well-fed Burgundy, Catherine sat back to play the role of proud mother as Charles received splendid homage from his subjects in Dijon and Mâcon.* The ceremonial entrée prepared by the citizens of Lyons, however, was a particularly satisfying personal triumph. It was this same city, she could hardly have forgotten, that had so thoroughly humiliated her on the occasion of her previous formal visit sixteen years earlier. This time, there was no mummery to celebrate goddesses of the hunt. Instead, the living tableaux invoked justice and the domestic virtues, and the great triumphal arch erected in front of the cathedral bore the garlanded legend: *"Catherinae M. Reginae Pacificae."*

The happy spirit of the voyage was shattered in Valence, where the Court arrived on August 22, 1564. Word had been received that Elizabeth of Spain, not yet twenty, had just been prematurely delivered of stillborn twins. Catherine hid her sorrow and wrote her daughter a long, cheering letter assuring her that she was still young enough to bear many other children. But the news from Madrid also served to remind Catherine of the anticipated meeting with Elizabeth's husband. Despite their never having met and although their wide correspondence reveals only the warmest cordiality,

---

* Another, unscheduled vital statistic marked the visit to Dijon. Mlle de Limeuil, who had been assigned to Condé, gave birth to a child which she insisted, over his denial, he had fathered. Her punishment, not for sinning but for carelessness, was expulsion from the Court.

Catherine and her son-in-law detested each other. Ever since she assumed the Regency, Philip had appointed himself as the Church's principal protector in Europe, a posture that in his eyes sanctioned not only his brutal repression of the Netherlands and the activities of the Inquisition's courts in Spain, but also his right to meddle as he chose in the internal affairs of France. Some well-meaning French Catholics conceded that right—indeed, one of them wrote that "if the King of Spain does not put his hand to the oar, in less than a year France will have become heretical"—but Catherine was not taken in. She could see, as did Philip, the pattern of the Hapsburg holdings: Spain; in the north, the Netherlands; to the east, the Catholic Rhineland and the mosaic of the Empire; to the south, all of Italy save Savoy, Venice, and Rome. In the center was France, the sole obstacle to universal rule over the continent.

Catherine could not hope to match Philip's soldiers or his treasury, but she could attempt to ensnare him in a web of matrimonial bonds. That, in fact, had been the purpose of bringing the royal children along for him to see. She had already launched a campaign to pair Marguerite off with his son, Carlos. For Anjou, she had in mind Philip's sister, Juana, who should command an appropriate dowry. For Charles himself, she had selected the eldest daughter of Philip's cousin, the Austrian Emperor.

Covering a leisurely six leagues a day, the cortège made its way across Provence. Nîmes, Aix, Arles, and Avignon all paid homage to their new king, although in each of these ancient cities the Catholics urged him to greater firmness and zeal, while the Huguenots sought private audiences to assail him with their grievances. For all of Catherine's intentions, France was far from pacified.

A stop was made in the little town of Salon for the express purpose of calling on its most illustrious citizen, Michael of Nostradamus. The old man welcomed the King and the Queen Mother into his study, fussed with his compasses, mirrors, and quadrants, and confirmed his prediction that all of Catherine's sons would wear a crown. Marseilles, which had greeted Catherine as a bride, prepared something special for her return. Two fleets of galleys, fully manned and equipped with mock cannons, were to give battle in the harbor, but Anjou, who was to command one of them, showed an early disposition to seasickness. In Carcassonne, which was reached shortly after Christmas, a heavy ten-day snowfall marooned the procession. Charles did not mind; as Catherine described in a letter to a friend, he and his pages built a fort in which they withstood a determined siege by the gentlemen of the guard.

During the months since his mother-in-law had left Paris, Philip had become increasingly wary of meeting her. He had used Elizabeth's weakened condition to put off the date. Now, when Catherine reached Toulouse on February 2, 1565, she received word that Philip had decided not to come at all, but to send the Duke of Alva in his stead. This was doubly distressing news, not only as a personal slight to her but because Catherine knew Alva's reputation as the most arrogant, inflexible of Philip's ministers. Nevertheless, she resolved to make the best of it.

The long-awaited reunion finally took place on June 30, on the banks of the Bidassoa River not far from the point where Francis I had crossed on his way home from Spanish captivity. As a witness described it, "Their Majesties of France, having heard that the Queen of Spain was to cross the river which separates the two kingdoms, dined full early and straight away set out for the said river, adjoining which they had caused two leafy bowers to be built, about two leagues distant from Saint-Jean-de-Luz; where they, being come, waited some two hours for her approach in a heat so desperate that five or six soldiers died, suffocated in their armor. At last, toward two o'clock, the court of the Queen was beheld coming near. Then the Queen Mother, seized with a great joy, crossed the river and found herself face to face with whom she had so long desired. Their salutations and embraces ended, they seated themselves in the boat and . . . the troops gave forth a cannonade as furious as it was possible to hear, at which the Spaniards were amazed."

Catherine had prepared a welcoming picnic on a grassy, shaded island in the river. The guests arrived "after a voyage accompanied by continuous music from several marine gods singing and reciting verses" and were seated at round tables scattered under the trees. After a feast of "hams and tongues and pastries and all sorts of fruits, salads, sweetmeats and a great abundance of good wine" served by the ladies of the Court dressed as peasant girls in satin and gold, the entertainment consisted of "satyrs playing instruments and a band of nymphs whose beauty and whose jewels dimmed the stars." Inevitably, however, just as they had begun their performance, "envious fortune, unable to bear its glory, sent such a terrible rainstorm that the confusion of the night retreat by boat gave the next morning as many good stories to laugh at as the festival had given thrills of pleasure."

A more serious disappointment marked Catherine's first conversation with her daughter. Elizabeth had been a shy, pliable girl of fourteen when she had left home to marry Philip, but the intervening years had added to her education. Catherine noted the change and commented, "How Spanish you have become, my dearest." Elizabeth replied, "I admit it. It is my duty to be so." And she added, "But I am still your daughter, the same whom you and my father sent off to Spain."

The meeting with Alva also foundered. The Duke was fifty-seven years old then, a tall, erect man who owed his spareness to a hard lifetime's service of God and his other two masters. For the first of them, Charles V, he had campaigned against enemies in Hungary, in Tunis and Algiers, in Catalonia and Navarre. Philip he had represented as governor of the Netherlands, where he proudly conceded having ordered the execution of 18,000 unrepentant heretics. Somber, with hard eyes and a drawn mouth over his trimmed beard, he had patience neither for Catherine's undistinguished paternal lineage nor for her accommodating attitude toward Huguenots. The two met on a blazing afternoon in the gallery of the palace which Catherine was occupying in Bayonne. As they paced back and forth, she began, as Alva reported to Philip, to talk "at incredible speed, touching one subject after another." All of them had to do with the marriages she was proposing. The Spaniard listened impatiently and, when he could, interrupted to bring up the topic of religion. "France must be cleared," he said, "of this vicious sect."

Catherine feigned to misunderstand and started to discuss a possible alliance against the Turks, but Alva brought the subject back to the Huguenots.

"Since you understand so well the evil from which France is suffering," she said, "tell me the remedy."

"Madame," Alva replied, "who knows better than yourself?"

"The King your Master," Catherine said ironically, "knows better than I everything that passes in France. What means would he employ?"

Alva ticked off words of advice. First of all, eliminate the leaders; the head of a salmon, he noted, is worth more than the heads of a thousand frogs. Second, rescind all edicts of toleration; they only encourage greater license. Third, banish all seditious preachers. Fourth, make the penalties for harboring heretics more stringent. "When I spoke of these things with the late King your husband," he added, "His Majesty was of my mind in the matter. If all good Catholics would unite to do what should be done, there would not remain one soul to break bread with that blasphemous brood."

"You can rest assured," Catherine replied frostily, "that I am not unmindful of my husband's counsel, and you can tell your master of the goodwill we bear toward the Faith and of our desire to do all things that will further the true service of God."

Subsequent meetings between Alva and Catherine reached the same impasse. He refused to entertain any discussion of marriages until the religious problem was resolved. She could not concede that any religious problem existed without opening France to Philip's interference. Although Catherine's program of masques, suppers, promenades, banquets, and ballets unfolded as planned, no progress was made. Finally, the Court made preparations to continue its progress. Charles wept at the prospect of his sister's departure and had to be told that "Kings do not shed tears." Catherine wrote that "my daughter the Queen parted from us on the third of July, I went on the same day to sleep at Irun that I might have the joy of seeing her as long as I could. We talked of nothing but caresses and good cheer, for in truth the chief reason for the meeting was to have this consolation—to see the Queen my daughter."

If that, in truth, had not been Catherine's chief reason, it did turn out to be her sole satisfaction. Assessing the political consequences of the conference in Bayonne, the Spanish Cardinal Gravella noted that "it was merely the meeting of a mother and daughter."

Not only did Catherine's talks with Alva fail to achieve their purpose, but they complicated her domestic problems as well. The strict secrecy in which the meetings had been held aroused the suspicion of the Huguenots, and subsequent reassurances only served to persuade them that some sort of alliance against them had indeed been concluded. The mood became apparent soon after the Court began its homeward journey. In Rennes, violent street fights marred the festivities. In La Rochelle, a white silk ribbon was stretched across the main gate; before he could enter, Charles had to dismount, bare his head, and swear to uphold the freedom of the city. It was a tradition dating back to the Middle Ages, but the presence of seven thousand Huguenots gave it a new significance.

Despite these warnings, Catherine resolved to wind up her two-year expedition with a grand, formal reconciliation to be held in Moulins, the old capital of the Bourbons. She summoned the Guises and Coligny, who for the sake of harmony had been excluded from the *voyage,* and ordered them to make up their differences. To encourage the process, she arranged for the Cardinal of Lorraine to be lodged in the same house as Coligny and told each that she would hold him responsible for the safety of the other. She also took measures to discourage the private settlement of grievances. Gentlemen were forbidden under any circumstances to put their hands to their swords. Lackeys and pages were disarmed. Lanterns were required to be hung in dim doorways, and no one was permitted to walk the streets at night without a light.

Catherine had also planned the program to make the most of national unity. The aged Chancellor, Michel de l'Hôpital, rose to tell the assembled notables that, based on what he had seen during the tour of the provinces, the fundamental evil in France was the bad administration of justice. Offices were traditionally sold to purchasers who used them to their own advantage, transmitted them to their heirs or resold them to other aspirants. All this was well known, and there was little dissent when the Chancellor proposed drastic reforms. Nevertheless, Catherine followed the debate with particular pleasure because Anjou, her favorite son, was for the first time participating in the royal council. Barely fourteen years old, he had already caught the attention of the Venetian, Giovanni Michiele, who found him graceful in manner and movement, admirably talented, intelligent, handsome, and affable—everything which his older royal brother Charles was not.

The subject of religion could not, however, be avoided forever. As soon as it was broached, by a delegation from Dijon complaining about the Protestants' holding of private worship in their homes, the old personal animosities flared up. The Spanish ambassador reported home that "the people here do not like each other," and Philip himself pressed Catherine to take the advice Alva had given her on how to deal with heretics. Her reply was to write that "so far as concerns the agreements I have made with my subjects in regard to which [Spain] seems to be so much troubled, after I have seen the combats so many times renewed, the pitched battles, the cities taken by assault, all to no profit except to ruin me and to make me lose every day the best of my subjects, I prefer to do what I have done rather than to lose the rest of my kingdom." And she added, under the circumstances more out of hope than conviction: "And God has made me so happy that, instead of the ruin which I saw threatening me, I now live in repose and my kingdom is building up again more and more every day."

IV

Despite Catherine's assertion, troubles with Spain continued. Three years after the death of Henry II, France had sent a small contingent of colonists, all of them Huguenots, to the New World, where they established a toehold on the coast of Florida. The idea had originated with Coligny, who hoped that the new settlement would become a refuge for his co-religionists, and it was approved by Catherine as a challenge to Spain's prosperous American empire. Fort Caroline, as the settlement had been named, had survived for three years when, in September, 1565, a Spanish fleet of eight ships swooped down on it. After shelling the fort to pieces, the Spaniards easily rounded up the settlers, tried them for piracy, and put them to death. With a bow to his mother-in-law, Philip ordered placards put around their necks, reading "Hung not as Frenchmen but as Lutherans."

The second clash occurred closer to home but again involved Coligny. Like all French Huguenots, he had watched and encouraged the attempts of the Netherlands to throw off Spanish rule. For him, however, more than religious solidarity was involved because one of the Dutch leaders, the Count of Horn, was his cousin and another, the Count of Egmont, was a close friend. In midsummer of 1566, the insurrection erupted, starting in Antwerp where the cathedral was pillaged and spreading rapidly into the entire province. Philip's predictable reaction was to order the Duke of Alva to march northward with a force of 20,000 and restore order. The shortest route lay across France, but Catherine refused to give her permission. Such a move, she told Philip, would provoke her subjects to "such a fright as might light a fire hard to put out." Undaunted, Alva took his army by sea to Genoa, then over the Alps and through Lorraine and Luxembourg. Egmont and Horn were captured, tried, and executed.

Before Alva's departure, Coligny had persuaded Catherine to prepare for possible treachery on Philip's part by raising her own army of Swiss mercenaries. His hope was to be able to use them in support of his Dutch friends, but the swiftness of the Duke, who had taken only eight weeks to reach Brussels and another three to dispose of the rebellion, defeated his plan. Rather, the sudden appearance of two armies, one skirting the border of France and the other advancing toward Paris, threw the excited Huguenots into a panic. Surely all this was evidence of some evil design plotted against them at Bayonne. A meeting was held at Coligny's castle in Châtillon where, despite his last-minute efforts, hotter heads were allowed to prevail.

The Huguenot plan was nothing less than to seize the
King and take over the country by forcing him to appoint
Condé, as First Prince of the Blood, to be his principal ad-
viser. Catherine, who was staying with her children in her
castle of Monceaux some fifty miles from Paris, was warned
of the plot but refused to believe that Coligny would be a
party to such treason. "There has been," she wrote to her
daughter Elizabeth, "some talk without foundation that
those of the Religion mean to make a stir, but, thank God,
we are as peaceful as we could wish."

However, on the morning of September 22 some suspi-
cious-looking horsemen were seen gathering in the woods
where Charles was accustomed to hunt. A messenger arrived
from Alva in Brussels, bearing both details of the conspiracy
gathered by the Duke's spies and his own offer of assistance.
Catherine wisely wanted no part of the assistance but moved
the Court to the relative safety of the neighboring walled city
of Meaux. As reports arrived of armed men converging and
shutting off the escape routes, the Council spent two days
inconclusively debating the best course of action. Finally, the
colonel commanding the Swiss troops, Ludwig Pfeiffer,
broke the deadlock. "May it please Your Majesty," he told
Charles, "to entrust your person and that of your mother to
us. With the points of our pikes we will open a path wide
enough for you to pass through the army of your enemies."
There was considerable opposition to this proposal, possibly
because, as the Venetian Correro noted, the Swiss looked like
"a set of baggage-porters, the most villainous-looking gang
I have ever seen." Nevertheless, Catherine agreed. The
Court slipped out of Meaux at four o'clock in the morning
and arrived in Paris after nightfall, tired, hot, hungry,
humiliated, and, as far as Catherine was concerned, filled
with unforgiving rage at Coligny.

The Huguenot cavalry reached Paris, too, and in their
frustration set fire to the Sainte-Chapelle before setting up

camp outside of the city. From her sanctuary in the Louvre, Catherine dispatched a herald to order them to lay down their arms and come before the King as the rebels they were. Their reply was to seize the towns on the Seine above and below the city in order to starve it into submission. Fighting broke out in the suburbs, so close to the gates that windmills in the faubourgs of Saint-Honoré and Saint-Martin were burned. Churches for miles around were plundered of their altar vessels, and Huguenot gentlemen fashioned themselves shirts and handkerchiefs out of the silk and lace of sacramental garments. Forced loans were extracted from small merchants, and those who would not pay were constrained into forced labor. But the very thoroughness of the Huguenots only served to defeat their purpose. Fearful of having them confiscated, thousands of peasants drove their cattle and carried their grain into the city.

In the confusion, the royal forces slapped together an army which met the main Huguenot force in the shadow of the abbey church of Saint-Denis on November 10, 1567. Like other set battles of the religious wars, it was a ragged, badly disciplined affair distinguished only by the fact that it claimed the life of the Constable, Anne de Montmorency. Although in his seventy-fifth year, the old man was in the thick of the battle and already bleeding from five wounds when a Scottish volunteer named Robert Stuart knocked him to the ground and pointed a pistol at his head. Accustomed from previous campaigning to be taken for ransom, Montmorency looked up and said, "But I am the Constable." "And that," replied Stuart as he fired, "is why I am killing you."

Despite the fact that they had held their own, Condé ordered his troops to pull back from the battlefield, first to the Marne and then to Pont-à-Mousson on the German border where he expected to gather reinforcements. Catherine employed the respite to start negotiations which dragged out for months. Neither side had either stomach or money for more fighting, but neither was prepared to make substantial concessions. The resulting agreement, signed at Longjumeau on March 23, 1568, was therefore universally considered to be more of a cease-fire than a peace treaty. Some of the Huguenot captains, whom campaigning had taken far from home, did not even bother to disband their troops.

The hostilities which resumed within three months were marked by a new level of cruelty. On both sides, soldiers were systematically slaughtered after surrendering. In towns that were captured, magistrates were hung and priests butchered. Tombs were opened to retrieve the lead linings of their coffins, which were melted down for cannonballs. Violence even reached to the high seas: when a Huguenot fleet intercepted seven Portuguese ships bound for Brazil and discovered that they were carrying sixty-nine Jesuit priests, they were all thrown overboard. So commonplace were the rapes, mutilations, and mass executions that even Theodore Beza, who had inherited Calvin's mantle, was moved to caution his brethren: "Certainly defense by arms is just and necessary, but the arms have been so badly used that we must pray God that He will teach us to handle them in a more holy manner. May His Church be rather an assembly of martyrs than a refuge for murderers and brigands." François de la Noue, who as a Huguenot field commander was one of the most dedicated of the brigands, put it more simply: "We fought the first war like angels," he wrote, "the second like men, and the third like devils."

The other distinguishing characteristic of that third war was the appearance of a new commander in chief of the royal forces. Over the objections of her counselors and the unspoken resentment of her eldest son, Catherine had forced the appointment of the now sixteen-year-old Anjou. His baptism of fire at the battle of Jarnac on March 13, 1569, was the occasion for both a clear Catholic victory and the

Illustration in widely circulated Catholic pamphlet depicts exotic atrocities allegedly committed by Huguenots, such as using eviscerated victim as a makeshift feeding trough.

death of Condé.* A proud Catherine rewarded him with a magnificent pageant at which the entire Court presented its congratulations, although Gaspard of Tavannes was later to describe in his *Memoirs* how, on the morning of the battle, he had been obliged to shake Anjou out of bed because 10,000 troops were awaiting his command.

The victory at Jarnac was celebrated with bonfires and *Te Deums* across France, but the Huguenots were far from being beaten. Retreating into the vast stretches of countryside they controlled, they waited for volunteers from the Lutheran states of Germany to replenish their ranks. Elizabeth of England, whom it suited to see Catherine embroiled in civil war, advanced a loan—although she required Condé's widow to pledge her jewels as security. Catherine left the Louvre to follow the armies, moving her headquarters as the scene of action changed and ignoring Philip's repeated offers of help. Six months after Jarnac, Anjou inflicted another defeat on the Huguenots, again with the discreet help of Tavannes. Once more the enemy escaped, this time because Charles, consumed with jealousy of his brother's triumphs, refused to let the army pursue them.

The war which was chewing up money and men, and was now dividing the royal children, dragged into its second year with no prospect of success. Over the protests of the Guises, the Papal Nuncio, and Philip's ubiquitous representatives, Catherine let Coligny know that she was ready to sue for peace. She knew that the price she would have to pay, in terms of concessions and privileges, would infuriate her Catholic subjects to greater violence. That had been the unremitting pattern of the last ten years. But at least she had learned that armed force would not achieve pacification. Clearly, another instrument was needed.

* When told the news, Mlle de Limeuil, now married to a prosperous banker named Scipion Sardini, had a one-word comment: *"Enfin!"* ("Finally!").

V

A respected French nineteenth-century scholar, Hector de La Ferrière, was once asked whether he would undertake a definitive biography of Marguerite de Valois—Queen Margot. He replied—with a wistful smile, one imagines—"It is a remarkable story. But alas, Monsieur, I have no time for such diversions."

Half Medici, half Valois, the granddaughter of both Francis I and Lorenzo de' Medici, she was born on May 14, 1553, and brought up along with all the royal and near-royal brats, at Amboise. More diligent than the rest, she applied herself to her studies, learning Latin as well as Italian and Spanish, both of which she spoke "as if she had been born and nourished in those countries." Brantôme, her most extravagant admirer, relates that she was ". . . most eloquent and beautifully spoken in her high grave conversation, but also charmingly graceful in her kind and pleasant wit." She was also, he says, "versed in learning, both sacred and profane, and delighted by books." This predilection, which was to last through a long and stormy life, was confirmed by another observer who noted that "when she set about reading a book, however long and thick, she never stopped for a moment till the end of it, and oftentimes she abandoned sleep and food for its sake."

Nor were the less formal aspects of her education neglected. As a wide-eyed, observant child, she witnessed the butchery which followed the failure of La Renaudie's plot; later, she could not help but be aware of the incessant goings-on of the *escadron volant*. She herself is credited with starting her amatory career at the age of eleven or twelve. Among her conquests at this period were, reputedly, two of her own brothers. This is probably a libel, although she had made allusion to something of this sort in her *Memoirs,* and even Brantôme relates that Catherine obliged her to drink at every meal a potion of sorrel, an onionlike vegetable reputed to cool "hot, boiling blood."

That there indeed was something special about her was noticed early. Giovanni Michieli wrote in 1561, when Margot was eight years old, that "by her grace, her beauty, and her spirit, she promises to become a very rare and fine princess, far superior to her two sisters." A decade later a Polish visitor to the court—Laski, the Paladin of Siradia—met her for the first time and announced, "After such beauty, I wish to see no more." Montaigne, who knew her well and dedicated the first edition of his *Essays* to her, described her as "one of those divine, supernatural and extraordinary beauties that one sometimes sees shining like stars through the veils of an earthly body."

Early portraits of her do show a very pretty girl, but with cheeks a trifle too chubby and a chin too firm to achieve the status of divinity. What does come unmistakably across the span of four centuries is a look in the eyes and a set to the features. Margot was, as her mother had feared, an extraordinarily sexy girl.

She had other attributes as well. She loved music and managed to maintain, however straitened her circumstances were to become, at least a lute player or two within her personal household. In addition to taking delight in books, she was herself a first-rate writer—her *Memoirs* are far more valuable as literature than as historical source. And, as might be expected, she was something of a style-setter, not only in fashion but in manners as well. Gossip had it, for instance, that she habitually slept on black sheets, the better to set off the whiteness of her body.

Whatever their color, it is conceded that the sheets suffered considerable wear and tear because, of all the women in France, Margot turned out to be a scorned, unsatisfied wife. As Noel Williams, the most gentlemanly and sympathetic of her biographers, explains: "United to a hubsand who treated her in this manner, unable to turn for aid or counsel to her mother or brothers, it is scarcely surprising that Marguerite should have succumbed to the temptations which surrounded her, and that she should have begun to indulge in highly dangerous flirtations." These flirtations, and their thundering consequences, will be examined in due course. But first it is necessary to trace the events that led to Margot's marital disaster.

VI

From Catherine's point of view, equating as ever her own personal dynastic aspirations to France's national interest, the most desirable match for Margot had been Don Carlos, the heir apparent to King Philip's thirty-three thrones and dignities. It was, in fact, so desirable as to have been one of the first projects to claim Catherine's attention after the death of Francis II. Using the coronation of Charles IX as a pretext, she had commissioned portraits of all the members of the family and sent them off to her daughter, Elizabeth, in Madrid. Elizabeth had written back: "Everyone here found the paintings to be the handsomest in the world, and especially that of my little sister. . . . The prince [Don Carlos] came to me after having seen them and told me three or four times, 'Mas hermosa es la pequeña' ['The prettiest is the little one']. I assured him that she was in truth very attractive, and when Mme de Clermont [Elizabeth's matron of honor] explained that she could be his, he began to laugh. Even the King found her very pretty and asked me whether she was tall."

Despite his amiability, Philip had no serious interest in Margot. He already had one Daughter of France, and saw no need to burden his house with another. Rather, his plan at the time was to marry Don Carlos off to the recently widowed Mary Stuart, thus adding support to her claims upon the English throne and putting pressure on its Protestant Queen. The prospect of the daughter-in-law she had cast off climbing upon a throne she had singled out for her own so irritated Catherine that she dashed off another letter to Elizabeth, urging her to do all in her power to defeat the project. It was, she wrote, not so much a matter of state as of Elizabeth's self-interest. If the marriage were to take place and Philip should then die, Elizabeth would become a dowager queen under a reigning Mary Stuart and her swarm of Guise relations—a disagreeable position which Catherine herself had experienced at first hand. The Stuart marriage did not take place, but Catherine's own strenuous efforts on behalf of Margot, which had culminated in the failure of the great meeting at Bayonne, proved no more successful. In the end, the unfortunate Carlos married no one. Mentally deranged since childhood, he grew progressively more unstable and became involved in a plot to murder his father. Placed in confinement in 1568, he died six months later, having just turned twenty-three.

Like any prudent mother with an eligible daughter, Catherine had kept other irons in the fire. One of them involved an alliance with Rudolph of Hungary, the son of the Austrian Emperor. From the paucity of Catherine's correspondence on this subject, and because Margot does not so much as mention Rudolph's name in her *Memoirs,* it is reasonable to assume that the proposal received a firm turndown from the prospective bridegroom's family. Another project, which dragged on for more than a decade, would have placed Margot on the throne of Portugal as the consort of King Sebastian. Even by the standards of the day this would have been a strange marriage because Sebastian, born posthumously and raised by a strict order of monks, was a religious fanatic whose consuming ambition was to lead a crusade against the Mohammedans. To this end, he turned over the government of the country to the Jesuits and prepared himself with a regimen of martial exercises, prayer, severe asceticism, and sexual abstinence. Nevertheless, diplomats with offers and counteroffers shuttled between the two countries—the French ambassador to Lisbon was Jean Nicot, whose more lasting contribution was the introduction of tobacco to France—until Charles IX lost patience and called off the negotiations. As for Sebastian, who had not been consulted, his wish was eventually granted, if only briefly. He assembled an army and led it as far as al-Kasr El Kebir in Morocco, where his troops were annihilated and he himself was killed in his first major encounter with the infidels.

While Catherine was engaged on her behalf, Margot behaved as the perfect, dutiful daughter—dutiful or perhaps fearful, for she noted in her *Memoirs,* "I had been brought up in such awe of the Queen, my mother, that not only did I not dare to speak to her, but if she only so much as looked at me I trembled with fear lest I had done something to displease her." She did, however, express her own preference to the extent of selecting a lover. He was the handsomest, most virile young man at the Court, graceful, carefree, and fully aware of his effect on women. "There was not a single heart," wrote a diarist of the period, "which could hold out against that face; he could persuade them without having to say a word." Unfortunately for Margot, he was also a Guise —Henry, the eldest son of the Duke Francis who had been assassinated in 1563.

Possibly because Henry had inherited in full measure his family's arrogance, or possibly because Margot's passion exceeded even her fear of her mother, the young couple took little precaution to hide their liaison. Henry of Guise was seen coming in and out of Margot's private apartments; notes and letters passed between the lovers. Gossips claimed to

have surprised the pair, "coupling like young dogs" in remote corners of the Louvre. Davila wrote in his *History of
the Civil Wars in France* that "their intimacy was so public
that rumor ran that they had been secretly married."

What happened when Catherine and Charles IX found
out about the affair is not described in Margot's *Memoirs,*
in Catherine's correspondence, nor in any other primary
French source. The account that has been accepted is contained in a letter dated July 7, 1570, and written to Philip II
by Francés de Álava, his ambassador-spy to France: "A well-
informed source has assured me that on the twenty-seventh
of the previous month, at five o'clock in the morning, the
King, wearing his nightgown, betook himself to the apartment of his mother, whom he found already awake. . . .
They sent for Madame Marguerite, who arrived in a half
hour with a companion." The companion was sent away
and a guard placed at the door. The Queen then spoke to
Madame Marguerite for about a quarter of an hour, after
which, Álava continues, "I am assured that the mother took
her hand to her daughter, and that her son did likewise to
the extent that she was rendered senseless, and remained in
that condition for an hour, after which the mother still
would not let her return to her own apartment"—presumably until the damage to her face and clothing could be repaired. It is possible that Álava embroidered somewhat to
amuse his master, and later French accounts add still more
unlikely notes,* but the fact is that Margot's first great love
was abruptly terminated. Shortly after the incident described
by the Spanish ambassador, Henry Duke of Guise was married to the Princess of Porcien, recently widowed and many
years his senior.

There had, all along, been still another prospective bride-

---

* According to one of them, Charles IX ordered his bastard half brother—
the son of Henry II and Lady Flemming—to arrange for the assassination
of Henry of Guise. The plot, if it existed, failed; but how different history
would have been had it succeeded.

groom for Margot. Indeed, that marriage had been informally arranged by her father, Henry II, when she and the husband-to-be—Henry of Navarre—were both six years old. This Henry was the son of Antoine of Navarre, and the only crown he could therefore bring into the family was from that tiny kingdom in the Pyrenees. This, at the time, seemed ample enough. Henry had just signed the Treaty of Cateau-Cambrésis, which at last offered the prospect of peace; he himself was in good health and could look forward to a long reign; there were more than enough other sons and daughters to marry off.

All this, of course, had changed with his death. Peace had been short-lived, and it was shattered by a different, more cruel kind of internecine war. From the moment she had assumed the regency upon the death of her eldest son, Catherine had tried and—whatever her detractors say—had largely succeeded in playing a balancing game between the rival religions and their supporters. The attempts to marry Margot off to Carlos, to Sebastian, to Rudolph of Hungary—all of them good Catholics—had been gambits in that game. By 1570, however, many factors made it desirable to reach some sort of accord with the Huguenots. Despite her late husband's wishes, Catherine had not at first seriously considered the young Navarre as a potential son-in-law. Nor did his crown attract her now. But he had another qualification: his mother, Jeanne d'Albret, wife of the late Antoine, was the acknowledged spiritual and political leader of the French Huguenot movement, and her son was the heir apparent to that position. Knowing Navarre to be a happy-go-lucky youth with an eye for pretty girls and a taste for worldly pleasures entirely out of keeping with his mother's stern example, Catherine did not think she would have any trouble securing his agreement to take Margot for a wife. Persuading his mother, however, was another matter.

Jeanne d'Albret was ten years younger than Catherine, but she looked and acted as if she were at least that much her senior. The daughter of Francis I's sister, Marguerite, she had been a frivolous and gay young princess whom a courtier had described as having "a humor so jovial that one could never be bored when in her presence." She had also early shown a streak of stubbornness. Commanded by her royal uncle to marry the German Duke of Cleves, she had flatly refused and had to be carried bodily to the altar—an indignity that only hardened her resolve, for that union was in due course annulled for nonconsummation. Her marriage to Antoine of Bourbon was, by contrast, a romantic match. An observer described Jeanne, newly wed, as "having no pleasure or occupation except in talking about or writing to [her husband]. She does it in company and in private . . . the waters cannot quench the flame of her love." For his part, Antoine, who had sworn to be "the gentlest, most affectionate of husbands," replied with tender letters of his own, expressing in one of them his pleasure at the anticipation of "lying warmly beside you." But Antoine was, for all his vows, an incurable philanderer. Jeanne did not especially blame Catherine for exploiting this affliction to her own purposes—*la belle Rouet* was just the last of a parading regiment. A fiercely proud woman quick to take offense at the least imagined slight to her position, what she would not forgive the Queen Mother was her role in the embarrassing circumstances of Antoine's death—that, and, of course, Catherine's duplicity in dealing with the legitimate aspirations of the Huguenots.

Unlike Antoine who changed religion seven times, Jeanne publicly embraced the teachings of Calvin on Christmas Day, 1560, and thereafter never wavered. On the contrary, the breakup of her marriage and the death of her husband only served to channel all her strength into the cause. For some people, the acceptance of a moral commitment has an ennobling effect, softening the hard edges of their character and enhancing their capacity to understand others without compromising their own convictions. In the case of Jeanne d'Albret, the opposite happened. Ardor modulated into fanaticism and then repression, to the extent that her tiny kingdom of Navarre became a miniature replica in reverse of the provinces writhing under Philip II's Christian custody: priests and nuns were hounded down; churches were destroyed and the Catholic ritual forbidden; subjects who persisted in the error of their ways were despoiled of their possessions. Agrippa d'Aubigné, the most impassioned of the Huguenot chroniclers, once described her as having "a mind powerful enough to guide the highest affairs, a heart impervious to all adversity, and of woman only the sex." She looked the part, too: small of stature, frail, but erect in a permanent attitude of righteousness and defiance; a narrow face with cold, unmoving eyes; thin lips which soured her words with sarcasm.

The two women had known each other slightly at Court during the last years of Francis I's reign and under Henry II. Although no direct evidence exists, it is likely that Jeanne, of impeccable royal blood herself and inordinately proud of it, was among the chief detractors of the Florentine grocer's daughter. Certainly the prospect of marrying off her only son and heir to one of the daughters of the Italian woman— and moreover a daughter who was already, it was freely said, soiled at the edges—could hardly have been tempting.

Skilled diplomat that she was, Catherine did not immediately reveal her principal objective. Rather, the negotiations that began in 1569 and were carried on entirely through intermediaries ranged over an extensive agenda. There was, first of all, the need to arrange an armistice, for the sporadic fighting which marked the wars of religion had again broken out. There was the question of what concessions the crown would make to the free exercise of religion. Though she was arguing from weakness, Jeanne d'Albret found herself winning point after point—to the extent that Monluc, who had faithfully discharged his duties to God and country by slaughtering as many Huguenots as he could catch, complained: "We defeat them again and again, but the edicts are always to their advantage."

Despite her success, or perhaps because she understood Catherine's strategy, Jeanne remained adamant on one point. Under no circumstance would she leave home and come to Court, as the Queen Mother repeatedly suggested. In a letter to Catherine, she wrote: "I cannot imagine why you should find it necessary to say that you want to see me and my children, but not in order to do us harm. Forgive me if I laugh when I read these letters, for you are allaying a fear I have never felt. I have never thought, as some say, that you fed on little children."

For her part, Catherine had never openly brought up the question of the marriage, but merely implied that it was a *fait accompli* which in due course would seal all the other agreements. Toward the end of 1571, the gossip from Paris was full of details about preparations for the ceremony, the gathering of a trousseau, the extent of the dowry. There were other reports that Catherine, dubious of her ability to persuade young Navarre to abjure Protestantism, had petitioned the Pope to grant a special dispensation for the marriage. Most disquieting to Jeanne, there was talk that the question of the annulment of her own first marriage to the Duke of Cleves had been reopened. A revocation of that annulment would have invalidated her marriage to Antoine and consequently would have branded Henry of Navarre as illegitimate. As such, the revocation would have eliminated him as First Prince of the Blood and possible successor to the throne of France.

Perhaps it was this threat, reinforced by Catherine's patient but unwavering single-mindedness, that finally induced Jeanne to agree to a personal meeting. Sensitive as ever to the nuances of time and place, the Queen Mother had chosen as site for the meeting neither Paris nor Blois, where the Court was in residence, but Chenonceaux. It was therefore in that most perfect of Loire castles, whose setting and architectural lines almost preclude discord of any kind, that the two ladies at last met on February 14, 1572. Giovanni Maria Petrucci, the Florentine legate, was an eyewitness: "The Queen Mother had scarcely crossed the threshold when the Queen of Navarre arrived. Embraces and salutations were exchanged . . . and the Queen of Navarre asked at once for something to eat. Immediately afterward the two Queens retired into a room alone. The Queen of Navarre is said to have thanked God for the honor Their Majesties wished for her son . . . but that she needed to discuss the particulars more fully."

In fact, the Queen of Navarre had not come alone but had brought along her daughter, Catherine, who was an impressionable but safe thirteen years old. Her son had been prudently left at home, and it is through her letters to him that the discussions—and even more revealingly her own maternal-political conflicts—can most clearly be followed. After her first conversations with Catherine, she wrote: "My son, the long dispatch I am sending contains details of the exchange I have had with the Queen Mother and Madame [the formal title for Margot, who had accompanied her mother]. . . . Since the matter must be played by ear I urge you not to leave Béarn until you receive word from me. If you are already en route, find some pretext to return." Having reiterated this concern, which suggests that she had few illusions about her son's strength of character, Jeanne spells out her own strategy: "Madame has paid me great honor . . . assuring me that she favors your suit. Given her influence with the King and her mother . . . if she embraces the Religion, we can count ourselves the luckiest persons in the world, and not only our family but the whole kingdom of France. . . . When you next write, please tell me to sound out Madame on her religious views, emphasizing that this is the only thing holding you back, so that when I show it to her she will tend more to believe that such is your will."

The rest of the letter trails off into petty complaints about real or imagined slights ("I was constantly pressed to come, but nobody is in any hurry to see me now that I am here"), and further exhortations ("I beg of you, my son, to pray to God, make a point of attending sermons and prayers . . . and not to forget to write what I mentioned above"). The original document also contains a postscript, penned in a thirteen-year-old's hand: "Monsieur, I have seen Madame and found her very beautiful. I wish you could see her. I spoke of you in such a way that you are in her good graces. . . . She was kind to me and gave me a little dog I like very much."

Jeanne was not as easy to win over as her daughter, or as ingenuous. On the contrary, as she saw that Catherine had anticipated her strategy, she became shriller and, fatal for a negotiator, less able to control her composure. Her letter of March 8 reads: "My son, I am in agony, in such extreme suffering that if I had not been prepared, it would overcome me. . . . I am being obliged to negotiate quite contrary to my hopes—and to their promises. I am not free to talk with either the King or Madame, only with the Queen Mother. . . . I only see Madame in the Queen's quarters, whence she never stirs except at hours impossible for me to visit her. I have not yet shown Madame your letter, but I shall do so. I mentioned it to her but, being very cautious, she answered in general terms, expressing obedience and reverence for you and for me too, in case she becomes your wife. . . . I have remonstrated on three separate occasions with the Queen. But all she does is mock me, and afterward tells others exactly the opposite of what I have said, with the result that they blame me. . . . She treats me so shamefully that you might say that the patience I manage to maintain surpasses that of Griselda herself."

The letter goes into considerable detail, with entire paragraphs which would fit smoothly into psychiatric texts: "I am sure that if you knew the pain I feel you would pity me, for they treat me with all the harshness in the world and without the gravity the issue merits. I am determined not to let anger get the best of me, and my patience is miraculous to behold. I know that I will need it even more than in the past, and I have braced myself. I fear that I may fall sick, for I do not feel well at all."

Regarding Marguerite, Jeanne concedes to her son that she is "beautiful, discreet and graceful," but adds that "she has grown up in the most vicious and corrupt atmosphere imaginable. I cannot see that anyone escapes its poison." And she continues, in terms hardly calculated to deter an adventuresome young man: "Not for anything on earth would I have you come to live here. Although I knew it was bad, I find it even worse than I feared. Here it is the women who make advances to the men, rather than the other way around. If you were here you would never escape without special intervention from God."

The letter ends: "You have doubtless realized that their main object, my son, is to separate you from God and from me. You can understand my anxiety for you. I beg you, pray to God." The signature, somewhat redundantly, is *"votre bonne mère et meilleure amie"* ("your good mother and best friend").

Whether Jeanne d'Albret ever seriously expected that Margot would become a Huguenot in order to marry her son is questionable. Being as evangelical as the most fiery of her pastors, she undoubtedly would have liked to see it happen. There is also little question that Catherine might have intimated that such a course of action was possible. Given Jeanne's intransigent refusal to agree to any sort of meeting, Catherine may in fact have done more than just drop a hint. She had, of course, no such intention. Her whole purpose was to gain a Huguenot son-in-law, not to lose a daughter to the ranks of Reform. As for Margot, she seems not to have given the prospect a thought. According to the Florentine Petrucci, Jeanne apparently penetrated the defenses established around Margot to the extent of asking about her intentions. "Two days ago," he wrote, "the Queen of Navarre said to Madame that she wished to know whether she would be content to follow the religion of the Prince. Madame replied with great wisdom that if it pleased God she would not fail in obedience to her and to the Prince in all reasonable ways, but that even if he were King of the whole world she would never change her religion. Thereupon [the Queen of Navarre] said, 'The marriage shall not take place.' So they parted with little satisfaction on either side."

But they did not part irrevocably, for Jeanne did not take the course that had been open to her from the moment of her arrival: to pack her bags and go home. Despite the lengthy complaints about her suffering and humiliation, she had at no point been under duress. That she chose to stay, and eventually agreed to the marriage, is a testament to Catherine's shrewd reading of her character. More accurately than Jeanne herself, the Queen Mother had weighed her religious conviction against her ambition for her son and had correctly guessed which way the scales would tilt.

For her part, Jeanne d'Albret fashioned a peculiar face-saving rationalization which assumed that it was she who had championed and pushed the marriage through against stiff opposition. This idea was expressed in a letter to Queen Elizabeth of England, a fellow Protestant monarch whom she had never met: "Madame, Events which order the destiny of great personages are usually so beset with difficulties that it is impossible to divine their conclusion. Such has been the cause, Madame, why I have not sooner informed you of the matters which I came to negotiate at this court. This uncertainty had not its rise, Madame, in the want of goodwill manifested by those chiefly concerned, but through the evil practices and devices of turbulent men, who opposed thus both the public weal and their own private welfare. Despite these impediments, He, who cares especially for those who rest on His wisdom and providence, has looked down upon me with paternal favor, and has at length disposed the hearts of all to take final and determinate resolution to complete the marriage proposed between Madame Marguerite and my son. . . . Although the Evil One, since my arrival here, raised in many the spirit of dissension and opposition, God has manifested His gracious goodness to the overthrow of their malicious intent and has inspired those animated with benevolence, lovers of concord and repose, to accomplish this union."

With her side of the story recorded for posterity, and the formal marriage contract signed on April 11, the Queen of Navarre took leave of Catherine to begin preparing for the wedding. By mid-May, she was established in Paris and sallying forth on daily shopping expeditions. Anne d'Este, mother of the dashing Duke Henry, wrote to a friend: "The Queen of Navarre is here, not in very good health but very courageous. She is wearing more pearls than ever." Catherine was away from Paris, but before leaving she had requested the Comte de Retz, one of her close friends, to look after Jeanne. Partly to thank her, and partly just to chat, the Queen of Navarre wrote to the Queen Mother on May 23: "I have seen your Tuileries fountains, when M de Retz invited me to a private supper. I have found many things for our wedding in this city during my excursions with him. I am in good form awaiting your arrival."

Despite her cheerfulness, it was the last letter Jeanne d'Albret wrote. Coming home from a shopping trip on June 4, she felt ill and went immediately to bed. In the morning, she woke up complaining of fever and a pain in the upper right-hand side of her body. Four days later, she died.

The conviction that Jeanne d'Albret was poisoned by Catherine de' Medici is an article of faith among Huguenot historians. The accusation first appeared in 1574—two years after the fact—in a scurrilous and completely discredited account entitled *Discours Merveilleux de la Vie, Actions et Déportemens de Catherine de Médicis,* which even detailed the *modus operandi*. It appears that the Queen Mother, aware of Jeanne's fondness for perfumed gloves, arranged to have a pair skillfully poisoned by René Bianco, her personal perfumer and fellow Florentine. As conclusive evidence, the author points to the autopsy, when, supposedly, the Queen Mother refused to permit the victim's head to be opened, lest the poison which had accumulated there be discovered. In point of fact, the head was opened during the autopsy as was the chest which revealed advanced tubercular lesions. More convincing is the negative evidence of the entire diplomatic corps attached to the French Court. Not a single dispatch reporting on the death of Jeanne d'Albret even suggests that it was due to anything but natural causes. Nevertheless, the myth has persisted to the present day, and it is preserved by the guides at the Château of Blois who delight in showing visitors to Catherine's small, paneled study the secret compartment in which she kept her collection of poisons.

VII

Before leaving Chenonceaux, Jeanne wrote a final letter to her son, reporting on the successful outcome of the negotiations. Because he was now expected to present himself at Court, she also set down some rules of behavior for him. The list begins with commonplace concerns: be gracious, speak politely but not obsequiously, remember that the first impression you make on arrival is important. But the last item catches the eye: "That is all I have to say except for this: train your hair to stand up properly, and be sure there are no lice in it." The time has come to meet the fought-over bridegroom—and Prince of the Blood—who needed such a reminder.

The kingdom of Navarre was a political anomaly on the map of Europe, a feudal fiefdom that had broken away from the enormous empire of Charlemagne and sat saddlelike across the peaks of the western Pyrenees. Over the centuries, Spain had nibbled away and finally swallowed entirely the half of the kingdom that lay on her side of the mountains. But the other half, largely surrounded by France, had been allowed to retain its independence as a permanent ally. This arrangement had proved doubly advantageous to France. First, it permitted her to recruit the regiments of Gascon and Béarnais infantry that had formed the core of the French armies during the interminable Italian wars; second, it provided nuptial candidates of acceptable rank when foreign alliances were not available. Thus, Francis I's own sister, Marguerite, had been married off to Henry d'Albret, King of Navarre, and the stubborn Jeanne d'Albret, sole child of that couple, had been given to Antoine of Bourbon.

The arrangement had not worked out so well as far as the King of Navarre was concerned. His powerful ally had been unable to help him achieve his life's ambition of retrieving the half of his kingdom lost to the Spaniards; his wife turned out to be a refined intellectual whom he could hardly understand; his son-in-law was a woman-chasing scoundrel who preferred the fleshpots of the Court to the simpler, ruder life at Pau in Navarre. And, to top everything off, Jeanne's first child, a boy, had died before his second birthday. The cause has never been satisfactorily established, but old Henry blamed it on the training methods—*"délicatesses françaises"* ("French delicacies"), he scornfully called them—instituted by the child's governess, who had been one of his wife's ladies-in-waiting. When Jeanne gave birth to another son, on December 14, 1553, Henry determined that he would himself supervise the child's upbringing.

Immediately upon the boy's birth, his grandfather rubbed his lips with garlic—a taste that evidently lingered, because both of his wives, at an interval of thirty years, complained that he stank. Historians also note that seven wet nurses were tried and rejected before one could be found whose milk

agreed with him. In other respects, however, young Navarre*
was treated exactly like any peasant lad of his age. In good
weather and bad, he spent his days outdoors, barefoot and
bareheaded. Even after old Henry's death, Jeanne, now left
in charge of the household because of Antoine's almost constant absences, did not countermand his wishes. Rather, as
her own affairs began to take her away from Pau, her son
was left free to acquire skills calculated to serve him better
in the barnyard and hayloft than in the drawing room.

In retrospect, there may have been purpose to Jeanne's
behavior—possibly she was so prescient as to prepare Navarre
for the strenuous life that lay ahead of him, or perhaps only
so simple as to raise her own son as differently as possible
from Catherine's pampered, hothouse brood. When Navarre
turned thirteen, firsthand exploration of nature was supplemented with more formal studies under the humanist Flo-
rent Chrétien. Maternal supervision became stricter. Upon
finding, one day, that her son had more money than he
should have, Jeanne demanded an explanation; Navarre's
admission that he had won it playing at dice earned him a
whipping.† To supplement the object lessons of Plutarch,
Caesar, and the rest, the Queen of Navarre began taking the
boy along with her as she traveled about her domains, attending to administrative matters. In order to round out his education as a sixteenth-century princeling, she also gave him
his first military command, in 1568. It was hardly a taxing
assignment—to pacify some fractious subjects who had already been defeated into submission—but the fourteen-year-

---

* His given name was Henry, but because of the plethora of other Henrys
in this narrative, he will be referred to as Navarre.
† Eventually, if not at the time, Navarre himself came to value such
disciplinary measures. There exists a letter that he wrote to the governess
of his own son, then six years old: "You have not reported beating my
son. . . . Please understand that I wish you to do so every time he
stubbornly persists in wrongdoing, for I know well, from my own experience with the best mother in the world, that there is nothing that can do
him more good."

old Navarre handled it with precocious good judgment. Rather than picking out the leaders and making an example of them, he assembled the rebels and pointed out the futility of resistance by force, offering instead to act as their advocate in the future.

Of personal charm, he seemed to have more than his share. A contemporary description, borne out by several portraits dating to this period of his life, notes: "His hair is a little red, yet the ladies think him no less agreeable on that account; his face is finely shaped, his nose neither too large nor too small, his eyes full of sweetness, his skin brown but clear, and his whole countenance animated with an uncommon vivacity." On a less superficial level, assessments of him are less trustworthy because most of them were composed years later and in the obvious light of the man that he became rather than the youth that he was. Nonetheless, there is the word of the Venetian Correro, who, in 1569, reported that he was "a young man full of wit, very carefully brought up in the new religion by his mother. The general opinion is that he will become the scourge of our times unless God applies some remedy."

For a young man who had just been accorded the hand of the most desirable princess in the world, Navarre appeared to be in no great hurry to present himself at Court. From Pau, where he had received the news, he wandered first to Nérac in order to take leisurely farewell of his young lady of the moment, a gardener's daughter appropriately named Fleurette. He was still on the route to Paris on June 13 when a courier reached him with the news that he was no longer merely the heir apparent to Navarre, but its King. The saddened cortege continued along, its ranks swollen by Huguenot leaders from all over France who had set aside their arms if not their animosities in order to attend the wedding. On July 9 they finally entered the capital, and Margot noted in her *Memoirs:* "Wearing mourning for the Queen his Mother, the King of Navarre arrived, accompanied by eight hundred gentlemen, also all in black, and was received with great honors by the King and the whole court."

The summer of 1572 was excessively hot in Paris, adding to the tension caused by the presence of the Huguenot hierarchy in what was the most fiercely Catholic city in the country. The civil wars had dragged on for a decade, long enough for almost every member of the rival camps to have suffered personal loss or pain at the hands of the other. Despite the happy nature of the occasion Catherine had arranged, men forcibly thrown together seized the opportunity to extract redress for long-nurtured wrongs.

July stretched into August, and still no date had been set for the wedding. Nor could it be set, because Catherine had not been able to persuade the Pope to grant his dispensation. To help him along, she had carefully avoided raising the issue of the bridegroom's refusal to change his religion and merely sought a ruling on the question of the couple's consanguinity. But His Holiness had not been taken in and in fact raised anew the question of finding a more suitable, which is to say Catholic, husband for Margot. Seeing her plans in danger of collapsing, and sensing also the mood of the city, Catherine acted with decision. A letter from the French ambassador in Rome was delivered to the Cardinal of Bourbon, who was to perform the ceremony, assuring him that pontifical authorization was on the way. Another letter, from Catherine, went to the governor of the city of Lyons, prohibiting him expressly in the King's name from "letting pass through any courier whatever coming from Rome." The letter to Lyons was dated August 14 and would take a fast rider three days to deliver. The wedding, it was announced, would take place on August 18.*

* Catherine was, as usual, thorough, because the governor of Lyons also received orders not to permit any courier to proceed southward to Rome *after* August 18 unless he had special royal credentials. Catherine wanted to be the first to inform the Pope of the marriage and to do it in her own words. She did so in a letter dated August 19, 1572.

The bride described the ceremony in her *Memoirs:* "Our wedding took place . . . in such triumph and magnificence as no other person of my rank had known until then; the King of Navarre and his troop having changed from mourning into very rich and handsome costume . . . I, in royal garb, with crown and ermine stole, leading the procession, the precious stones in my crown flashing, and my great blue cloak with four trains carried by three princesses; the stands which had been put up as usual for the weddings of Daughters of France, from the Bishop's residence to Notre-Dame, covered and draped in cloth of gold; the people packed together down below to watch the wedding procession and all the Court passing above them. So we arrived at the cathedral porch, where the Cardinal of Bourbon was officiating, and when he had received us and we had said the usual words customary in such cases we passed along the stands to the platform separating the nave from the choir, where there are two flights of stairs, one to go down into the choir, the other leading out of the church through the nave. The King of Navarre went out by those of the nave, we . . ."

Here Margot's narrative of her wedding, so attentive to detail, stops abruptly and is never resumed. The reason, in all likelihood, is that she did not wish to have to explain the highly irregular nature of the ritual that was followed.

Because the couple's prospective mothers-in-law, in their months of negotiation, had not resolved the question of religion, it had been necessary for them to agree upon a compromise in order to permit the wedding to take place. As a devout Huguenot, Navarre would neither hear the Mass nor kneel before the High Altar. As an equally devout Catholic, Margot would do both. The actual ceremony, therefore, would be performed outdoors, as the bride described. Afterward, she entered the cathedral where the nuptial Mass was celebrated, while her bridegroom strolled out into the cloister and passed the time—three full hours—chatting and joking with friends. Margot also fails to mention two other sig-

nificant details about her wedding. The first is that diplomats
from all the Catholic nations pointedly were absent. The
second, firmly fixed in legend, is that when the Cardinal
asked her for her assent, the Duke of Guise, her former
suitor and lover, "rose and stood up in front of the other
noblemen to take a closer look at Marguerite's face and
eyes." For a moment she remained speechless and motionless, whereupon her brother, the King, brusquely reached
over and pushed her head down.

The festivities that followed the wedding were as bizarre
and disquieting as the ceremony itself. On the surface, they
resembled dozens of other elaborate pieces of mechanized
spectacle which Catherine had produced in the past—artificial rocks, marine monsters, mythological heroes, and the
inevitable pliant maidens of the *escadron volant*.

But those theatricals had been largely allegorical diversions. The ones celebrating this highly political marriage
seemed themselves to convey a pointed political message.
Thus, one of them revealed a setting that showed Paradise
on one side and Hell, lit by sulphurous smoking fires, on the
other. As the action opened, three armed knights—Navarre
and two other Huguenot nobles—strode on stage and attempted to force their way into Paradise and the Elysian
Fields that lay beyond. Their right to enter was challenged
by three other knights—King Charles IX and his two
brothers—who repelled them and pushed them into Hell,
where costumed devils took them prisoner. Then Mercury
and Cupid, suspended on wires, descended to center stage,
recited verses of praise to the victors, and entreated the
nymphs who had been lounging in the Elysian Fields to
come out and intercede in favor of the vanquished knights.
After a ballet which is described in contemporary accounts
only as "very diverting and lasting a good hour," the King
and his brothers allowed themselves to be persuaded and
forced open the gates to permit Navarre and his companions
to come out. Lest the point of the story be lost, the account

concludes: "Thereby it was shown that the King relegated the Huguenots to Hell, whence they were permitted to escape only through the intercession of love."

The explanation was unnecessary, for the animosity and mutual mistrust which had been building, and which the peculiar wedding ceremony itself had only served to point up, now could almost be tasted in the air. Even the King, who as usual had merely read the words and enacted the mummery prepared for him by his mother, became aware of it and ordered soldiers of his own guard to patrol the streets of the city. The Guises, present in full force as honored wedding guests, did not bother hiding their satisfaction at the turn of events.

The following day, Thursday the 21st of August, the governor of Paris abruptly left the city, delegating his duty of maintaining order and tranquility to underlings. Since he was a Catholic, his departure not only set off new flights of rumors, but gave them a point of immediacy. Nevertheless, the program of diversions rolled on, with another pageant in which the King and his brothers appeared as Amazons to do battle with Navarre and his friends, cast this time in the humiliating role of Turks.

While the guests at the Louvre watched the performance move to its predictable conclusion, some four hundred yards away in the Rue des Poulies a renegade Huguenot adventurer and hired killer named Maurevert entered a house that belonged to a retainer of the Duke of Guise.

VIII

As the new senior member of the Huguenot leadership, Gaspard de Coligny, the Admiral of France, had accompanied Navarre to Paris for the wedding. He knew Catherine too well, and over too many years, to delude himself into believing that any lasting goodwill toward his cause had caused her to press for the alliance. Nor did he place great confidence in Navarre's ability to resist either the pressures or the temptations that would be prepared for him. Nevertheless, the occasion presented opportunity. As he wrote home: "My dearest, my well-beloved wife, Today was completed the marriage of the King's sister with the King of Navarre. The next three or four days will be passed in pleasure and in banqueting, after which the King, so he assures me, will give up several days to the hearing of the divers complaints which arise in many parts of the kingdom . . . in which matters I am constrained to labor to the utmost of my power. And although I have the greatest wish to see you, I think we should both of us feel a strong remorse if I failed in care and duty upon this business. Were I only to consult my own deeds, I had far rather be with you than sojourn here at this Court. . . . At Paris, this eighteenth of August 1572."

In fact, Coligny had already spent considerable time with the King, on this and earlier occasions, and had established a relationship that prompted the twenty-two-year-old monarch to call him *"mon père"* ("my father"). The choice of those particular words could be ascribed to the difference in their ages or to Coligny's habitually grave and measured manner. Whether the King himself perceived that they might have other significance as well is uncertain. To Catherine, however, no other salutation could have set off more urgent alarms. The circle of fierce protectiveness she had forged around her children, and especially her sons, had not been challenged since the death of Francis II twelve years earlier. Neither had her own prerogative to rule. Indeed, the two had long since become synonymous in her mind. To rule for her children; to rule through her children—the distinction was purely in the choice of preposition.

During those twelve years, Coligny had sometimes been

an ally, sometimes an adversary. In that respect, he was no different from the Bourbons, the Montmorencys, even the Guises after she had tamed them. Charles had grown up to be an erratic, moody youth given to solitary pastimes and fits of unreasoning anger. But still he was a properly wise monarch and good son; he always did exactly what his mother wished him to do. And never had he called any of the older men around him *"mon père."*

Nor had any of the puppets, Huguenot or Catholic, whom Catherine had learned to manipulate ever shown the boldness Coligny now displayed. The respites between the religious wars had been occupied with flirtations, on the part of both camps, with foreign powers. The Catholics, and notably the Guises themselves, had early learned that they had good friends in Madrid as well, of course, as in Rome. But their Roman friends, with the decline of the papacy's political power, could do little more than cause annoyances and muddy the waters from time to time. And their Spanish friends were too powerful and too clearly France's archrivals in Europe to be entirely trusted—at least for the present. As for the Huguenots, they could look to the German Lutheran princelings, who were on the whole too unimportant and weak to make desirable allies. Or they could reach across the Channel, where Elizabeth always seemed to promise more than she was willing to deliver—either of her own person as a much-sought bride or of her military assistance. Finally, there was, lying just north of France, the Netherlands. A Spanish province whose subjects were predominantly and militantly Protestant, the territory was a perennial thorn in the side of Philip II of Spain and a promising opportunity in the eyes of Coligny. As he saw the situation, and as he tried to make King Charles IX see it, powerful intervention by France in the Netherlands would be a blow against Spain. Such action would be relatively easy because the invading troops would be welcomed by the populace as liberators. And it would be profitable for both France and its King, for the first would gain the rich trade of the Low Countries, and the second would become the most powerful sovereign of Christendom.

Coligny had begun pressing his campaign several months before the wedding and had even set its main points down in terms which even the King could be expected to understand ("The cure for civil wars is to employ the warlike parts of the nation upon foreign territory. . . ."). The King did understand—at least the part about becoming the most powerful ruler of Christendom—and gave his approval, but Catherine managed to postpone the final decision for a week during which she persuaded her son to reverse it.

But Coligny was not ready to give up. On the contrary, an attempt to regain the royal approval was among the matters for which, according to his letter to his wife, he felt "constrained to labor to the utmost of my power." Once again, he went through his arguments, only to find that the Queen Mother had done her work well. Not only were the other members of the royal Council opposed to the plan, but the King, too, refused this time to grant permission. Turning to Catherine and speaking slowly and without anger, Coligny then said, "Madame, if the King renounces going into this war, may God grant him that he not find himself faced with another which he undoubtedly will not be able to renounce as easily."

Whether this was a veiled threat to unleash another civil war, or more likely the melancholy promise that such a war was inevitable, it was also Coligny's own death sentence. On Friday August 22, at eleven o'clock in the morning, he left the Louvre and, as he did each day, walked through the Rue des Poulies to the Hôtel de Béthizy, where he had been staying since his arrival in Paris. As he passed through the narrow street, the thick curtains of a window on the ground floor of one of the houses parted slightly and a shot rang out. Clutching at his left arm, he looked at the window from which a puff of smoke drifted and said, "See how honest men are treated in France." Two of his companions rushed into the house, but all they found was the weapon, an arquebus, left lying on a table.

Others carried the bleeding Coligny home. Someone was sent to notify the King, who was playing tennis. Breaking his racket in rage, Charles IX cursed and shouted, "More trouble? Am I never to have peace?" Another messenger went to find Ambroise Paré, who had attended Henry II upon his fatal illness. The surgeon found that the shot had mangled the index finger of Coligny's right hand and then had lodged itself near the elbow of the left arm. Working rapidly, he amputated the last joint of the finger with a pair of scissors but managed to save the arm by extracting the spent ball. Then he dressed his patient's wounds and ordered him to rest.

This was easier said than done, for even before Paré had finished his work Coligny's house had filled up with anxious visitors. The first to be received were Navarre and some of the principal Huguenot chiefs. There was no question in their minds about who was responsible for the attempt; that the house where the murderer had been hidden was owned by a Guise retainer was proof enough. Moreover, who in Paris had better or more public reason to see Coligny dead than the Guises, who had sworn blood revenge against him nine years earlier over the assassination of Duke Francis? With some difficulty Coligny persuaded his friends not to take justice into their own hands, but the more impetuous of his followers could not be restrained from marching to the Duke of Guise's imposing *hôtel* and hurling stones at the windows. Next came Marshal Cossé and other representatives of the Court. To their questions Coligny was more direct, replying that "I suspect Messieurs de Guise. I make no accusation, but by the grace of God I have no other enemies." And he added, "It is true that this wound grieves me in that I am unable to show the King how much I wished to serve him. I could wish that he would be pleased to hear from me for a few minutes, for I have things to say that touch him closely and I think there is no other man who dare say them."

With this statement Catherine would have agreed wholeheartedly. She had spent the morning urging her son the King not to rush off, as he had wished, to his self-chosen father's bedside. It would be a sign of greater honor, she finally persuaded him, if the entire Court, herself included, were to pay its respects to him *en masse*.

They arrived late in the afternoon and crowded the sickroom. Tearful and shaking with childish emotion, the King told Coligny: "You have to bear the pain, but I bear the shame. Yet I will take a revenge so dreadful that it should never be wiped out of the memory of man." To which Catherine added, "It is not you who are wounded, but all of France." Then Coligny launched into a lengthy speech in which he recalled the main events of his life, reaffirmed his loyalty, and came to the point, which was another appeal to permit the war in Flanders to start. "You have pledged yourself to undertake it," he reminded the King. "If you go no farther, you expose the kingdom to an obvious danger."

The King reassured him: "I shall punish those that did it."

Coligny replied: "They are not far to seek. The signs are plain enough."

Sensing the danger of this new direction, Catherine interrupted him solicitously: "It surely is unwise for a sick man to talk so much." The medical men took their cue and began fussing with the dressings. The courtiers edged out of the room, but only after the King had assured Coligny that he would personally guarantee his future safety.

There is, unfortunately, no first-hand account of what passed between mother and royal son on the way back to the Louvre. Catherine had, for the moment, averted catastrophe. But for how long?

Millions of words have been written about the events that followed the bungled assassination of Coligny and culminated eventually in what was thereafter to be known as the Massacre of St. Bartholomew's Eve. Until the planned and institutionalized horrors of our own century, no single episode in the history of Europe so revulsed humanity and frightened it with the awesome consequences of its own capacity to do evil.* Certainly, no event became more inextricably associated with Catherine de' Medici and history's generally unfavorable judgment of her. Whether, as her detractors hold, she intended the wholesale slaughter of Huguenots, or even the decimation of their leaders, is questionable. Coligny, however, was another matter. No close student of Machiavelli could have failed to remember the pertinent passage, which appears in a discussion of the circumstances under which a prince may properly resort to cruelty: "It can be said to be well employed when it is used on occasion only, dictated by the necessity of retaining power, and on condition that one has no further recourse to it except in the interest of the nation."

To Catherine, this condition was amply satisfied by Coligny's continued existence. If she lost her son to him, as appeared inevitable, she lost everything. Thus, he had to be removed. And if, in the course of removing him, she could not only protect herself but also get rid of a powerful rival faction which had caused France—which is to say herself—trouble in the past, that was all for the better.

Catherine's plan, in which she enlisted the aid of her son, the Duke of Anjou, had been simply to ask the Guises to get rid of Coligny for her. Very little persuasion on her part was needed. Indeed, the Duke Henry agreed so readily that he even suggested that his mother be permitted to fire the fatal shot—how could anyone miss at so short a range?—in order to squeeze out the last drop of revenge. In making the pro-

---

* This is true to the extent that four hundred years after the fact, on August 24, 1972, the French daily *Le Monde* published a front-page editorial recalling the event and using it as a plea for greater tolerance and mutual understanding.

posal Catherine had anticipated that suspicion would instantly point to the Guises, as in fact it did. With the Huguenots' hatred and resentment already tuned to a high pitch, the cowardly murder of their hero would set off a wave of fury which would wipe out the Guises, and with them all trace of her and Anjou's participation. It had been a simple scheme—so simple that a scholar closer to Catherine's own day and its prevailing climate of political morals saw through it immediately. In his *Considérations Politiques sur les Coups d'État,* which was published in 1639, Gabriel Naudé accurately described the circumstances leading up to the attack on Coligny, and then proceeded to deplore the plan's failure—i.e., that the Guises were permitted to survive.

The irony that they owed their survival to the dreadful aim of their own hired assassin was not lost on Catherine, but she now had a more serious problem to ponder—the most serious problem of her life. The King had probably already decided that the Guises were to blame for the attempt on Coligny, or he would do so as soon as he realized that no one else had sufficient motive. He did not yet know of her own complicity, but he was bound to find out, if not from the Guises then from Coligny himself. The injured man's remark about not having to look very far for the culprit suggested that he knew or had guessed. In any case, it was too large and far too dangerous a secret to keep buried.* Given the King's unstable, violent nature, there was no telling what he might do. For herself, she could envisage dismissal and exile; Charles would probably stop short of matricide. But as for Anjou, whom Charles loathed as pathologically as she herself adored him, she could easily see her elder son throttling his brother with his own bare hands.

On that short trip from Coligny's bedside to the Louvre,

---

* Assuming that they would succeed, the conspirators took few precautions. The arquebus used by Maurevert, for instance, had been borrowed from a royal guard and still bore its identifying insignia when Coligny's companions found it.

Catherine decided that the only possible solution was to whip Charles into unreasoning, inhuman fury, and then turn it away from herself and Anjou.

In order to escape from prying eyes, Catherine requested the members of the Council of State, now acting as a council of murder, to meet her in a shaded corner of the new Tuileries gardens which she had ordered to be laid out for herself along the Seine a half mile from the royal palace. One by one they arrived: the Duke of Nevers, formerly Louis of Gonzaga; the Comte de Retz, whose family name was Gondi; René de Biragues, Keeper of the Seals, who until recently had been merely Signor Renato Birago; the Marshal Tavannes, faithfully serving his fourth successive king of France—all old trusted friends of Catherine and all save one, as French historians pointedly note, Italians.*

The problem was not to decide what to do—bad luck had left them no choice—but how to secure Charles's sanction for their act. Tavannes's suggestion—that the King be reassured that he was more freely permitted to move against his subjects by extralegal measures than they could be allowed to use against him—merely showed that he had better stick to soldiering as a career. The Italians understood that they would have to turn the King inside out, to make him believe that Coligny, his beloved father, the man he had sworn not only to protect but to avenge, was in reality the leader of a deep conspiracy to remove him from the throne. There was no dearth of evidence about the intentions of the hotheads among the Huguenots; they had been stomping through the streets, threatening to impale any Guisards they could catch. At dinner the previous night, a certain Huguenot named Pardaillan had lost his Gascon temper and, glaring across the table at the King, had threatened to avenge Coligny himself if no one else had the stomach for it. There was the

* Two other members of the Council were absent: the Cardinal of Lorraine, who was on business in Rome, and Gaspard de Coligny, who was there in spirit if not in person.

report of a spy, Bouchevannes, who had penetrated the inner councils of the Huguenots and had sent word that they were arming for war.

Catherine, who knew her son better than the others, outlined the plan. She instructed de Retz, chosen because he had once been Charles's tutor and still enjoyed his confidence, to paint for him a picture of France on the brink of a rebellion that would sweep its king off his throne and into exile and disgrace.

As de Retz talked, intentionally using the simple locutions of a teacher instructing a slow student, he introduced a new and disturbing idea. Yes, everyone knew that the Guises had plotted the death of the Admiral. But what if they had not acted alone? What if others proved to have been implicated?

This was the cue for the part Catherine had written for herself. She calmly told her son that she and Anjou had worked together with the Guises in planning the assassination. She did not confess to complicity; she took credit for it. Standing over him, her eyes never leaving his face and her voice a monotone of contempt, she repeated again all the charges against Coligny—his role in the murder of the old Francis of Guise; his treasonable dealings with England and with the Germans; the criminal folly of the Flanders adventures, which would bring Spain down upon France; his twisted ambition to become ruler of a Huguenot France which would have no use for a Christian monarch. He, Charles, had been too blind and stupid to see where his good friend and "father" was leading him. But she, his mother, had once again recognized the danger. Unlike him, she had acted. Was he perhaps afraid of the Huguenots? She was not afraid. His brother, Anjou, was not afraid.

All else had been prelude. This was the sting. It was not necessary for her to remind Charles of Anjou's great military triumphs; they poisoned his waking moments and infested his nights.

Very well, Catherine concluded, if he was not prepared to

protect the lives of his mother and his brother, who had risked them on his behalf, they would have no choice but to depart from France and leave him alone.

Now it was de Retz's turn again. The smooth voice painted an entirely different picture, in which the King of France stuns and impresses the entire world with the swiftness and resolution he shows in cleansing his country of its enemies.

The eloquence was wasted on Charles who, still looking at his mother, interrupted: "Very well, then, by God's death let it be so. But kill them all so that none will be left to reproach me." And as he fled out of the room, he repeated over his shoulder, "Kill them all. Kill them all."

This was more than Catherine had asked for, and far more than she was prepared to undertake. Aside from the sheer impracticability of the enterprise, many of the Huguenots were not even remotely involved in politics. Some, like Ramus, were great scholars; others were poets, lawyers, merchants, or simple citizens. Furthermore, Catherine had no wish to sweep the board clear for the Guises and their Catholic allies. She insisted that her new son-in-law, Navarre, and his young cousin, Louis de Condé, be spared. That they deserved immunity as her guests in the Louvre had nothing to do with her decision; she simply did not want to eliminate the Bourbons as another potential countervailing force.

The actual job of drawing up the list, according to some of those who participated in the process, took longer than the time needed to persuade the King to give the order. In the end, Catherine by her own later admission proposed "five or six names." Because others had been less restrained, it became clear that the combined military forces at the disposal of the Crown—the Swiss Guards, the Guises' followers, the free-lance volunteers—were inadequate to the task. Claude Marcel, the former Provost of Paris and a man known for his dislike of Huguenots, was therefore summoned and asked how many men he could raise. How much time did he have, he asked, boasting that in a month he could collect

100,000 or more. "What about tomorrow?" He promised to provide 20,000, all volunteers recruited from the working classes.

By ten o'clock on the evening of Saturday, August 23, order had been restored inside the Louvre to the extent that Charles was able to hold his habitual *coucher*. Crowded about his bedchamber stood the lords whose position had dictated their being housed in the palace. Catholics and Huguenots alike, they played their roles in the traditional ceremony of exchanging pleasantries and helping the King prepare for the night. This ultimate treachery and dissimulation, more than the slaughter itself, inspired the great historian Michelet to scornful indignation: "Abominable fate! The knife that had served them with the King's bread was to be thrust into their heart; the officers and captains of the guard, their boon companions of the evening, were to be their executioners in the morning. This was the word of the King of France, a word respected among infidels, respected as far as the end of the world! The word of a gentleman, of a feudal host—the ultimate security upon which one left or unloaded one's weapons on crossing the drawbridge! All these ancient holy things of France broken and destroyed and honor itself assassinated!"

As the gentlemen were ushering themselves out of the royal chamber, Charles noticed Francis de la Rochefoucauld, a friend of long standing with whom he had spent many days hunting. Aware of what awaited, he said, "Foucauld, stay with me. Let us talk nonsense for the rest of the night." But his friend had an assignation with his mistress, so he begged off. "My little master," he said, "it is time for sleep and going to bed."

"You can sleep with my valets," Charles said.

"Impossible. Their feet stink." Rochefoucauld was one of the first to be butchered in the morning.

By prearrangement, the signal for the attack was to come at four in the morning with the ringing of the great bell of the church of Saint-Germain l'Auxerrois, which still stands facing the facade of the Louvre. But no chance was taken that the first, most important victim would again cheat fate.

Between two and three o'clock in the morning, after making sure that his patient was comfortable, Ambroise Paré left the Hôtel de Béthizy. Shortly afterward, hoofbeats followed by heavy hammering on the door shattered the night's silence. One servant who tried to bar entry into the house was killed in the doorway; another, who had rushed upstairs, was cut down on the staircase. Seven men-at-arms raced past him and into Coligny's bedroom. Moments later, the voice of Henry of Guise boomed out from downstairs: "Have you done?" And the reply came, "It is over." "Well, throw him down here so we may see for ourselves." With this, the body of the mortally wounded but still living Admiral was hoisted and thrown, head first, out of the window. One of Guise's men, the Chevalier d'Angoulême, took out his handkerchief and wiped the blood off the face of the motionless figure on the cobblestones. "Yes, it is he," he said and kicked the body. Guise looked down for a moment and turned away. As he did so another of his men, Petrucci, kneeled and cut off the head, which he carried back to the Louvre.

There, in the Queen Mother's apartments, a drama of a different sort was playing out. According to custom, Catherine's daughters had attended her own *coucher*. As Margot recalls in her *Memoirs:* "I was at the Queen my mother's, seated on a coffer next to my sister [the Princess Claude] who was looking terribly sad. The Queen my mother, who was talking to some others, saw me there and told me to go to bed. As I was curtseying to her, my sister took my arm and stopped me, crying bitterly, and said to me, 'My good sister, do not go there!' which frightened me dreadfully. The Queen my mother, noticing this, called my sister over and scolded her very angrily, forbidding her to tell me anything. My sister answered that there was no point in sending me there to be sacrificed like that, and no doubt that if they discovered anything they would take their revenge on me. The Queen my mother replied that . . . whatever happened I must go, for fear that otherwise they might suspect something, which would interfere with the plan."

Still unsuspecting, Margot found out what was happening soon enough: "As soon as I was in my dressing room . . . my husband, who had already gone to bed, told me to do so too, which I did. I found his bed surrounded by thirty or forty Huguenots whom I did not yet know, since I had only been married a very few days. All night they did nothing but talk of the accident that had befallen the Admiral, resolving that as soon as day broke they would demand justice from the King against M de Guise, and that if he did not accord it they would take it upon themselves."

Eyewitness accounts of the massacre which began at dawn on the Day of St. Bartholomew—ironically, the patron of healers—abound, but there is nothing edifying about them. No sooner had Claude Marcel's twenty thousand volunteers taken to the streets of Paris than they were joined by other volunteers: second sons murdering their elder brothers to stand nearer their inheritances; neighbors at last permitted to express a long-nurtured grudge; the poor venting their resentment on the rich; the weak ganging up on the strong. The list, so carefully drawn up, may as well never have been compiled, for it certainly did not contain the name of a small girl who was stripped of her clothes and dragged through the blood of her butchered parents; or those of a lady and her maid who, fleeing the mob, clung to the piers of a bridge over the river until their hands were chopped off at the wrists; or of another woman who attempted to escape disguised as a nun but was betrayed by the red slippers she had forgotten to take off. Only a very few men such as Don Diego de Cuñiga, Philip II's ambassador to France, found some peculiar sense in the mindlessness, for he reported to his master: "As I write they are killing them all; they are stripping them naked, dragging them through the streets, plundering the houses, and sparing not even the children. May God be blessed who has converted the French princes to His cause."

In the streets of Paris, the bodies of the dead and dying piled up faster than they could be carted away. Even had they wanted to, neither the King nor the Queen Mother could control the mob. On the afternoon of the 25th, as sheer arm-weariness threatened to end the butchery, an electrifying report spread through the city: a Franciscan monk had, with his own eyes, seen a hawthorn bush at the cemetery of the Innocents, "a dead thorn, dry and quite spoilt," burst into bloom overnight. This miracle, this certain sign that Heaven was pleased with their efforts, rejuvenated the servants of God to fresh exertions on His behalf. Thereafter, other divine manifestations materialized as needed: a new star of the East appeared, holy statues were seen to shed tears of gratitude.

On Tuesday the 26th, a splendid procession made its way from the Louvre to the Palace of Justice: the King, followed by his family and his entire Court, was on his way to dispense justice regarding the events of the previous three days. The Queen Mother, attended by the glorious, exquisitely gowned ladies of the *escadron volant,* seemed particularly animated and interested in the grim spectacle: "They indulged themselves," noted one writer, "in the lewd pleasure of gazing at certain signs of masculinity on the naked corpses."

Because the observer was a Protestant, his comment cannot be entirely accepted. But nowhere, neither in her own letters nor through any number of intermediates she could have chosen, did Catherine show the slightest remorse or regret for what had happened. While her son addressed the assembled Parlement to denounce the Huguenot conspiracy and declare himself the sole author of their punishment, she sat contentedly at his side. "She looked," the ambassador of the Duke of Savoy reported, "a younger woman by ten years, and gave me the impression of a person who has come out of a serious illness, or escaped a great danger."

Religion had played no part other than pretext in the massacre; no high Church figure was permitted to participate in the deliberations or was even given advance notice. Nevertheless, having caused the brutal death of several thousand innocent people,* Catherine sought to collect political credit for her piety. To Philip II's ambassador, she said, "Come, am I, after all, such a bad Christian? Go back to your master—tell him what you have seen, tell him what you have heard." And lest his report not be adequate, she herself wrote a letter to his master: "My son, I have no doubt that you will share our joy at God's goodness in giving my son the King the means to rid himself of subjects rebellious equally to God and to himself, and that it pleased Him to preserve us all from the cruelty of their hands, for which we feel assured you will praise God with us, both for our sakes and for the good which will result to all Christendom. . . ."

It is said that, upon receiving this letter, the Spanish monarch was heard to laugh in public for the first and only time of his life.

The Pope, Gregory XIII, had already received word of the attempt on Coligny, but when the full extent of Divine intercession reached Rome his joy spilled over. The messengers who had brought the glad tidings were richly rewarded; victorious salvoes were fired off by the cannons of the Castel Sant'Angelo; *Te Deums* were ordered in the churches, and the Pope himself led fifty-three cardinals to celebrate a solemn mass at the altar of San Luigi dei Francesi. Charles IX, who had previously been dismissed as the insignificant son of a dangerous, unreliable mother, was elevated to the status of "an avenging angel, divinely sent."

In Protestant Europe, reaction was predictably different.

---

* Estimates vary according to their source, but the most credible reconstructions place the number of the dead—in Paris alone—at somewhere between four thousand and eight thousand.

Among the German princelings and in the Swiss cantons, the "avenging angel" and his mother were branded as treacherous, heartless criminals. Frenchmen were insulted and threatened; pictures appeared glorifying Coligny, while others depicted in hideous detail scenes of the massacre in Paris. None of this worried Catherine; time and money would patch up misunderstandings. England, however, was another matter. She had sent a special emissary, La Mothe-Fénelon, with a carefully prepared explanation for her "dear sister," but his mission had gone wrong from the start. After being allowed to cool his heels for several days, Fénelon was permitted to appear before the Queen, who along with her entire Court, was dressed in deep mourning. Before he could even begin his speech, Elizabeth had snapped at him: "Are the common rumors true?" Rattled, Fénelon attempted to assure her that "good understanding between France and England would in no wise be cooled or diminished." Elizabeth interrupted to voice her concern that "a King who had abandoned his own subjects would not hesitate also to desert his allies." Fénelon tried to change the subject by reminding her of her promise to stand as godmother to Charles's expected child. The Queen replied that not only would she herself not venture to France but that she would not risk the life of anyone she valued in so unsafe a country.

After Fénelon's report reached her, Catherine attempted to soothe matters herself. Sorting through the papers which had been taken from Coligny's study, she gathered together some notes in which he urged Charles to move against Flanders on the grounds that if she did not, England surely would. "Here is your noble friend. You can see how well he loved England." Sir Francis Walsingham, Queen Elizabeth's ambassador in Paris, read the papers and replied with dignity, "Madam, he loved France."

Within France, the Huguenot forces were in near-total disarray. A few of their leaders had managed to escape from the Parisian trap; a number of others had for one reason or another rejected the invitation to attend the blood-soaked wedding. But their spiritual leaders, Jeanne d'Albret and Coligny, were dead, and their new titular leader was a captive—and not only a captive, but not even any longer a Huguenot. Charles IX had obeyed his mother and spared the lives of Henry of Navarre and of his cousin, Louis de Condé. That she wanted them to survive was her business; but if they were to remain his subjects, the subjects of the Very Christian King of France, they would do so on his terms. As soon as blood had begun to spill in the streets, the two young men had been taken by armed guards and led to the royal chamber. There, they were given a simple choice: convert or be killed.

On September 29, 1572, in an elaborate ritual held in the same church of Saint-Germain l'Auxerrois, Henry of Navarre was inducted into the highest chivalric order of the realm, the Order of St. Michael. As he rose from his knees and walked away from the altar and back to his place, Catherine turned to the seats occupied by the foreign ambassadors and laughed out loud.

IX

If Margot is to be believed, it was actually her quick thinking that saved Navarre's life. She relates that five or six days after the massacre, ". . . as we were about to attend Holy Communion, the Queen my mother asked me to swear whether the King my husband was in fact a man. For if he was not, then it would be possible for her to arrange a divorce for me. I begged her to believe that I was not sufficiently experienced to be able to tell her what she wanted to know, but that in any case, since she had given me in marriage to him, I wished to remain his wife. For I had very little doubt that in trying to separate us they were planning to do him some harm. . . ."

Although there is no direct substantiation for this story, it is wholly in character with Margot's standards of behavior. She had many qualities including vanity, haughtiness, and a disposition toward nymphomania that were less than exemplary, but cruelty and dishonesty were not among them. Years later, when political exigency forced her to be cordial to someone she detested, she agreed only with reluctance, saying, "I will make good cheer for him. But I promise you that directly he appears and as long as he stays, I shall wear a garment that I have never yet worn—dissimulation and hypocrisy."

Only a few months older than her new husband, she possessed from first-hand experience a far keener grasp of politics, especially as practiced by her own family. Possibly, too, she felt sorry for the young man who, despite his late mother's admonitions, cut such a poor figure at the Valois Court. His ill-fitting, unfashionable, and frequently less than immaculate clothes set him apart, as did the fact that no amount of brushing could prevent his hair from standing up straight, against all the dictates of fashion. Worse, whatever social standing he had commanded had been stripped from him, for along with his forced conversion to Catholicism, Catherine had ordered him to abdicate his crown of Navarre, to ban Huguenotry from his possessions, and to turn over their government to a regent of her choice. Without a title, jobless, powerless to act, he was little more than an errand boy, waiting on the Queen Mother's pleasure. Margot's pride if not her compassion would have held her back from lashing out at so defenseless a figure. Furthermore, Margot had, strictly speaking, intimated the truth to her mother; Navarre himself later testified that "being young and of warm blood" they did indeed consummate their marriage, not just once for the record but in ample measure. But as can often happen between healthy, uninhibited, sensual people, the more earnestly they tried the more they discovered that they did not enjoy together what each found pleasurable and rewarding in different company. Rather, the bond between them took a form which, for a man and a woman, was rare in the sixteenth century—and rarer still at the Valois Court. They became good friends.

For her part, Catherine had little confidence in either of them. Of her youngest daughter, she once said, "She has been the bane of my existence, the source of all my earthly woes"—which may have been her way of conceding that of all her children and close associates, Margot was the one who could unerringly see through her schemes. As for Navarre, his primary usefulness to her as a son-in-law had vanished with whatever hope there had been, before St. Bartholomew, for a reconciliation with the Huguenots. Still, a tame, captive Prince of the Blood could be worth something in the future.

The opportunity to test his tameness came sooner than Catherine might have wished, for less than four months after they had, in theory, been rendered helpless, the Huguenots again challenged the authority of the crown. They took by force the town of La Rochelle, unseated the royal authorities, and proclaimed freedom of conscience within its walls. It was little more than a token gesture, commensurate with the poor forces they could muster, but Catherine could not afford to ignore it. Of immediate concern was not only her new position as staunch upholder of the faith, but also the geographic fact that La Rochelle was a seaport, one of the most secure in France, and readily accessible to English arms and men should Elizabeth decide to carry her own game of balance of power onto the continent. She already had the needed pretext: the citizens of La Rochelle had written her that they were prepared to acknowledge her as their "sovereign queen and natural princess" if she would protect "her people which have belonged to her from all eternity."

The Duke of Anjou, as Lieutenant-General of the kingdom, was given the task of dealing with the insurgents.

Valorous and handsome he undoubtedly looked to Catherine during the grand departure of the army from Paris, but the sight that gave her at least equal satisfaction was Navarre, wearing the royal Catholic colors as he rode off to war against his former Huguenot subjects.

Along with everyone else in France, Catherine believed in Anjou's military genius. This time, however, the experienced old Marshal Tavannes was too ill to take the field alongside the Duke, and what should have been for a skillful commander a week's decisive work dragged instead into a tedious siege more damaging to the attackers than the defenders. Fortunately for Catherine and for Anjou's reputation, events at the far opposite end of Europe provided a pretext to abandon the costly campaign, which she did by magnanimously granting to the citizens of La Rochelle the concessions they had by their own efforts preserved.

The opportune diversion took place in Poland, a region which, to those few Frenchmen who had heard of it at all, was associated with miserably cold weather, impenetrable forests, and fur-bedecked barbarians. But Catherine, whose ambition was to provide each of her sons with a throne of his own, had years earlier singled out the country for particular attention. Her choice had come about through simple elimination. Of all the ruling houses of Europe, the one closest to extinction was that of the Polish Jagellons. Sigismund Augustus II, Poland's reigning monarch, was elderly, childless, and in doubtful health. To be sure, Poland was not the equal of Spain, Austria, or even one of the larger, more prestigious Italian city-states. But in her nimble mind Catherine could visualize a new kingdom of Poland suddenly rejuvenated and concluding advantageous alliances of its own, inching westward to appropriate territories now held tenuously by the Hapsburgs.

On July 7, 1572, Sigismund Augustus satisfied expectations and passed away heirless, leaving the throne to be filled by election. The competition was hardly challenging—Ernest, one of the seemingly numberless Hapsburg archdukes, and Ivan the Terrible of Russia—but Catherine left nothing to chance. She had started her campaign a year earlier and made every promise she could think of: free trade between France and Poland; the gift of all of Anjou's patrimony to the Polish treasury; an expeditionary force to fight Russia, Poland's traditional enemy; the endowment of a Polish university in Cracow. A delegation of Polish notables was invited to France and treated to a mouth-watering taste of what they might henceforth expect on the banks of the Vistula. Among the festivities Catherine had invented for the occasion was a ballet in the course of which sixteen lovely maidens impersonated the provinces of France—Provence decked out in oranges and lemons, Champagne in sheafs of wheat, Burgundy in wine grapes. Margot, too, had risen to the occasion: when the Poles came to pay their respects to her, Adam Konarski, the Bishop of Posen, addressed her on their behalf in Latin, whereupon she "replied him so pertinently and eloquently, without any notes, having perfectly well understood his speech, that they called her a second Minerva." The election itself, held in May, 1573, was a formality. To the joyful if unintelligible shouts of approval of Warsaw's populace, it was announced that the Duke of Anjou had just become the new King of Poland.

Catherine had temporarily lost a son. But as the court that had accompanied Anjou as far as the French frontier headed back homeward, she discovered—or, rather, was forcefully reminded—that she had still another one. Nothing has thus far been said about him, her youngest, for the simple reason that he had not yet done anything worth mentioning. This, however, was about to change.

Hercules, Duke of Alençon, has not fared well at the hands of historians. "Vindictive," "despicable," "pitiable," are the adjectives that recur in the estimations of his character, and almost every physical description of him stresses his puny size, his scrawny legs, his swarthy skin, enormous bulbous nose, and hideously pockmarked face. Born in 1555, Alençon was scarcely four years old when his father died and his mother undertook the burden of government. Because she was at the same time too busy keeping peace between her older sons, Catherine had little time for the younger child and customarily left him alone for months on end in one royal residence or another. Gradually and apart from the Court he gathered a motley circle of his own: adventurers, men of doubtful political leanings, available women, even alchemists and astrologers who had been attracted to France by Catherine's well-known predilection for these disciplines but had failed to win her favor. It mattered not at all to him what their private motives were so long as they demonstrated their personal loyalty, tolerated his appearance, and echoed his conviction that he, too, would somewhere, somehow become a king.

Had it not been for St. Bartholomew, Alençon might well have spun out his days in futile plotting and intrigue. But the shock of the Massacre, both in Paris and as it spread to the provinces, had for the first time cracked the foundation on which the French monarchy rested. Before, it had been a simple matter: *"Un Roi, une loi, une foi"* ("one King, one law, one faith"). But now, loyal patriotic men of honor questioned whether it was necessary to support their monarch in order to practice their faith and observe the law—indeed, whether it was possible to do all three simultaneously. Among those who answered the question in the negative were members of some of the oldest and noblest families in France. Still few in number and without an effective leader, these *Politiques,* as they came to be known, recognized what Catherine had known since childhood: that it was frequently expedient to disguise affairs of state as affairs of the Church. Loyal Catholics themselves, they could not see any purpose in changing religion. That, despite the zealots and opportunists on both sides, was not the issue. What mattered was the government of France, and on this score the *Politiques* were unanimous. They despised the Queen Mother, distrusted the King, and feared the Guises.

Should they be able to enlist him in their cause, Alençon would represent a precious potential asset to the *Politiques*. King Charles, though only twenty-three years old, had already begun to show the hereditary flaws of Catherine's male children. He was subject to hemorrhages, fevers, and fits of fainting and coughing so severe that the journey to accompany Anjou had to be conducted at a snail's pace. If he died, and it then proved possible to exclude Anjou from the line of succession by virtue of his position in Poland, the *Politiques* would have captured France.

Enlisting Alençon proved to be no problem, but keeping the fact from Catherine's spies was another matter. Again, there is no direct proof that she learned of this new plot, but the circumstantial evidence is persuasive. When, after Anjou's departure, Alençon asked that the title of Lieutenant-General of the kingdom be bestowed on him—as custom would dictate—the request was summarily refused. Furthermore, when the entire court had returned and settled down to its normal activities, Alençon found that he was as much of a prisoner, and under as close surveillance, as Navarre.

This was for Catherine a particularly trying and exasperating period. According to the Venetian Michieli, she daily demonstrated that she was "the most skillful personage of state" in Europe. She not only knew everything that went on in France but in all the other major powers as well. Counsellors she neither had nor required. She knew that her recent actions had incurred the hatred of her subjects and also of the English, Flemings, and Germans. On the morrow of St. Bartholomew, all of the Protestant foreigners who had been in Paris, at the University or elsewhere, had packed up and left. Nevertheless, she had worked tirelessly at appeasing their hatred and had, to a spectacular degree, succeeded. Now she worked even harder to prevent civil war from erupting in some other corner of France. The nation's treasury was, as ever, empty. Philip II was scheming across every one of his common borders with her; she had to anticipate and block his moves. She had, of course, to keep a constant eye on the Guises, for there was no group powerful enough to pit against them. On a busy day, her correspondence would amount to twenty or more letters, many of them composed in her own handwriting.

After forty years, during which she had not set foot outside of the country, she knew France and the French to their core, and knew just how they would want their king to comport himself. How much simpler if she could be, in fact, their king? But she wasn't and could never be. So, having tried with no success to train him for kingship, she sat down and wrote out in detail for Charles:

"I wish that you would select a certain hour on which to arise and, in order to satisfy your nobles, follow the example of your late father; when his vestments were brought to him, all the princes, seigneurs, captains, knights of the order, and gentlemen were ushered into his chamber, where he could see them and converse with them. This done, he would proceed to sit with the Council, accompanied by his four secretaries. . . . After that, I wish you would give an hour or two to listen to the dispatches and to those matters which cannot be settled without your presence, and that afterward you would proceed to hear Mass, as did your father and grandfather. And that all the gentlemen be permitted to accompany you there, and not, as I now see, only the archers of your guard. . . . And after dinner, at least twice a week, grant an audience, which is a matter that enormously satisfies your subjects. And afterward, when your work is done, come to see me or to the Queen in order that we may have a sense of court, which is something else that greatly pleases the French, who have been accustomed to it by your father and grandfather. . . . And during the afternoon, take yourself out on a promenade, on horseback, or on foot, in order to show yourself and satisfy the nobility. And leave time to spend with the younger people, preferably at some hearty exercise. . . ."

It is reasonable to assume that Charles was a moody, unpredictable young man who shunned human company and the social choreography of the Valois Court. In fact, he often wandered off into the woods for days on end, stalking boar alone on foot and armed with nothing but a spear. The only close friend he had in the world was his mistress, the Huguenot Marie Touchet. His hobby, if that is the proper term for it, was to play at being a blacksmith; he had his own fully equipped forge into which he would lock himself, to emerge blackened, singed, and on the point of total exhaustion.

One wonders, therefore, to what extent Catherine would have permitted him to exercise the duties of a king even if he were willing to observe its social trappings. Another of the Venetians, Cavalli, who had known her well and long, observed: "All of her actions have always been guided and regulated by an unquenchable passion which she could not fully hide even while her husband was still alive: the passion to rule."

Cavalli also noted that she was "indefatigable in the transaction of affairs." This preoccupation did not, however, prevent her from throwing herself enthusiastically into other pursuits as well. In appearance she was, as one of her biographers diplomatically puts it, "a Juno in the fullness of bloom." Nevertheless, she still traveled constantly, over bad roads and in foul weather. She continued to hunt, even though a head injury sustained during a fall in 1574 had required trepanning. When engaged in conversation, she was apt to start walking with such briskness that her companion, male or female, had difficulty keeping up with her. Even when sitting she could not remain idle but would work at intricate embroideries, which Brantôme insists were "as perfect as it was possible to be." She ate well and with hearty appetite. The diarist, L'Estoile, reports that she nearly succumbed to indigestion from having partaken too freely of a dish of artichoke hearts and cocks' combs. With the years, her youthful prudery mellowed to the extent that, when once shown a prize of war—a gigantically bored cannon that the Huguenots had nicknamed "the Queen Mother"—her obvious amusement embarrassed the officers accompanying her. She was fifty-three years old, had brought into the world ten children, and had governed France single-handed for thirteen years. She had outlived and generally outwitted a full generation of adversaries—Hapsburgs, Guises, Montmorencys, Bourbons, d'Albrets.

And now, at what should have been the apogee of her career, she was obliged to cope with the antics of irresponsible, self-indulgent adolescents who had not the least idea of what mischief they could cause. Navarre—former King, bridegroom, son-in-law, and whatever else—was just nineteen years old. His wife, her own Margot, was twenty. Alençon, who was likely at any moment to spark off a war without realizing what he was doing, was eighteen. The new Duke of Guise, for all his fancy ways with women and his pretentions to descent from Charlemagne, was twenty-one.

Catherine handled them all precisely as she felt they deserved. Navarre, who should have been her most resolute opponent, was the easiest. Whether through fear, dissimulation, or plain indifference, he had given her the least trouble. He smiled a great deal, was amused or amusing as required, played tennis with Guise when asked to—and suffered such insulting treatment at his hands that the Florentine ambassador could not help but comment on it. Catherine detached for special service with him one of the most accomplished members of the *escadron volant,* Charlotte de Beaune Semblançay, Baroness of Sauves.

It is a pity that more is not known about Mme de Sauves. There is a single Clouet portrait of her which reveals a face more agreeable and animated than sensuous. There are the bare biographical details that she was the granddaughter of one of Francis I's superintendents of finance, that she was married to Simon de Fizes, a minor Court functionary, and thereby had probably come to Catherine's attention. There are mentions of her as taking part in some of the pageants and ballets which Catherine produced. But none of it explains her extraordinary skill at her job or, as will be seen, her sheer durability.

Her assignment was to ingratiate herself with Navarre, presumably by the same means that the *Belle Rouet* had successfully used on his father, Antoine, and thereafter to be in a position to report his plans to the Queen Mother. The best testimonial to how quickly and thoroughly she carried out her assignment comes from Margot herself. Writing in her *Memoirs,* she complains that "Mme de Sauves so completely ensnared my husband that we no longer slept together, nor even conversed."

This success encouraged Catherine to ask for something more difficult. Could Mme de Sauves, while keeping Navarre still ensnared, also capture the affection of her own son, Alençon? The object, of course, was not to brighten Alençon's life but to create a source of friction between the two young men and thus complicate any joint scheme they could be hatching. Again, Mme de Sauves was successful, as Navarre himself later conceded: "Our first falling-out," he recalled about his relations with Alençon, "began when we were both prisoners at the Court. Bored and not knowing how to occupy ourselves, we would let quails loose in my chambers and attempt to catch them. When that palled, we took to caressing the ladies in such random fashion that both of us became enamored of the same beauty, who was Mme de Sauves. She would swear her affection for me and at the same time make disparaging remarks about him. And she would do this even in his presence, which enraged him."

Margot, as her mother suspected, needed no help to get into trouble. Hardly the sort of woman who would passively suffer the theft of her husband, she set out to select a lover for herself. There was no end of willing volunteers, but Margot naturally settled on the one candidate who, at the moment, enjoyed the greatest popularity and renown in this line of endeavor. His name was Joseph de Boniface de La Môle, and, on the surface at least, he appeared singularly unsuited for his reputation. One of Alençon's questionable companions, he was, first of all, in his middle forties—well-preserved, but still of a doddering age for a courtier. His accent betrayed him as being a Provençal, but beyond that no one seemed to know who he was or what he had done. Another oddity about him was that he detested the outdoors. All three of his favorite pastimes—the other two were dancing and attending Mass, which he sometimes did five or six times a day—could most comfortably be enjoyed within four walls.*

Alençon hovered over the romance even after it had blossomed into open gossip. His motives as ever were confused, but chief among them was a complicated plan whereby he and Navarre would escape, join a band of Huguenot troops stationed nearby, and then either flee to Flanders, where they would raise an army, or immediately return, confront Catherine, and demand the King's abdication in favor of Alençon. La Môle's function was first to gain Margot's cooperation, which he tried to do in the only way he knew, and then to act as messenger between the conspirators and the waiting troops.

Like most of Alençon's ideas, it was foolish and ill-conceived. Margot would probably have agreed to help him even without La Môle's ministrations. Tactical considerations were left vague: the Huguenot forces, led by a cavalry officer named Chaumont-Quitry, showed up several days too soon, and numbering five hundred men rather than the expected ten thousand. Fortunately, they were not called upon to do

---

* King Charles IX, who was not wholly humorless, is reported to have said: "It is always easy to know how many affairs La Môle is carrying on. Just count his Masses."

anything. Even as they were waiting—in the wrong place—
the would-be escapees were unconvincingly trying to explain
their innocence to the Queen Mother, who had been kept
fully informed of the developing scheme by Mme de Sauves.

It would not do, Catherine realized, to let the world know
that her son and son-in-law had been caught conspiring
against their King and against herself. Alençon was therefore presented with a written statement that began: "Having
heard that some imposter has sown and spread false rumors
against me," and went on to place the entire blame of the
affair on La Môle. He signed it eagerly.

Navarre, thanks to Margot's help, was at least spared this
humiliation. As she recalled, "The King my husband, having
none of his councillors available, charged me to put his defense in writing, so that his evidence would harm neither
himself nor anyone else. God granted that I did so to his
complete satisfaction." The defense which Margot composed for her husband was not a confession but a plea
for royal clemency, directed to Catherine. It recalled the
happy prospects of his marriage and how they were shattered
by the Massacre; it reminded the Queen Mother that most of
his friends had been butchered even though they were
innocent. It described in detail the ignominies which he
daily had endured during his enforced stay at Court—
ignominies which until Margot set them down on paper
he himself had not dared to complain about. And it ended:
"That is, Madam, all I know. I very humbly beg you to
consider whether I did not have just and sufficient reasons
for going away; and may it please yourself and the King in
future to treat me as I am, having no other desire than to be
your very humble, very faithful and obedient servant."
Whether because of its eloquence, its naked truthfulness, or
because she considered one confession adequate, Catherine
accepted the document—to which Navarre's sole contribution was his scrawled signature—without changing a word.

La Môle, accused by his friend and patron, was tortured

into making a confession of his own which conveniently implicated two of the leading *Politiques,* the Marshals Cossé and Montmorency. Despite their rank, they were sentenced to prison terms, more as a warning to others than as punishment for their misdeeds. Then, his usefulness over, La Môle along with his accomplice, an equally murky Piedmontese adventurer named Hannibal Coconnas, were conveyed to the Place de Grève and beheaded. His last words on the scaffold, light-hearted in view of the physical abuse he had been obliged to endure, were: "God have mercy on my soul, and commend me well to the good graces of the Queen of Navarre and the ladies."

That should have been the end of the story, but diarists insist that there still remained one final chapter. It was the practice after executions to leave the heads of the victims on public display. But in the morning, the heads of La Môle and Coconnas had disappeared, never to be seen again. The reason they were gone, it was said, was that in the middle of the night a carriage had drawn up to the scaffold to permit two cloaked female figures to step out, collect their grisly trophies, and ride away. The figures were those of the Queen of Navarre and the Duchess of Nevers, Coconnas's mistress of the moment. And the reason the severed heads never turned up again is that the ladies had them embalmed and, with their own hands, buried them in consecrated ground.

King Charles's first reaction, when told of the plot and its failure, was to ask "Why couldn't they at least wait for me to die?" For months, his fits of coughing and sieges of fever had been so frequent that he was seldom able to leave his room. To add to these ills, he had also begun to suffer from frightful hallucinations: visions of torrents of blood and floating corpses. For days on end he allowed no one to approach him save his childhood nurse, to whom he would describe the horrors passing before his eyes. His clothes and bedsheets were covered with the blood that he continually coughed up. Papers were drawn up and shown to him, including a decree declaring Anjou's succession and his mother's right to the Regency during his own illness. He signed them without comprehension. During the interrogation of La Môle, Catherine tried to keep him abreast of her handling of the affair, but he did not even pretend to pay attention to her. On May 30, 1574, the doctors, who had long since resigned themselves to their helplessness, sent her word that the end could come at any hour.

Charles lay still as the royal family gathered around his bed. Then, as if waking up, he looked around and said, "Call my brother." Catherine gestured Alençon to approach. Charles looked past him and again repeated, "Send for my brother." Understanding only too well, Catherine ordered a guard to summon Navarre.

When he entered the room, Charles beckoned him to approach and embraced him. "You are losing a good friend," he said. "Had I believed all I was told you would not be alive now." Catherine started to interrupt, but Charles managed to raise his voice: "Madam, I do say it; it is the truth." He continued to speak from time to time, in barely audible tones. Then again to Navarre: "Believe me, brother, and love me. Pray God for me. . . . I rejoice that I leave no male child to wear the crown."

Catherine did not grieve excessively for her second son. One reason was that his terrible illness had lingered so long and left him so weak that there was little doubt about its outcome. Another reason may have been that Charles, alive and prey to hallucinations, was a final ghastly reminder of St. Bartholomew and her own direct participation in it. Catherine was not by nature a cruel or vicious woman. Although like any other sixteenth-century ruler, including her dear sister of England, she could easily rationalize the political necessity of eliminating a few political opponents in one fashion or another, she could not have remained entirely free of remorse at the runaway magnitude of the Massacre. But probably the most soothing balm to her grief was that

Charles's death brought to the throne her third and favorite son, Anjou, whom a Court observer had described two years earlier as the "right eye and the soul of the mother."

On the day after Charles's death, she wrote to Anjou in Poland: "I send you in great diligence a messenger to bring you piteous news for me who have seen so many of my children die. . . ." She fashioned out of her imagination a death scene that she knew would please Anjou: "No man ever died in fuller possession of his senses . . . and always talking of your goodness and that you had always loved him so much and obeyed him and never gave him pain but did the greatest services." Having thus patched over a lifetime's hatred between her two sons, she added, "Since it pleases God that I should be proved and visited by Him in such a way so often, I pray Him . . . to give me the consolation of seeing you very soon here and in good health, for if I should lose you, I should have myself buried with you alive because I could not bear this loss also."

As it turned out, history failed by a narrow margin to test this particular vow. There is no question, however, of Catherine's sincerity at the time that she made it, nor of the unnatural intensity of her love for Anjou—a love which not only drained all her maternal feelings, but so obsessed her that it remains one of the keys to understanding her complex character and political motivations.

Meanwhile, there was still France to run. A formal message under Catherine's name was delivered to all European heads of state: "Although I am oppressed by the natural sorrow of a mother over the loss of the most dear and precious thing in the world—a sorrow which makes me desire to leave all public affairs to find some tranquillity of life—nevertheless, persuaded by the pressing request which my son made to me in his last words to take up the office of Regent for the good of this Crown . . . I feel constrained to accept this office." It did not matter to Catherine that the recipients of this note, alerted by their ambassadors to the true details of Charles's dying hours, would see through it and might even manage a chuckle at the Queen Mother's yearning for a peaceful retreat. The only head of state whom she feared was Elizabeth of England, who, she was convinced, had lent her aid to Alençon's attempt to escape. In a separate, secret message, she instructed her ambassador in London to assure the Queen that, although offers of a large sum of money and the use of troops had been made to Alençon, she was convinced that these things had been done by reckless individuals acting on their own and without the consent or knowledge of the Queen. For his own information, Catherine also gave her ambassador her own view of the situation: "To tell you the truth, we are not in a condition to declare war against her and no more has she, I believe, decided to declare war against us, unless she should see a good opportunity."

In an attempt to demonstrate that no such opportunity existed, Catherine summoned Sir Roger North, the English ambassador, and staged a little performance for him. While she expanded on her assurances that she did not believe England was involved in any plot against her, Alençon walked into the room and declared that it would never enter his mind to make trouble for France, and that if foreigners should try to do so, he would always be glad to spend his life and his fortune in the service of the King his brother. Navarre, who had accompanied Alençon, then took the floor to announce that "there have never been any traitors in our family; so don't send anyone to try to suborn me." The effect of the demonstration was vitiated, however, for in reporting it to Elizabeth, North added: "Whilst they told their tale, Alençon held me fast by the hand, and the King of Navarre jogged me in the elbow to give me to understand that their meaning was not as they said."

Catherine had dispatched two messengers by different routes to carry the news of Charles's death to Anjou. They arrived in Cracow within a few hours of each other, having covered the distance of some eight hundred miles in seventeen days of hard riding. Anjou resolved to return to France even before he had finished reading the letters. His brief reign as King of Poland had been a strange and dissatisfying experience, not unlike the position of a beautiful prince put in charge of a large family of lumbering, affectionate bears —affectionate but not wholly convinced of the prince's sincere desire to remain in their midst. As King, Anjou had not even pretended to understand the complicated machinery of Polish government, which more nearly resembled an Asiatic oligarchy than a monarchy. His duties, to the delight of his subjects, were wholly ceremonial and consisted largely of presiding over field exercises in which horsemen could display the skills inherited from their ancestors and monotonously male banquets which ended only when the last guest could no longer accurately bend an elbow.

Anjou had already begun to make his preparations— Bellièvre, his secretary, had left for Vienna to arrange for safe passage through Austria, and one of Catherine's messengers had been dispatched back to Paris carrying Anjou's personal jewels and other valuables—when Count Tenczynski, the Grand Marshal of the Household, arrived to announce that under no circumstances would his subjects allow their beloved King to leave. Somebody else—anybody—could become king of France. He was theirs, forever.

That night's banquet was, by the King's order, gargantuan even by Cracovian standards. Great servings of venison and spiced meats followed one another, punctuated by volleys of toasts and still more toasts as the French members of the King's entourage seemed, for once, to enter into the spirit of the occasion. At one point Anjou leaned over to Tenczynski and slapped him on the back: "Still doubtful of me? Well, I'll soon be peacefully in my own bed, and you can then do likewise." He continued joking and feasting until his eyelids began to droop and his head to nod. Servants led him off to his apartment, helped him off with his clothes, and put him to bed. All the while, he continued talking to Tenczynski, who had insisted on accompanying him. But then his words became slurred and turned into a peaceful snore. The Grand Marshal drew the curtains around the bed, stayed for a few minutes to listen and finally tiptoed out. After he had gone, the door to an adjoining room opened quietly and three of Anjou's retainers entered, already booted and spurred. Two of them helped him back into his clothes while the third opened the iron cask attached to the royal bed and containing the crown jewels. Anjou started to voice an objection but was easily persuaded that the jewels had, after all, become his property. Passing through service staircases and past the deserted royal kitchens, the little party reached a gate where the watchman had already been told that the King was on his way to a very secret assignation with a lady whose name could not even be whispered, and they raced to a small chapel where horses stood waiting.

Through a pitch-black night they rode. At one point, when they appeared to be lost, they stumbled across a woodcutter's hut, woke him up and forced him at knife-point to direct them toward the frontier. Farther on, they crossed a wooden bridge and paused just long enough to destroy it in order to slow down pursuit. Nevertheless, after another full day and evening of riding, they were caught. Tenczynski, who had led the chase, had known all along that neither he nor the Poles could keep Anjou against his will. Still, he tried: "Sire, I beg you to return. You will find us always your most obedient subjects."

"Count," Anjou replied, "in going to claim the throne of France as my lawful inheritance, I do not renounce the other. When I have fulfilled my duty, you will see me again."

The Count tried one last time. "Sire, you will not find in France subjects as faithful as your Poles." That statement proved to be as true as Anjou's was false.

In Vienna, Anjou was received with all the pomp and honors due him not as King of Poland, but as Henry III, the name under which he had chosen to become King of France. As such, too, it was considered unsafe for him to travel through the Lutheran German principalities, which might be expected to harbor some resentment of his complicity in the Massacre. Instead, his homeward voyage would take him by way of Venice, Turin, the Alps, and into his new kingdom. In anticipation of what he proposed to make into a leisurely trip, he wrote a note to his good comrade, the Duke of Nevers: "My dear fellow, Here I am, having managed by the grace of God to get out of Cracow, and making merry. . . . I shall be in Venice in six days or thereabouts. . . . Wait for me there, since you are so close by; I can't think of a better Pantaloon than you. . . . Trusting that God will keep you and not let you die before I see you, I sign myself Henry, at present King of France, the same you formerly knew as Duke of Anjou." It might, in tone and intent, have been a letter from a too-rich, vacationing college boy of Scott Fitzgerald's day proposing a bit of fun to a fraternity brother.

The better to enjoy himself, Henry had inquired of Du Ferrier, the French ambassador in Venice, whether it would be possible for him to pass through incognito. That, the reply came, would be unthinkable—"Though Popes, Emperors, and Kings have sojourned in this city, they say that they have never been so delighted as at the prospect of seeing a King of France." The most elaborate of preparations had been made; princes had arrived from all over Italy. Gentlemen of advanced years lived in fear that they might expire before having paid homage to the French King.

The ceremonies began as Henry crossed into the Most Serene Republic at the little port of Marghera. Waiting to receive him was the entire Senate, all seventy members wearing their crimson robes. A choice of three gondolas, draped in black velvet, violet, and gold cloth, awaited. Henry boarded the golden one and, to the smooth rhythm of eight oarsmen, was borne slowly past what still remains, despite the ravages it has suffered, one of the most splendid, nerve-quickening stage settings created by Western Man. From a fleet that numbered more than one thousand, forty gondolas, each bearing a young patrician who was to serve on him personally, detached themselves and escorted the King to his lodgings in the Palazzo Foscarini. Every day which followed offered new honors and spectacles: a triumphal crossing of the Lagoon aboard the Doge's own ceremonial galley, the *Bucentaur;* participation in a session of the Senate, to which he was named a member; the obligatory visit to the studio of Titian, who was then ninety-seven years old; a night of fireworks so beautiful in their intricacy that the twenty-two-year-old King could not help but observe to someone standing next to him, "If only my mother were here to receive a share of these honors which I owe so entirely to her."

Despite this schedule, Henry managed to indulge his desire for anonymity, once at the expense of sixty dinner guests who waited in vain for him. Dressed in black, he roamed through the streets and bazaars like a latter-day Harun al-Rashid. He paid a visit to Veronica Franco, Titian's favorite model and the reigning courtesan of her day.* He purchased necklaces, gold charms, and great quantities of musk. He called on Paolo Veronese, then at the prime of his powers, and on Tintoretto, who, while disguised as a sailor aboard the *Bucentaur,* had done three sketches of him. To dispel the tedium of protocol, he visited the theater to see the famous company, *I Gelosi,* which he had requested be brought from Milan.

The visit to Venice dragged out for nearly a month, and was repeated in smaller scale in Mantua and again in Turin. Here, Henry was reunited with his Aunt Marguerite, whose marriage to the Duke of Savoy had been in part the occasion for the tournament which had cost Henry II his life. During his trip, Henry had spent lavishly, on himself and on gifts

---

* In this instance, his disguise failed him, not through any lack of precaution on his own part, but because the lady could not resist recording his visit in a sonnet.

which he bestowed at a whim. Now penniless, and having exhausted all of his abilities to borrow, he nevertheless wished to present his beloved aunt with a token of his gratitude for her welcome. As King of France, he therefore spontaneously made her a present of three fortress-cities that lay in his kingdom, just beyond the borders of Savoy. It was his first royal act and a presage of his reign.

X

Catherine had followed her son's slow progress with impatience and had written repeatedly to urge him to hurry. She willingly would have gone to meet him were it not that her full energies were engaged in preserving his kingdom for him. Not since the debacle of the Hundred Years' War was France in such a state of chaos and self-destructive folly. The Court swarmed with conspirators whose temporary, self-serving alliances had been made more complex by the death of Charles and the delayed arrival of the new King. What position would he take? Or would his mother permit him to take any position at all other than the one she dictated? The Guises had been quiet but hardly inactive. Catherine learned that the Duke Henry of Guise had approached Navarre and ingenuously offered his assistance if Navarre wished to be rid once and for all of Alençon—a process that would make Navarre, as First Prince of the Blood, heir apparent to the still-childless Henry III. She also learned that Navarre, to his credit, would have nothing to do with the scheme. Alençon himself, though outwardly contrite after his escapade, was a constant problem.

All these difficulties Catherine could, with the help of Mme de Sauves and her colleagues, manage. She had been doing it for nearly fifteen years. The more serious problem was that, for practical purposes, the Court had become detached from the rest of the country—a master mechanism whose control circuits had been severed. The expediency of capitulating to the Huguenots during the siege of La Rochelle had cost dearly. Other cities defied royal authority and proclaimed liberty of conscience for themselves. The *Politiques,* their ranks swollen by those who thought they detected a trend, entrenched themselves in south-central France and established what in effect was a kingdom within a kingdom. Elsewhere, in isolated villages and towns, local squires or even plain bully boys appointed themselves to positions of authority and defied the crown to unseat them.

They, and the Huguenots, would perhaps have been less secure in their defiance had it not been common knowledge that the national treasury was empty. Even as her son was passing out lavish gifts and replenishing his own jewel boxes with expensive new baubles, Catherine was haggling with bankers. The Duke of Florence turned down her request for 500,000 crowns at ten-percent interest. So did the Milanese. Even the merchant bankers of Lyons, accustomed to take risks, would not advance 300,000 *écus* at fifteen percent.*

The most disastrous immediate consequence of royal insolvency was the complete breakdown of discipline in the army. Not only could the unpaid troops not be relied upon to carry out orders and contain the spread of Huguenotry, but "the very soldiers put throughout the countryside to protect the people became an intolerable burden to them." It had happened before, in other countries as well as in France, but never at a more critical time.

For weeks, Catherine agonized between duties of state and the urge to see her son. Motherly love undoubtedly played a part in that urge, but so did another consideration. Henry

---

* It must be said that the need to apply austerity measures to her own expenses did not seriously occur to Catherine. The Court continued to consume money at its usual rate, and the Venetian ambassador reported that the expenses of burying Charles IX had amounted to 150,000 *écus.*

had not bothered to reply to any of her letters or even acknowledge receipt of the detailed advice they contained on what he should do now that he was King. It was essential that she have a long talk with him and, if necessary, clarify her own role in whatever plans he had begun to formulate. Finally, despite the opposition of her ministers, she decided to compromise. Taking the entire Court with her, including Alençon and Navarre, whom she obliged to ride in her own carriage like two schoolboys, she journeyed to Lyons, where she arrived on August 8, 1574.

Still moving at pleasure's pace, Henry made his appearance almost a month later, on September 5. As on all Medici-Valois family occasions, there was a great deal of crying and laughter, and for a brief time at least Catherine was a mother rather than a Queen Mother as she alternately embraced her son and held him at arm's length the better to look at him.

There was little question, judging by her other sons, why this one should have been her favorite. Morosini, a Venetian who was on hand to congratulate him on his return to France, left this description: "He has a noble carriage, a gracious presence, and the most beautiful hands of anyone, male or female, in France. His manner is at once gentle and rather serious, but he is capable of the most engaging affability when he chooses to display it." Portraits and medallions of Henry III fill in the details: a lean, thoughtful face, dark and lustrous eyes, a finely drawn mouth delicately balanced between a smile and a petulant frown.

Soon enough, though, he would give himself over to a way of life which prompted Jean Héritier, the principal present-day biographer of his mother, to describe him as "above all else a clinical psychological case." For the present, however, he was only a disappointment to everyone except Catherine. Judging by his behavior France could well have been a land at blissful peace. "The King," the Spanish envoy noted with clear disgust, "goes every night to balls and does nothing but dance. During four days he was dressed in mulberry satin with stockings, doublet and hose of the same color. The cloak was very much slashed and had all its folds set with buttons and adorned with ribbons, and he wore bracelets of coral on his arm." He might have added, as did the Venetian Morosini in his report that "he had his ears pierced in the fashion of women and, not content with a single ring on each of them, affects to wear several, with pendants encrusted with pearls and jewels."

On one score at least, Catherine could feel reassured. She had, as planned, held a long private discussion with her son about his views of kingship. Yes, he had given a great deal of thought to the matter and would insist that certain changes be instituted at once. For one thing, it had been the custom of courtiers to approach the King with their wants whenever it struck their fancy—when he was dressing in the morning or preparing to retire, when he was eating, bathing, or even sitting on his own elegant *siège percé*. This was an intolerable offense to royal dignity that would have to stop. Henceforth, all requests for royal favor would be presented in writing and deposited in a specially designated sack. Secretaries would then prepare a précis of the demands for the King's adjudication, at his leisure. There were a dozen other equally imperative reforms that he meant to put into practice immediately. No one, regardless of rank, for instance, could henceforth enter the royal chamber without prior permission; a rule was prescribed for the order and manner in which the King would eat and for the ritual whereby certain chosen nobles would in turn present him his napkin, his food, the basin of water to rinse his hands after eating.

Henry also had ideas about how to solve the Huguenot problem. His hosts in Vienna and Venice had diplomatically counseled him to show leniency, or at least flexibility, toward them. He had considered this advice and rejected it. The only way to treat heretics was to eliminate them. Since this could not be achieved by force, Henry proposed to do it in a

manner that had never for a moment occurred to his mother:
with the aid of divine assistance. There still existed in sixteenth-century France a number of small religious or mystic
orders which lived close lives and found expression in
peculiar practices of their own. One of them, the Brotherhood of the *Battus,* had preserved and refined the ancient
practice of mortifying the flesh. Henry joined the Brotherhood, learned its rites, and then ordered and led a mass
penitential procession such as had not been seen since the
Middle Ages. Hooded, shoeless, their shoulders laid bare,
members of the Brotherhood and of the Court alike paraded
through the streets of the ancient papal city of Avignon,
chanting psalms and carrying a lighted torch in one hand
and a whip in the other.

Whatever personal compulsion Henry thus satisfied, the
religious problem remained unaffected except for an inci-
dental benefit that came Catherine's way. The old Cardinal
of Lorraine, head of the Guise house and her archenemy for
fifteen years, could not permit a mere king to surpass him in
a display of devoutness and had therefore taken part in the
procession. But the exertion and the exposure to the cold
November night proved too much for him. He caught cold
and died. Catherine received the news as she was sitting
down to dine. "I really cannot believe this," she started to
say. "He was a great prelate and a wise one, and France, and
ourselves, have suffered a grievous loss in his death." Then
looking around the table at the faces she had known and
who had known her for so long, she stopped and continued,
"Now we shall have peace, for he is dead and people say he
was the one person that prevented it."

The pleasure of burying a well-hated enemy capped Catherine's joy at having Henry back. To be sure, as a king he
had proved to be a disaster. His new rules of protocol had
served only to offend and alienate loyal and trusted members
of the nobility. His public displays, whether of ostentation
or penitence, only further cast discredit on the institution of

the monarchy. His coronation, on February 13, 1575, had been a near-disgrace; midway through the long ceremony, he complained aloud that the crown was hurting his head. He had even ignored his mother's matrimonial find—a ready and waiting Swedish princess—and instead had chosen to marry Louise de Vaudemont, the pious, quiet, younger daughter of a cadet branch of the Lorraine family. But against all this, Catherine could balance the single fact that her own worst fear had not materialized. For the present at least, Henry III was not about to edge her from her position of tutelage.

XI

The mother's joy did not, however, extend to include the other members of the royal family. When they were children, Henry had amused himself by devising games that would turn his brothers and sisters against each other, to his own advantage. Now, as King, he continued to devise such games, but for perilously higher stakes. Convinced that his brother and brother-in-law were jointly plotting against him, he created opportunities to drive them apart, using as instrument his sister, Margot. Once, when riding with Navarre, he noticed Margot's private coach, unmistakable for its yellow velvet and silver brocade lining, halted before the house of a gentleman of the Court. Immediately, he ordered one of his followers to break into the house. It was empty, but the man reported, "The birds have been there, but they have flown." Navarre was only amused at such attempts to provoke his jealousy, but Catherine, to whom Henry personally reported the episode, took it less kindly. "As soon as she saw me," Margot wrote, "she commenced to spout out fire and to say everything that a most unmeasured anger could utter. I told her the truth, but she had no ear for the truth nor for reason. She wouldn't listen to me. Whether it was because her mind was filled with the falsehood or perhaps to please that son, whom out of affection and a sense of hope and fear she fairly worshipped as an idol, I do not know, but she would not stop moving around the room crying out loud and threatening me. And all of it was heard by the next room full of people."

But Margot was a young lady who could take care of herself. Among Henry's favorites was Louis de Clermont, squire of Bussy d'Amboise, who, at twenty-six, was a younger, bolder and, if it is possible, more virile version of La Môle. Bussy, as he was known at Court, had come from nowhere to become a walking, prancing legend at the Court. No major brawl was complete without him; the number of duels he had survived lay uncounted behind him. To anyone who would listen, he boasted that "I was born a simple gentleman, but there is an Emperor in my belly," and upon reading Plutarch's *Lives,* recently translated into French, he observed humbly, "There is nothing here that I could not have done myself." To repay her dear brother Henry, Margot set herself to detach Bussy from his service and enlist him in her own.

In her *Memoirs,* Margot describes the episode gingerly, as a purely cold-blooded maneuver to secure Bussy's multiple talents on behalf of her brother, Alençon. This she accomplished, but it would have been surprising indeed if the arrangement had been as strictly businesslike as she pretends. In fact, Bussy assumed his place on her list of lovers with such *panache* that it was impossible for the youngest page at Court to be unaware of it. Nevertheless, Henry ran to his mother in order to inform her of his sister's infamous behavior. By this time, however, Catherine had recognized the mounting danger. Rather than punishing Margot, she tried to explain to Henry: "It's troublemakers who put such ideas into your head. My daughter is unfortunate to be born in such an age. In my own time we talked freely to everybody and all the honest gentlemen who followed the King your father were ordinarily in the chamber of Madame Marguerite, your aunt, and in mine. Nobody thought it was strange as there was no reason to think it was strange. Bussy sees my daughter. . . . What is there to think about it? Do you know anything else?" Astonished and uncomprehending, the King persisted: "Madame, I only say what others are saying." Catherine tried again: "Who are these others, my son? They are people who want to get you into a quarrel with all your family."

But Henry, whether he understood or not, would not give up the game he had started. To repay Alençon for the theft of Bussy, he encouraged his own followers to heap ridicule on his younger brother's appearance, to mimic and belittle his personal ambitions. In his frustration, Alençon wailed, "I, the second person in this realm, am the most wretched human being in it." Matters could not continue indefinitely at this pitch. As Navarre wrote to a friend, "The Court is the strangest place you ever saw. We are nearly always ready to cut each other's throats. We carry daggers, mail coats, and often cuirasses under our jackets."

The break was precipitated unwittingly by Catherine herself. Alarmed by the virulence of the hatreds within her family, she banished Bussy from Paris—an order which he obeyed in his own fashion, riding leisurely through the city streets while wearing Margot's colors as a cockade in his hat. But a Bussy loose in the provinces proved far more useful to Alençon than one popping in and out of bedrooms in the Louvre. Before he left, Margot instructed him to gather a force of men in Dreux, a city that was one of Alençon's personal fiefdoms. She then arranged for Alençon himself to ride to a brothel on the Rue Saint-Marceau which he was known to frequent. While his coach stood waiting outside, Alençon entered the house, passed through a rear door and, disguised in cloak and muffler, scurried to a nearby gate of the city where a horse was waiting for him. "His departure," Marguerite relates, "was not discovered until nine o'clock in the evening. The King and the Queen my mother asked me why he had not come to supper with them. I told them I had not seen him since the afternoon. They sent to his rooms and were informed that he was not there. Then they ordered him to be sought in the rooms of all the ladies whom he used to visit. They searched the Palace, they searched the town, but in vain. The alarm then heightened. The King grew angry, furious, threatening, sending for all the princes and lords at court, and ordering them to take to horse and bring him back, dead or alive."

Many of the lords, mindful of Bussy's reputation, disobeyed the order, explaining to the King that although they would gladly lay down their lives for him, they also knew that he might one day turn against them if they dared to do harm to his royal brother. They would gladly go, they said, if the King would first find out whether the fugitive meant to do him any harm.

Alençon spared Henry the trouble. From refuge, he notified his brother that he had escaped "for the sake of my liberty and because I have been in daily expectation that His Majesty would take some resolution molded on the counsels of Cesare Borgia." He further informed Henry that he was assuming the self-imposed duties of "Governor-General for the King and Defender of the Liberties of the Commonwealth of France." The first of these duties, as the new Governor-General saw them, was to lead the troops assembled by Bussy on a ramble through France, throwing out the royal governors of every town he passed through and replacing them with his own men.

The flight had taken place on September 15, 1575. Daily thereafter, reports of masses of Huguenots and other malcontents falling into Alençon's ranks began arriving at the

Court. It was not his personal magnetism or the virtue of his cause that attracted them as much as the circumstance of his royal name.

Catherine, who had seen five kings on the throne of France, understood Frenchmen to perfection. She was convinced that so long as the Huguenots or even the *Politiques* could not legitimately wrap themselves with the banner of the lilies, the nation would never accept them as anything but usurpers. Alençon's defection had, for the first time since the outbreak of the wars, given them at least a hold on a corner of that banner.

Six days after Alençon's flight, Catherine climbed into her coach and, accompanied by Margot, whose influence over her younger brother was well known to her, undertook the humiliating task of attempting to bring him back. The chase assumed some of the characteristics of a comedy sequence, for neither the pursued nor therefore the pursuer had any specific destination in mind. Alençon traveled completely at random, borne on the breezes of euphoria. For the first time in his life people were cheering him, greeting him as a liberator, treating him seriously enough to prepare proclamations for him to sign—proclamations in which, had he read them, he would have discovered that he was proposing such sweeping reforms as complete religious toleration in France and the exclusion from affairs of state of all foreigners, presumably including his mother.

After nearly three weeks during which her anxiety over leaving Henry to manage alone can be measured by her writing forty-eight letters to him, Catherine finally caught up with Alençon at Chambord. The meeting had the customary aspects of a family reunion: when she stepped out of her coach, he rushed up to kneel on the ground before her and she tenderly embraced him "not without tears," an eyewitness noted. But his filial duty—or fear—had now been tempered by a taste of glory. No, he would not return home. Nor would he even listen to his mother until she had heard his terms: that the Marshals Montmorency and Cossé, who had been languishing in the Bastille since their arrest during his first attempted escape, be freed and restored to their titles and dignities; that the Château of Blois, which he well knew was a royal property, be turned over to his personal use. There were other demands, some petty and some so sweeping that even had she wanted to Catherine could not have satisfied them. The woman who for years had matched her diplomatic skills against Philip of Spain, Elizabeth, a handful of popes, and the rival factions within her own country therefore found herself obliged to sit down and negotiate in earnest with an irrational twenty-year-old adolescent who happened also to be her own son. Under the circumstances, she did well to persuade him to agree to a six-month truce— time enough to repair some of the harm he had caused.

But events had gone far beyond Alençon's ability to control them. His first defiance of his brother the King had been a signal to those French Huguenots who, after the Massacre, had sought refuge in the Lutheran lands across the Rhine. The subsequent proclamations he endorsed had facilitated their efforts to recruit a mercenary army. By the time the truce was declared—November, 1575—the first elements of that army had already begun crossing into France. Under the command of Duke John Casimir, the son of the Elector Palatine, eight thousand German cavalrymen, six thousand infantry from the cantons of Switzerland, and some seven thousand arquebusiers were marching westward and southward, plundering and burning as they cut their way to the Loire. Watching their easy success, the *Politiques* mounted an army of their own and put it at the disposal of their heaven-sent new leader. Without quite understanding how it had happened, Alençon found himself, early in 1576, at the head of thirty thousand men, waiting for his command to march on Paris. Again, Catherine was obliged to journey out and attempt to make peace.

This time, however, her bargaining position was almost

nonexistent. Confronted with his first crisis, Henry III had chosen to abdicate all responsibility. To his other pastimes, he added a sudden passion for literature and the contemplative life. Almost daily after dinner he would retire to a small, windowless room, taking with him four or five young poets and a few gentlemen and ladies of the Court. There, by the dim light of candles, one of the poets would speak in praise of one of the virtues, after which all the others in turn would argue against what had been said. The meetings of this so-called academy took precedence over all other matters. When one of his secretaries or ministers would find an opportunity to approach Henry and report on the progress of the enemy, he would be told that when the time was right a royal army of adequate size to wipe out the rebels would be sent to deal with them.

Catherine knew, and was aware that the Huguenots knew, that the King could not have collected three thousand men, much less thirty thousand to wipe out anyone. This could be offset in measure by judicious bluffing. But her own highly developed sense of balance warned her that the time had come to moderate the partiality she had shown toward her elder son. The results of her second meeting with Alençon reflect this concern, for the agreement she consented to was less the product of negotiation than of capitulation. The Peace of *Monsieur,** as it was called, was signed on May 6, 1576, and granted every demand made by the Huguenots. Free exercise of religion was to be permitted everywhere in the realm. Every local Parlement was to have a tribunal composed equally of Catholic and Reformed judges. The sentences of all those who had been executed because of religious differences since the death of Henry II were to be revoked. Alençon was granted the independent administration of the provinces of Touraine, Berry, and Anjou. On one

* So called because, according to Henry III's new rules of protocol, the King's younger brother was to be addressed as *Monsieur,* a custom that survived to the end of the French monarchy.

count only did Catherine hold fast. Alençon, or his counselors, had demanded that the instigators of the St. Bartholomew's Massacre be punished. Since this would condemn herself and Henry, Catherine persuaded Alençon to be satisfied instead with a formal declaration that all the victims of the Massacre had been innocent and, in reparation, that their families would be freed from the obligation of paying taxes.

In the midst of these great events of state, a domestic detail that was to have overwhelming consequences in the history of France went almost unnoticed. On February 4, 1576, the King of Navarre escaped from the Louvre.

During his four years of captivity, he had behaved in such erratic, servile manner that the true nature of his motives is still a matter of contention among historians. Most of them, including all those writing in French, tend to view him as "an eagle penned in among preening peacocks," presumably only waiting for the first opportunity to fly away. It is likely that this metaphor again pays more honor to the great man he was to become rather than the young prince he then was. Militating against it are the charms of Mme de Sauves and the bountiful pleasures of Court life after the austerity of a Calvinist upbringing. There is also the evidence of Agrippa d'Aubigné, the great Protestant scholar who challenged Navarre shortly before he escaped: "Sire," wrote the fiery old partisan who had known him since his boyhood, "can it be that the spirit of God is still within you? You cry to Him about the absence of your friends; they cry for your return. You have tears in your eyes; they have weapons in their hands. They fight your enemies; you serve them. They are on horseback; you are on your knees. . . ."

But the most persuasive evidence that Navarre was something less than an unwilling prisoner is the very manner in which he made his escape once he had decided to do so. He was out hunting with the Duke of Guise in the forest of Senlis just outside of Paris, a pastime he had engaged in dozens of times, when he managed to stray away from the rest of the party. As they continued to pursue the stag, he joined two waiting companions and, together with them, started riding south. No one pursued them, but L'Estoile, who relates the story, adds that "no word was spoken between them until they had reached the Loire." Once safely across, Navarre vowed never to return to Paris. "I have left two things behind me," he said. "The one is the Mass, the other is my wife. As for the first, I must try to do without it. As for the second, I mean to have her back."

He had not notified Margot of this resolve. As she relates the events prior to his departure, "Whether he was busy planning his escape or wanted to spend the short time remaining to him in the voluptuous presence of Mme de Sauves, my husband never had time to come and visit me. He came back to bed as usual at one or two o'clock in the morning, and as we slept in separate beds I did not hear him come in. And as he got up before I was awake, in order to attend the *lever* of the Queen, he did not remember to speak to me as he had promised, and left without even saying *A Dieu* to me."

XII

"The history of the next years was a succession of incoherent and inconclusive incidents, without consistency or continuity," writes the historian Ralph Roeder—a judgment a recital of the bare facts would support. Only in psychological terms do they make sense, and then only as the tangled middle section of a certain kind of family novel, after the character of the chief protagonists has been established, and before they begin gravitating toward their respective ordained ends.

Henry III rewarded his mother's efforts on his behalf with sarcasm such as he had heretofore only dared use on others.

Referring to her hard-won Peace of *Monsieur,* he told her he would gladly have given half his kingdom for peace, but he had not expected her to take him at his word. To underline his displeasure, he demanded that hencetorth he be shown all state dispatches before she was allowed to see them. Furthermore, he pointedly refused to talk to her at all for two months.

While he thus played at being both spoiled brat and King, it was she who suffered the brunt of public disapproval. The Venetian Michieli reported: "The blame of everything that happens is put on the Queen Mother, whence it comes about that, if at first she was little loved because she was a foreigner and an Italian, now, to tell the truth, she is hated because everybody knows that to keep herself in supreme authority, she has always fomented the discords and divisions of party . . . and always trying as far as she could to keep her sons, even when they were grown up, far from business and grave thoughts in order that they should put everything into her hands."

Another reason for the growing hatred of Catherine was that the list of her political enemies was becoming longer. The Huguenots had feared and mistrusted her since St. Bartholomew; there was almost no concession she could make that would erase those blood-soaked sentiments. But now, the very people who had, after the Massacre, proclaimed her a dedicated servant of the Faith, who had sung masses in her honor and compared her favorably with Joan of Arc, found reason to distrust her as well. The preface to the Peace of *Monsieur* had read: "In oblivion of the past. . . ." Ardent Catholics and those who, for their own purposes, purported to show the highest zeal in protecting the Church, interpreted the peace more as a warning that henceforth the Crown would look upon the Reformers with particular partiality.

A League of the Holy Trinity was founded, with the stated purpose of serving the Church and protecting it against all its enemies, including the royal family if that became necessary. Elements of such a league already existed in the form of small, local groups whose aggregate effect had been negligible because of a lack of central leadership. Ironically, these groups tore a leaf out of Calvin's *Institutes of the Christian Religion* and now organized themselves on a national basis. Henry, sensing the danger such a powerful force represented, sought to disarm it and perhaps even direct it to his own purposes by exercising his royal prerogative to declare himself its chief. His wish could not be denied, but underneath him another Henry—the Duke of Guise—began to conscript the loyalty of the Catholics to his own person. Equally important, Guise allowed himself to be persuaded to accept secret financial support from Philip II of Spain.

Meanwhile, Alençon had not the remotest idea of what to do with his good fortune. In the wake of the publication of the Peace that bore his name, he became a hero to Protestant forces all over Europe. The Dutch, writhing under the boots of their Spanish masters, offered him the title of Prince and Count of Holland and Zealand if he would lead them into open revolt. Alençon hesitated because he had conceived the notion of marrying one of Philip II's daughters and thereby securing a dowry which would make him an independent prince and finance his further career. The fact that the prospective bride was a daughter of his late sister, Elizabeth, and therefore his own niece, either slipped his mind or did not pose any problem to him. Philip replied to the suggestion in flattering but vague words. Meanwhile, he ordered the removal of the Governor of the Netherlands, whose sadistic measures of repression were the principal cause of discontent, and replaced him with his own bastard brother Don Juan, whose victory over the Turks at Lepanto had made him a hero in all Christendom. Rushing across France incognito to take up his new post, Juan quickly stilled the rebellion by means of broad concessions. As soon as this change was made, and the offer of the Holland and Zealand crown withdrawn, Philip destroyed Alençon's matrimonial plans by letting it be known that "a Christian cannot allow this kind of marriage which is more seeming for dogs."

Restless, rootless, driven to frenzy by ambition, yet unable to carry out or even formulate the simplest plan, Alençon was easily persuaded by Catherine to return home—particularly as Mme de Sauves, who had accompanied the Queen Mother, promised that, with Navarre gone, he would no longer have a competitor for her attention. Henry cemented the reconciliation by offering him the title of Lieutenant-General of the kingdom—the same honor that, had it been offered to him a year earlier when he had asked for it, would have precluded both his escape and its doleful consequences. He accepted the title, even though the price for it was that he would have to lead Catholic troops against his former Huguenot companions. Like a grotesque windup doll, he took on the task with such single-minded resolve that his campaign, formally recognized in history texts as the Sixth War of Religion, exceeded in bestiality anything that had been previously inflicted on the innocent civilians caught between the warring factions. Years later, an unimpeachable source* described, as just one of the acts of atrocity committed by Alençon's troops, how a group of soldiers caught six village girls, raped them to boredom, and then filled them up with gunpowder and set fire to them.

To celebrate her youngest son's victory, Catherine arranged what was to be the most memorable of her entertainments. The setting was Chenonceaux, whose gardens were for the occasion transformed into a vast open-air banqueting-hall—at a cost of 100,000 francs, which, L'Estoile notes, the Queen Mother personally raised as "loans" from members of the royal household. The nature of the diversion she had planned for the occasion was unmistakably indicated when, after the gentlemen guests were seated, the young ladies of the Court

* Sully, Henry IV's great minister, in his *Oeconomies Royales.*

came out to wait on them, naked to the waist and wearing their hair loose to their shoulders—the traditional fashion of brides on their wedding night.

But again, success frowned on Alençon. Jealous of his younger brother's military prowess and the attention lavished on him, Henry summarily stripped him of his title and encouraged the Court to mock him personally and belittle his achievements. Once more Alençon haunted the corridors of the Louvre, this time without Navarre's shoulder to cry on, and once more he escaped to pursue the crown which had so narrowly eluded him in Flanders.

In less than a year, Henry III's fling at kingship had succeeded in creating a powerful new threat to himself—the Holy League—in letting a raving, irresponsible Alençon loose where he might at any moment provoke Philip into declaring war against France, and in squandering money with such single-mindedness that there was no hope of raising an army to defend the country. Then, as abruptly as he had assumed the duties of state, he shrugged them off to devote himself to a new set of pleasures.

A different kind of gentleman began to appear, first at Court and then in the streets of Paris. They were all young, mostly of humble or uncertain origins, but all of them delicately handsome and ferociously devoted to the King. What distinguished them on sight was their style of dress: velvet toques under which they wore their hair "long, frizzed, and refrizzed by skilled arts," brilliantly colored linen doublets and shirts with a circular starched and pleated collar so wide that one had the impression of "seeing the head of Saint John upon the dish."* To less respectful observers, the collars, which became their trademark, looked even more like the white folded paper on which butchers were accustomed to display heads of veal. These *mignons* (darlings)—Maugiron, Quélus, Saint-Megrin, D'O, Livarot, Mauléon—almost over-

---

* They were, in fact, so wide that it was necessary to introduce the use of long-handed spoons in order to allow their wearers to feed themselves.

night came to symbolize in the minds of the people the
decadence, the political and spiritual bankruptcy of the monarchy. Their appearance in the streets, prancing and leaving
behind a delicate scent of violets, was the signal for sly
whistles, jeering cries of *piou-piou,* and vulgar, suggestive
gestures. Fresh doggerel appeared daily, celebrating their
doings. Thus, after one of them had been beaten in a fight
with an older courtier:

> *Quélus n'entend pas la manière*
> *De prendre les gens par devant,*
> *S'il l'eust pris, par derrière,*
> *Il luy eust fourré plus avant.*

> At fighting face-to-face,
> Quélus is not too gifted.
> He would have run a better race,
> If to the rear he'd shifted.

More appropriate, since the *mignons* were given not only
to transvestitism and pederasty but to any other sort of sexual
sport as well, were the opening lines of a pamphlet entitled
L'Île des Hermaphrodites:

> *Je ne suis mâle ni femelle*
> *Et si je suis bien en cervelle*
> *Lequel des deux je dois choisir*
> *Mais qu'importe à qui on ressemble*
> *Il vaut mieux les avoir ensemble*
> *On en reçoit double plaisir.*

> I am neither female nor male,
> Though I know I should choose only one
> But who cares! It is better
> To be both together,
> And that way have double the fun.

Inevitably, Margot had been drawn into the family's violent feuds. Enraged by her husband's escape, which he
wrongly accused her of abetting, Henry had chosen the

characteristically petty revenge of ordering that her favorite lady-in-waiting, Mlle de Thorigny, be removed permanently from Court. Margot learned of the plot just in time to arrange to save the poor girl as, tied and weighted with stones, she was about to be thrown into a river. As reward for this good deed, Henry ordered his sister locked up in her apartments and prohibited anyone from visiting her. Only Catherine dared defy this command. Margot relates how her mother came and begged her not to be angry but to make allowances for the King's actions—"You are intelligent and will therefore understand." She expressed the hope that, by God's will, Margot's confinement should not last long, and added, "If I myself don't come to see you too often, it is only in order not to arouse the King's suspicions, but believe me that I will not allow any harm to you, and will do my utmost to make peace."

"After she left me," Margot writes, "I remained thus for several months, without anyone, even my best friends, daring to visit me, afraid that if they did so they would be ruined. At Court, when all is well one is surrounded by people, but in adversity one is always alone. Persecution breaks up the best and most intimate friendships." To fill the long hours between her mother's visits, Margot relates that she found solace in the world of books: "In my sadness and solitude, I rediscovered the great gifts of study and devotion—gifts which, among the vanities and magnificence of my former good fortune, I had never truly tasted."

A pretty picture, but hardly convincing and not in conformance with the facts. For one thing, Alençon's return had brought Bussy d'Amboise back to Court—a Bussy who, if anything, was more self-assured and dashing than ever. Shortly after his arrival, he appeared at Mass escorted by six pages dressed in gold cloth and wearing their hair in neatly arranged curls. His own costume consisted of a shoddy, unadorned cloak suitable for an undertaker's assistant. After making sure that the King and his *mignons* had noticed

Catherine de' Medici in her middle forties, in widow's
costume she wore for the last three decades of her life

Polemical Huguenot drawing showing the ceremonial trappings of the Roman Church, including the papal tiara, being weighed and found wanting against the simple, unadorned austerity of the Bible

Facing page, two of Catherine's principal adversaries: Gaspard de Coligny and, *at far right,* her son-in-law, Philip II of Spain

At right, Jeanne d'Albret,
mother of Henry of Navarre

MUSÉE CARNAVALET—GIRAUDON

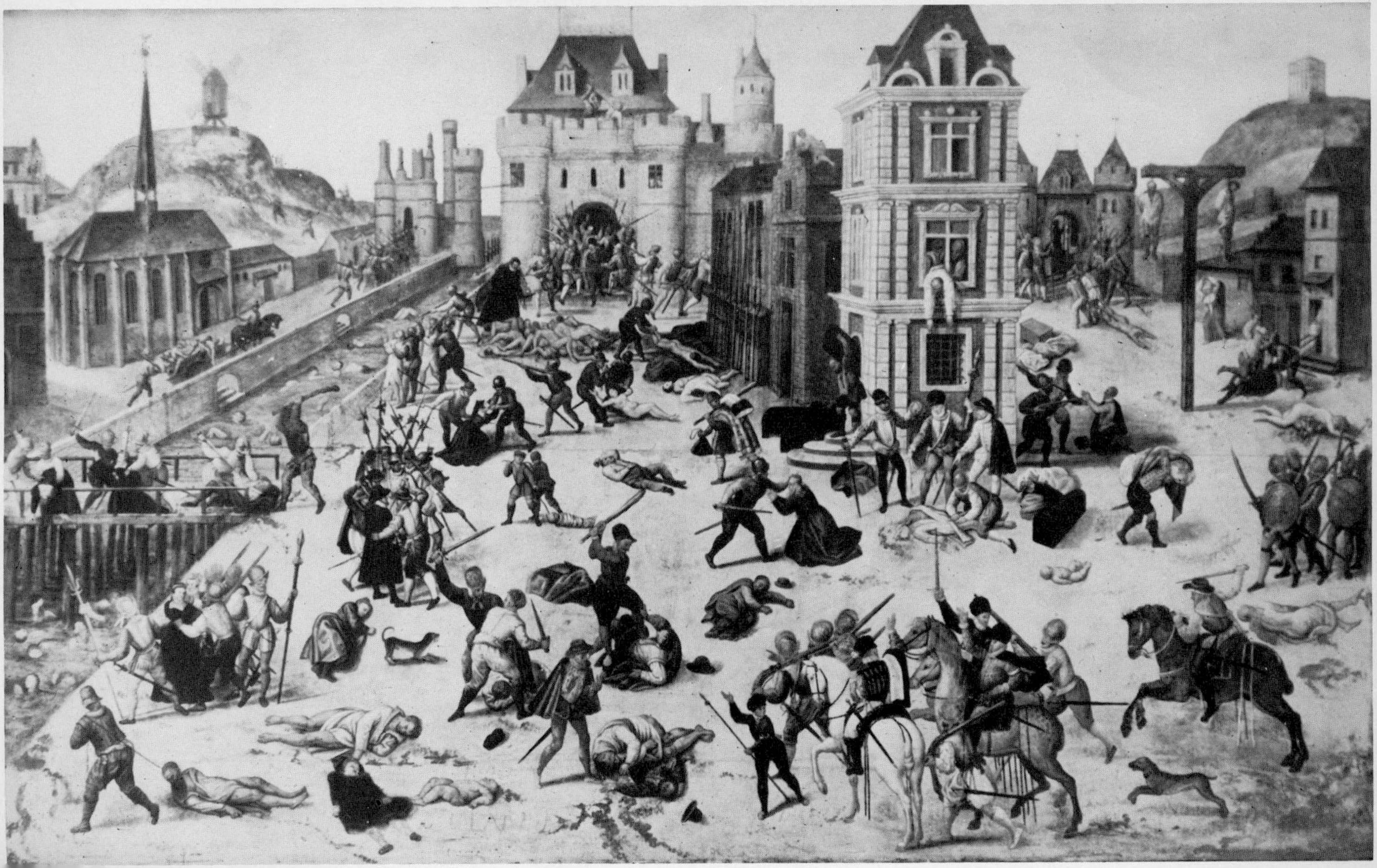

At left, contemporary view of
Saint Bartholomew's Massacre

Marguerite de Valois, as she
looked prior to her marriage

Charles IX, the second of Catherine's
sons to become King of France

Orgiastic scene of dancing, drinking, and backgammon showing Dutch engraver Johann Sadeler's view of an evening at the Valois Court

At top left, Mme Charlotte de Sauves, the most gifted member of Catherine's *escadron volant,* and two of her charges: the Duke of Alençon, *center,* and Henry of Navarre, as he looked at the time of his marriage to Marguerite

Tapestry presented to Catherine showing procession leaving Anet, at rear; Catherine in sedan chair at center

Other scenes recalling some of her entertainments: in foreground, *at left*, Henry III and, *at right*, Alençon

Above, portrait of Henry III by the engraver Wierix; *facing page*, reception in Venice on Henry's homeward voyage from Poland in 1574, and a performance by *I Gelosi*, the *commedia dell'Arte* company which he admired and subsequently brought to France

MUSÉES NATIONAUX

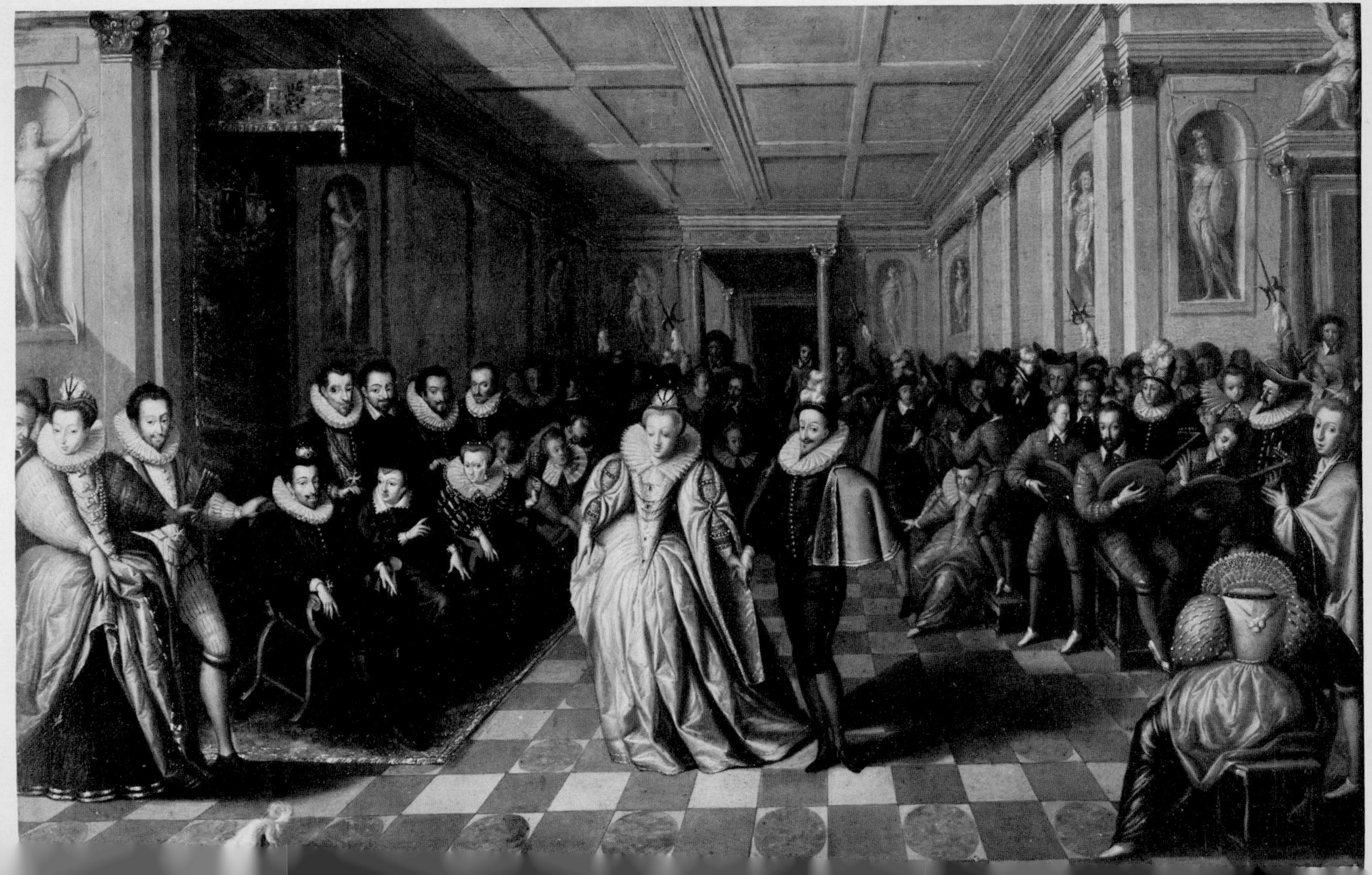

At left, the celebrated Ball for the Duke of Joyeuse showing Henry III seated far left, his mother, second person to the right, and three of the Guise brothers standing behind them; *above,* Henry of Navarre, *left,* and Henry, Duke of Guise; *right,* the cover page of a typical political pamphlet of the period (see page 241 of the text)

Marguerite de Valois, as she looked on her return to social life in Paris

Catherine's last portrait, undated but probably done when she was 66

A procession of the Holy League in Paris. Contemporary accounts suggest that the event may have taken place just as it is shown.

Henry IV entrusting the regency to Marie de' Medici from the well-known and very fictional cycle she commissioned Rubens to paint him, he shrugged his shoulders and observed loudly: "What then is there left for gentlemen to wear, when valets start to dress like gentlemen?" On another occasion, after Bussy had publicly called one of the *mignons* a "royal bed warmer," Henry ordered him to make peace with the aggrieved young man by embracing him. Looking his monarch in the eye, Bussy asked, "No more than that, Sire?"

In addition to having Bussy as a diversion from her contemplative pursuits, Margot had also resumed her political activities. During one of Catherine's clandestine visits to her, the Queen Mother had casually asked Margot to patch up her differences with Navarre, who on his return home had resumed both his throne and the leadership of the Huguenots. Catherine's motive was to pave the way for a possible political reconciliation, but the solicitude she expressed was that of a concerned mother. "These are little quarrels between husband and wife," she told Margot, "which can easily be mended. I know that with a few gentle letters you will regain his heart." Margot, rising to the part of dutiful daughter, had promised to do her best. What she had not bothered to tell her mother was that, from the time of his return home, she had already started corresponding secretly with Navarre.

On another occasion, when Henry had consented to pardon her in order that she could accompany Catherine on the journey to bring Alençon back to Court, she had seen through his motives as well. "As soon as he had my brother back at court again, he would find some excuse for making war on the Huguenots, in order that they should not enjoy what with bitter regrets and by force he had been compelled to grant them."

After events proved that she had been only too accurate a prophet, Margot had sought to atone for the disservice she had done Alençon, and at the same time pay back Henry for the humiliations he had heaped on her. Using poor health— a rash of erysipelas on one arm—as a pretext, she had asked

Henry's permission to travel to Spa, in what is now Belgium, in order to take the curative waters. The trip had been a complete success, both medically and personally. Everywhere she had gone, she had charmed her hosts. Only reluctantly had she been allowed to make her way home, and then only after assuring everyone that her younger brother was preparing to come among them, bringing wise and just rule.

XIII

As her children were playing out their deadly games, it was Catherine's turn to act again. She knew how wise and just Alençon's rule was likely to be; even then he was raising the troops—the customary bandits and cutthroats—which he hoped would secure the throne for him. She knew what kind of king Henry III had turned out to be. The knowledge did not cause her to adore him any less uncritically; it only strengthened her conviction that he needed her help. She now also knew, although this knowledge did not increase the affection she had for her, how effective a political instrument Margot could be. But above all she knew that France in the sense in which she understood the term—as a large, powerful, single geographic entity ruled by the Valois-Medici dynasty—was in extreme peril. Bountiful as the land was, much of it lay untilled or unharvested because people were fearful to venture into a countryside ravaged by marauders who took what they wanted, and killed or maimed those who attempted to interfere. Commerce and trade slowed as cities, Catholic or Reformed, locked their gates and trusted no stranger. Now in her fifty-ninth year, hobbled by obesity and rheumatism, uncertain about her reception in hostile territory, Catherine again undertook a great journey to preserve France for her family. To this end, no fatigue was too great, no risk too frightening, no falsehood too black.

The surest key to her plan was Navarre. She had known this eight years earlier when she had been determined to detach him from his mother and make him a bridegroom. Events unforeseen had thwarted the achievement of her purpose then, but her judgment had been right. That first time, she had required him to come to her in order to claim his bride. This time, she would go to him and bring the bride with her.

Thanks to the painstaking work of scholars who have collected, compared, and cross-checked letters, royal household accounts, diaries, memoirs, and diplomatic reports, we are able to follow their progress, and Margot's subsequent stay with her husband, on a day-to-day basis.

The Queen of Navarre and the Queen Mother took formal leave of the King on the morning of August 2, 1578, at Ollainville, a secluded mansion south of Paris which he had originally purchased for his Queen, but had subsequently appropriated for his own use and that of his *mignons*. Slowed down by their respective trains which together numbered more than three hundred people, the two ladies moved leisurely through Étampes, Orléans, Blois, Chenonceaux, where they rested for three days, Tours, Poitiers, Cognac, and eventually reached Bordeaux, where Navarre had promised to meet them, on September 19.

Margot made her triumphal entry alone. Riding a white palfrey and dressed in a gown of her favorite golden orange silk, cut low enough to set off the fair white shoulders and breasts of which she was proud, she lived up to her reputation as "the most superb, refined woman in France, peerless in the elegance and daring of her taste." She also, in her responses to the many welcoming speeches by the city's officials, justified her intellectual fame. Brantôme, for once an eyewitness rather than a collector of gossip, describes how "to one after another she replied—which I myself heard since by her orders I was close to her on the platform—so eloquently, wisely, and spontaneously, with such grace and majesty . . . that the same evening the President [of the local Law Court] came up to me in the Queen Mother's chamber, telling me that he had never heard better speeches in his life, although he had often had the pleasure of listening to her predecessors, the Queens Marguerite [Francis I's sister] and Jeanne d'Albret, but that in eloquence they were no match at all for this Queen Marguerite, who was truly her mother's daughter."

Catherine's answer, according to Brantôme, was that "even though she was her own daughter, she could honestly say that she was the most accomplished princess in the world." Effacing herself in order to place Margot in the fullest view was central to Catherine's strategy. Although she had brought along her most accomplished diplomats and a select detachment of the *escadron volant*—including the invaluable Mme de Sauves—it was Margot who was her principal attraction. Like a shrewd, practiced trader, she proposed to tempt the potential buyer by showing off the best merchandise she had to offer. Shakespeare, who based his *Love's Labor's Lost* on Margot's reunion with Navarre, saw through her game. In the play, he has one of the chief advisers to the Princess of France urge her to:

> Consider whom the king your father sends*
> To whom he sends, and what's his embassy:
> Yourself, held precious in the world's esteem . . .
> Be now as prodigal of all dear grace
> As Nature was in making graces dear
> When she did starve the general world beside,
> And prodigally gave them all to you.
> —Act 2, sc. 1.

The two Queens' visit to Bordeaux was a personal triumph, marred only by the apparent lack of interest on the part of

* In the play, the Princess is daughter to the King, rather than his sister—an immaterial difference.

their prospective customer. Although he had written them warm letters of invitation and expressed impatience at seeing them, Navarre still made no move to stir out of Nérac, his capital. Catherine, while waiting, wrote to Henry reassuring him that everything was going well and that Margot in particular was being cooperative: "It is three days now that she is closeted with her maids, one with a razor, the other with balms, and the third with water." She described in detail the hours of soaking in perfumed baths, the plucking of the eyebrows into fashionable shape, the massages and pummelings. And, aware of Henry's unpredictable fits of jealousy, she was careful to add: "You are her heart, her everything . . . [A]ll these charms are at your service." Meanwhile, Catherine was also sending emissaries to Nérac, in effect asking Navarre what was keeping him away. Like a tomcat on the trail, eager but cautious, he protested that Bordeaux was too far and too dangerous for him. Would the ladies consider a meeting place closer to his own borders? Anxious and impatient, Catherine agreed to any arrangements that suited him. Thus it was that the reunion of the King of Navarre and his wife—and his mother-in-law—took place on October 2, 1578, in an isolated manor house halfway between the villages of Macaire and La Réole.

Catherine was, on the whole, pleased with the results of this first meeting. She wrote that night to Henry that she had every reason to believe that "my journey will be of help to you." To be sure, Navarre was not convinced of their good intentions—he had ridden up surrounded by a body of "more than five hundred gentlemen, well-mounted." Once reassured, however, he demonstrated "the greatest grace and pleasure possible" at seeing them. He consented to travel in her carriage on the short ride into La Réole, where he had ordered accommodations prepared for them—"one for me, and another across the street where they will lodge and sleep together."

Other differences were not so easy to resolve. Catherine

247

had a long agenda of concessions she wished to extract from Navarre. He, in turn, had as many demands to make, and he could not afford to make any compromises in return because his claim to leadership of the Reform was already clouded by his long residence at Court. The two fenced for six days and agreed to meet again later during the month. Navarre returned home, while Margot proceeded to Agen, an ancient city that belonged to her as part of her personal endowment.

Through October and November, the two Queens and their movable Court traveled from town to town. Navarre joined them for a few days, then vanished again. It was a peculiar way to conduct negotiations, but it suited Navarre's purposes. As the English ambassador reported: "The Queen Mother and her old and grave counselors are at the end of their Latin; they find him [Navarre] to be furthest out of danger when they think he is already in their snare."

Navarre had obviously learned a great deal during his years of observing Catherine at work, but there were still tricks of patience she could have taught him were it not for her constant concern over having left Henry alone in Paris. To forestall some impetuous, irreparable action on his part, she filled her letters to him with feigned impatience of her own: "Hour by hour I try to hasten things; we do not waste time. . . . I am furious and annoyed at having been here three days without hearing any news from the King of Navarre. . . . What does he take me for, showing no respect for me?" She even made a rare reference to her own personal discomfort, complaining of "the suffering I have endured in taking such a long journey in such a bad season," adding that "if he had any consideration for my person he would act differently." And always she came back to her central theme: "Through it all I have tried to act gently and kindly . . . knowing that this is what you would want."

For Margot, unencumbered by concern for Henry, the

trip was an altogether delightful experience for several reasons. First, the splendid reception she had received in Bordeaux was repeated on a smaller scale in every town she visited. Second, she sincerely believed that her mission was important and in a good cause, for she wrote to a close friend: "I am determined to do everything in my power which will not be prejudicial to my husband in order to bring him to conform himself to the will of the King . . . in whatever will be for the peace and tranquillity of the state. You must believe that I will do this and that there is nothing dearer to me than this; for I would prefer death to war." And finally, she was happy to be reunited with her husband, even if thus far only on a hit-and-miss basis. There was, despite Catherine's observation regarding sleeping arrangements, little sexual attraction between the two; for all the good they did her, Margot could have saved herself the trouble of the massages, baths, and depilation. Navarre may have initially observed the conjugal niceties—it would have been out of character if he had not—but soon thereafter his roving eye had swept across the offerings of the *escadron volant* and found an agreeable landing site. It was not Mme de Sauves this time, who perhaps reminded him of more bitter days, but a young Spanish beauty named Victoria de Ayala, newly recruited to the ranks. As Margot noted in her *Memoirs:* "The King my husband has fallen deeply in love with Dayelle." But she adds: "In spite of this, he treated me with great honor and friendship, as much as I could have wished. From our very first meeting he told me of all the tricks that had been played on him at Court in order that we should be on bad terms. He realized that this had been done solely in order to disrupt the friendship between my brother [Alençon] and himself, and to ruin all three of us, and he showed great pleasure that we were together again."

Eventually, Catherine's patience outlasted Navarre's. Having raised every objection and invoked every delay he could, he finally made it a condition that the negotiations be carried on in Nérac, his own city. When Catherine agreed, there was nothing left for him to ask. On December 15, 1578, the royal party cross the border into Navarre. Catherine rode discreetly in the rear, permitting the King and his wife to lead the procession. It was Margot's first opportunity to behold her subjects, and theirs to look at her in the flesh.

Good Gascons all, they rose to the occasion. The reigning poet laureate, Salluste du Bertras, had composed an elaborate ode of welcome in his native dialect. Margot listened politely but uncomprehendingly. When the verses were translated to her as an invocation bidding the Nightingale to ". . . greet with a sweet song the most beautiful woman in the world," she impulsively removed her embroidered scarf and pressed it on the young lady who had been chosen to recite. At the feast that followed the reception, hospitality and goodwill more than compensated for the absence of the exotic refinements of Paris. There were great platters of trout, freshly caught in the icy mountain streams, braces of quail and pheasant roasted on spits, mounds of peaches, plums, and apricots, and tuns of Jurançon wine to wash everything down. Good, simple food led to good, simple pleasures. The two Courts, the one predominantly feminine and the other exclusively male, had approached each other only gingerly. Now, taking their cue from their respective leaders, they mingled with the happy relief of guests at a party after the ice has been broken. As the evening's dancing progressed, young gallants snuffed out the candles one by one until the rooms were dim enough to permit what later was described as "deeds of dishonor."

The older of Navarre's subjects, whom Catherine described as "grave men with cast-iron countenances" disapproved of such worldly excesses. Many had not yet brought themselves to trust entirely the young son of Jeanne d'Albret. To be sure, she had trained him well, but he had suffered perilously long exposure to the temptations of Babylon. And no one could forget the sorry performance of his father, Antoine de Bourbon, who had changed allegiances and religions with the effortlessness of a chameleon.

It was Catherine who, in the end, bore the weight of the old men's suspicions and resentment. The negotiations which had begun shortly after her arrival in Nérac became a protracted haggle. Sessions started each morning after the Queen Mother had heard Mass, broke for hasty meals, and continued until well past midnight. The Huguenots spelled each other in relays; Catherine, seemingly gaining in energy as she threw herself into her favorite sport, held down her side of the table virtually alone. Finally on February 28, the Articles of Nérac were drawn up, signed by the Queen Mother and Navarre, and dispatched to the King for his ratification. Catherine's position throughout the talks had been that "as mother of the King she wanted also to show herself as the mother of the people, and that she had devoted herself to contenting all her subjects, leaving aside everything that might lead to the renewal of the troubles." There is no question that this was an accurate statement of her true feelings, but the division between her subjects had long since grown too deep to be bridged over by any signatures on a sheet of paper. Catherine was realistic enough to know this, too. The twenty-seven clauses of the agreement she had just concluded were as fragile as the good will of the Huguenots and of the Catholic Holy League. But for the moment she had accomplished her objectives. Navarre had promised her to observe the peace; she believed him and wrote Henry as much: "He spoke with complete sincerity or else I am the most mistaken woman in the world." Furthermore, she had regained her son-in-law, for Margot agreed to remain in Nérac, "resolute never to leave her husband again." With this promise and the couple's warm farewells, she turned north for the long homeward journey.

XIV

Even without the additional inducement of her husband's company, the castle in Nérac was the sort of place that Margot would have found difficult to leave. It had originally been built in the fifteenth century as a fortress, a simple hollow square cornered by four circular towers. Long since, however, feudal severity had yielded to the gentler accents of the Renaissance. Only one of the four wings, relieved by two smaller towers flanking the entrance to the inner courtyard, had remained intact as a souvenir of the past. The others had been replaced with loggias in the graceful Italian style. The former guards' gallery, measuring sixty feet by twenty, had become a handsome reception room. Above it, occupying a sunny corner, were the King's apartments. A staircase led directly to gardens stretching to the bank of a placid stream, the Baise, which formed a lazy half loop around the castle. Great laurels and cypresses planted in long avenues provided shade, a place for quiet walks or discreet privacy.

Before Margot's arrival, the interior had displayed the typical bare, unkempt look of bachelor's quarters, but, as Navarre's household expense ledgers reveal, this situation was quickly remedied. Tapestries were ordered, new furniture and paintings purchased. A greenhouse was built so that there would be fresh oranges at the table. Other entries testify to the tastes of the new lady of the house: "For violinists and other musicians summoned by the King: thirty *livres;*" "To Paul of Padua, chief comedian of his troupe, ninety *livres;*" "Idem to Marco Antonio Scottivilli and Massimiano Milanino, Italian comedians."

Recalling her days at Nérac, Margot wrote: "Our Court was so delightful and agreeable that we did not envy that of

France. We had with us a number of my ladies and maids-in-waiting. The King my husband had in his service a fine company of lords and gentlemen, as accomplished as the most gallant courtiers I had known at Court; there was nothing to reproach them except that they were Huguenots. But of this difference in religion there was never any discussion. On their side, the King and his sister went off to listen to their preachers; I and my suite attended Mass in a chapel which stood in the park. As we came out, we all went for walks together. . . . The rest of the days were passed in all manner of harmless pleasures, and we usually attended balls during the afternoon and evening."

The harmless pleasures consisted of tennis, skittles, recitations, and impromptu theatricals. But never far from the surface was the favorite game of all—the game of love. Margot so thawed the Huguenots that Sully, one of the most serious-minded of all and Navarre's chief minister, ruefully noted in his memoirs: "Life at Court was so gentle and pleasant that one spoke only of pastimes, pleasures, and love, to the extent that I, too, participated and took a mistress like all the others."*

Only d'Aubigné, who had shamed Navarre into leaving the Louvre in the first place, resisted temptation. Describing the social climate in Nérac, he wrote: "Such luxury draws vice as heat draws serpents. Both spirits and arms have grown rusty while the Queen of Navarre has been there. She taught our King her husband that a cavalier lacks spirit unless he is in love."

But the cavalier was only too eager to learn. After years during which his clothes, casual and worn for days on end, had been his badge, he suddenly began to pay attention to his wardrobe. His personal expenses for 1579 include such items as doublets of silk and satin, yellow breeches, shirts of the finest Holland linen, scarlet riding cloaks, and Spanish

* Or, as Shakespeare put it in *Love's Labor's Lost*, Cupid thumped them all "with his bird-bolt under the left pap."

felt hats. In that same description of life at Nérac, d'Aubigné also reveals something of Margot's character, as well as his own, by noting that the Queen of Navarre "claimed that to make love openly was virtuous, but to do it in secret was vicious." Margot had amply demonstrated this code by the manner in which she had conducted her own life. But in her sense of it, the term "love" carried far more meaning than the narrow carnality which d'Aubigné intended to convey. One of her favorite books in the small library she gathered at Nérac was *L'Honneste Amour,* a French version of Marsilio Ficino's adaptation of Plato's *Symposium* which the translator had dedicated to her. Doubly removed from its original and weighted with Renaissance and Christianized concepts, *L'Honneste Amour* presented a perfect state of being where love expressed itself equally in the celebration of physical beauty and the observance of spiritual nobility. Although her own natural impulses did not always permit her to observe this delicate balance, Margot attempted to pattern her life after this book. She memorized whole sections of it and discussed it enthusiastically with the poets and scholars—including for a time the young Michel de Montaigne—who were only too happy to be invited to spend time at her Court. Whatever their intellectual appraisal of *L'Honneste Amour,* it suited Margot to perfection. She could remain on the terms of warmest friendship with Navarre while at the same time finding two young, handsome gentlemen of his suite and successively falling madly in love with them. But when Navarre himself became ill of a fever, she could forget dancers, lovers, and everything else and remain by his bedside for seventeen days, nursing him gently back to health.

It all might have gone on indefinitely, but the times were unfortunately not propitious for neo-Platonic idylls. Navarre had been genuinely sincere when he had assured Catherine of his wish for peace, but Henry III, goaded by the Duke of Guise and the Holy League, felt no such desire. Sporadic violence broke out again and inevitably provoked some of the other Huguenot leaders into retaliation. Margot found herself, not for the first time, caught in the middle. Although a devout Catholic, her first allegiance was to her husband. She recalls that "I had several times informed the King and the Queen my mother of the situation, asking them to improve it by giving some satisfaction to the King my husband; but they had taken no notice, apparently convinced that [they] would be able to bring the Huguenots to their knees. As my advice was ignored, matters went from bad to worse, until it came to fighting."

Nor were her efforts as a peacemaker more successful with the other side: "In spite of all my efforts, to my very great regret, I was unable to prevent the conflict from spreading. . . . I discussed it with my husband and all the members of his Council, trying to prevent it, pointing out to them what little profit this war would bring them. But although the King my husband did me the honor of placing a great deal of faith and confidence in me, and the leaders of the Religion admitted that I had a certain amount of common sense, I still could not persuade them to what, in due course, at their own expense, they had to admit was the truth."

The truth, as she had foreseen, was a full-scale resumption of the civil war, which erupted again in April, 1580. Attempting to forestall it, Catherine had written to Navarre: "I cannot believe that you want to ruin this kingdom as well as your own, yet this is what it will mean if this war breaks out again. I beg you to believe me and you will see what a difference there is between the counsels of a mother who loves you and those who do not." And she added, defending Henry, "What occasion has the King given you to do this? He asks only that you observe what you have already sworn to."

With no hope in his heart, Navarre replied directly to the King, describing "the misery to which we have been reduced through the fault of your ministers and officers," and going

on to list the Huguenot cities that had been taken in contra-
vention of the peace, the inhabitants massacred, the women
raped, and the children held for ransom. As Margot had
foreseen, it was impossible for him to remain neutral once
fighting had begun. His position as leader of the Huguenot
forces had been compromised in turn by his marriage, by
the style of life he had adopted, and especially by his open,
fair-minded dealings with Catherine. He knew that not only
was he obliged to go to war, but that he would have to
achieve a success spectacular enough to disarm his detractors
and reassert his claim to primacy.

The target he chose was the city of Cahors, a wealthy
Catholic stronghold so situated on a steep, rocky hill and
surrounded on three sides by the Lot river that it had remained impregnable through all the previous wars. Days
were spent in preparation for the campaign, but before leaving he took time to compose a letter to Margot: "My dear,
we are so closely united that our hearts and wills are but one.
. . . It is with extreme regret that instead of the contentment
I hoped to give you, as well as a certain amount of pleasure
in this country, precisely the opposite is the case, and you
have the displeasure of seeing me in such an unfortunate
situation. God knows who is to blame. . . ." As a man, even
more than as a soldier, the King of Navarre was beginning
to grow up.

The taking of Cahors was all that an ambitious, courageous commander could have hoped for. Navarre and his
troops, some fifteen hundred men in all, reached the foot of
the hill on which the city stood as night was falling and a
great summer thunderstorm threatened. Exhorting his men
that "their only retreat should be that of their souls from
their bodies," he led the charge up the hill and managed to
plant two huge *pétards*—primitive powder-filled bombs—
which exploded and breached the walls. From there, it was
uphill through the narrow streets of the city, fighting house
by house and snatching a mouthful of food or water as they

fought. Always in the front rank, Navarre ignored bullets and pike thrusts that dented his armor, hardly sleeping during the five days it required to bring the town's garrison to surrender. No one watching him or hearing the tale retold would ever doubt again that this in truth was the son of the good Jeanne, in whose veins ran the pure blood of Navarre, and on whose chest the symbol of the Religion could with full justice and confidence be emblazoned. Typical of the new Navarre who was emerging out of the chrysalis of the court fool was his first act after accepting the city's surrender. Himself exhausted, he sent a note to the wife of one of his commanders: "Madame de Batz, Although I am still covered with blood and powder, I will not undress until I tell you that your husband is safe and sound. Throughout, he was never farther from me than the length of his halberd. . . ."

In Paris, the news of the taking of Cahors caused predictable dismay, but a more interesting reaction came from another European capital. Philip II had watched the renewed outbreak of civil war with satisfaction—another bloodletting to hasten the death of France as a nation. He was pleased that the financial support he was providing to the Duke of Guise and the Holy League—which they in turn used to hire mercenaries—was accomplishing its purpose. But now another intriguing possibility presented itself. Navarre, whom Philip had dismissed as a fop and a coward, had proved that he could offer a fair match for Henry III's forces. Why not attempt to make him an ally of Spain? This would place Philip in the peculiar position of financing both sides of another country's internal war, but if it contributed to the disintegration of France, it was gold well spent—gold that Philip's American colonies seemed to produce in an unending stream. Dressed in the unrelieved black affected by their master, Spanish envoys arrived in Nérac to press with insistence Philip's proposal. Navarre would give his sister in marriage to the Spanish King. In exchange, and as his new brother-in-law, Philip would restore to Navarre the long-lost half of his kingdom—the ancient dream of the d'Albrets. In addition, if Navarre was inclined to enlarge his territories at the expense of France, Philip could be counted on for assistance in that endeavor as well. And, as an added inducement, Philip reminded Navarre that Spain's influence with the Pope was such that it would be a simple matter to procure an annulment of Navarre's marriage to Margot, after which a match could be arranged with one of Philip's own daughters—the bride whom Alençon had sought in vain.

The proposal was attractive, but also traitorous. Guise had accepted to do Philip's work for far less reward. Navarre flatly refused.

But even as he was earning his spurs in the twin worlds of war and international affairs, Navarre permitted neither to interfere with another of his major pursuits. Regrettably, the delectable "Dayelle" had left Nérac with Catherine and the other ladies of the *escadron*. But Margot had brought her own train of maids-in-waiting, including a Mlle de Rebours who soon found ways to console Navarre for his loss. Margot deplored his choice, not out of pique or jealousy but because she knew the girl well and considered her malicious and not very bright. Navarre was persuaded to drop her, sampled several others, but finally settled upon an even more unfortunate choice: Mlle Françoise de Montmorency, fifth daughter of the Baron of Fosseux, who inevitably earned the nickname of "La Fosseuse" ("the grave-digger"). Again, Margot objected to her husband's choice, still not out of jealousy but for the very sensible reason that La Fosseuse was not quite fourteen years old.

Navarre was himself still only in his late twenties, but apparently he fell genuinely in love with the girl—as completely and as easily as he was to fall in love with a dozen others. Nevertheless, there was something not quite right about the King of Navarre dandling the young girl on his knee and feeding her, by hand, sweetmeats and tender morsels that he ordered expressly for her. The entire relationship, and the Court's attitude toward it, was summed up with Gallic perfection by the historian Jean Mariejol, who noted that Navarre's private receipt books showed a payment of 140 *écus* to Pierre de Montmorency, Baron of Fosseux "for good and sufficient reasons," and added the comment, "Hé! Oui."

It appears from Margot's account of her husband's affair with La Fosseuse that, at the beginning, it was limited to "only such familiarities as might with all propriety be permitted." Taking advantage of this peaceful state of affairs, Margot decided to try presenting her husband with an heir. She journeyed to Bagnères-de-Bigorre, a Pyrénées village whose natural hot springs were reputed to help promote fertility, and wrote to Catherine: "I am at the baths at Bagnères, whither I have come to see whether I shall be so fortunate as to increase the number of your subjects. Several persons have found them beneficial. I shall not fail, on my return to Nérac, to acquaint you with the benefit I have received."

Margot did not become pregnant, then or for that matter at any time of her life. But it seems that, during her month's absence, the bounds of propriety had been stretched beyond redemption, for on her return to Nérac her husband informed her that, without the benefits of baths of any kind, La Fosseuse had developed a lingering *"mal à l'estomac."* When, by May, 1581, it became increasingly awkward to account for the persistence and peculiar symptoms of this stomach-ache, Navarre turned to Margot for help—to take care of La Fosseuse, and if possible to "undo that which she had done." It was too late for that, but Margot loyally offered to do what she could. "As everyone," she writes, "was talking about the girl's pregnancy, not only at Court but throughout the country, I decided to speak to her. Taking her into my room, I said, 'Despite your having estranged yourself from me, and of people telling me that you have been trying to make trouble between the King my husband and myself, the

friendship which I bear you and the respect I have for your family still do not permit me to refuse you assistance in helping you out of the unfortunate position in which you have placed yourself. I beg you therefore not to deny me, nor ruin both your reputation and my own. Be assured, on the contrary, that my concern for you is like that of a mother's.'"
Margot then proposed that La Fosseuse go with her to an isolated country house belonging to her husband, pointing out that an epidemic then threatening Nérac would provide a convincing reason for their departure. "I will take with us," she continued, "only the attendants which you may wish me to. Meanwhile, my husband will go hunting in the opposite direction, and will not return until after your delivery. In this fashion, we will put a stop to the scandalous talk, which is as painful to me as it must be to you."

But La Fosseuse would have none of it. Rather than being grateful for Margot's offer of assistance, the young girl assumed a pose of injured innocence and promised that she would herself give the lie to those who had been talking about her. "She said she knew very well," Margot continued, "that for some time I had no longer liked her and was only seeking a pretext to ruin her. And, shouting as loudly as I had been speaking gently, she stormed out of my room and went directly to the King, who was so furious over the manner in which I had treated his little girl that we remained on bad terms for the several months until the end of her pregnancy."

What Navarre had in mind as an alternative is not clear, but in due course nature took over. "We were sleeping," Margot continues, "in the same room but in different beds, as was our custom, when the doctor brought my husband the news that her pains had begun. Not knowing what to do, afraid on the one hand that everything would be discovered and on the other hand that she would not be properly looked after, for he loved her dearly, he finally decided to admit everything to me, and begged me to go to her aid. I replied that I honored him too much to take offense at anything which he may have done, and that I would look after her as if she were my own daughter. Meanwhile, I urged him to get up and go hunting, taking everyone with him in order to put a stop to the gossiping." True to her word, she then went to her young rival and saw her through her labor. The mother came out of it in good health, but as for the child, "God willed that it be a daughter, who moreover was stillborn."

Margot made no allusion to the fact, but her relief must have been great that it had turned out that way, for Navarre had long let it be known that if any of his mistresses should present him with a male heir, he would divorce the barren Margot and legitimize the child.

But this was not quite the end of the story. Exhausted from her long day's work, Margot had gone back to bed, where Navarre found her upon his return from the hunt. "Although I had taken trouble to have her [La Fosseuse] properly nursed, my husband asked me to get up and go to her. When I told him that I had already done everything necessary and could do no more, he became extremely angry with me. This greatly displeased me as I did not think that my behavior merited this reward."

Not long after this episode, which occurred in November, 1581, Margot resolved to return to Paris. Taken alone, the affair with La Fosseuse and Navarre's inexcusable behavior would probably not have prompted her to leave. There were, however, several other reasons that had been nagging at her. Her personal finances, based on the revenues from her hereditary properties, were in a dismal state and could only be corrected by the King. Moreover, for all of her delight in the simple life of Nérac, she could not help but miss at least a little the splendors and gaieties of the Louvre. Now that Navarre had established himself as a dangerous opponent, both the King and Catherine had repeatedly asked her to come back, if only to deprive his Court of the prestige which she as a Daughter of France represented. And last, though ranking higher in her own list, the man she was currently in love with, the handsome Jacques de Chanvallon, was in Paris.

Navarre attempted to persuade her to stay. "Being most anxious to deter me from making this trip to France," she wrote, "he treated me somewhat more kindly." But her mind was made up, and on January 29, 1582, she left Nérac. Navarre accompanied her as far as Saint-Maixant, near Poitiers. Meanwhile Catherine, who had advanced her daughter 1,500 *écus* to pay for her *voyage,* took advantage of the opportunity to see Navarre again and to make one last not very hopeful attempt to persuade him to come to Paris as well.* The three met and spent two days together, but there was little common ground left between them. As they were parting, a number of Navarre's gentlemen companions courteously saluted the Queen Mother and asked whether she had any final words or commands for them. "What I have to tell you," Catherine replied, "is that you are destroying the King of Navarre and yourselves." The words were said in disappointment and some anger and marked perhaps the first public crack in the indomitable will that had sustained her since the day she had first set foot in France a half century earlier.

The Paris to which the two Queens returned on May 28, 1582, was a city enormously different from the one Margot had left four years earlier. The sullenness and resentment of its citizens against the King could be smelled in the streets as distinctly as the garbage that lay uncollected. As he retreated from responsibility and deeper into himself, the two sides of his character—the bizarre morbidity and the manic debauchery—reached grotesque proportions. Public processions of flagellants, including one during which nine hun-

---

* To this end, she had written Margot to be sure to bring La Fosseuse back with her, hoping that this additional bait might lure her husband the rest of the way. This might have worked on a younger Navarre, but not any more.

dred men, women, and children, "naked as on the day they were born" trailed the King through the streets, became a commonplace sight. When public ridicule finally put a stop to these processions,* Henry affected a new costume consisting of a long black cape and a wide ebony collar adorned with carved ivory skulls. He redoubled his pilgrimages, sometimes marching for hours on his knees until he would fall over in exhaustion. He built a mock monastery in the forest of Vincennes where he would hide away for days on end, accompanied by a dozen fellow hermits—five cardinals, four bishops, and three dukes—and their servants. Observing it all, the Papal Nuncio reported home that "I am forced to believe that this King wants to serve God if God will do what he wants, but not otherwise."

Henry appeared to have a sense for what would most surely affront his subjects. Italy and Italians had been in low repute since his mother's arrival in France and especially since her elevation of her friends—Gondis, Biragos, Sardinis —to positions of power and wealth. In the face of this unpopularity, Henry commissioned the acting company that had so amused him in Venice, *I Gelosi,* to come to France. Their repertory of *commèdia dell'arte* was typically broad in humor and occasionally bawdy in theme but nothing like the royal entertainments which Catherine had been staging for years. Nevertheless, the Parlement of Paris issued an order forbidding them from performing. Applauding this decision, L'Estoile noted, "Their comedies taught nothing but fornication and adultery, and served as a school of licentiousness to the young people of both sexes. And in truth, their example was so pernicious that young ladies affected the manner of soldiers, parading their bare, shining

* A bit of popular verse, typical of many, ran:

> "After having pillaged France
> And put her people to the rack
> Isn't it fine penitence
> To wear a dripping sack?"

chests and shaking their breasts with perpetual motion like a clock, or better yet like the bellows which ironsmiths used on the fires of their forges." Henry rescinded the order of the Parlement, personally paid the fine of 10,000 *livres* which it had imposed, and ordered the company to resume its performances. Well might the clergy have fulminated against this affront to decency, for as L'Estoile further notes, "There was such a jam of people that the four best preachers in Paris put together could not attract as many."

The *Gelosi* could not, however, be blamed for other feminine wiles that according to Brantôme became fashionable—such as the practice, affected by some of the ladies at court, of decorating their pubic hair with colored ribbons for the surprise and amusement of their swains. Nor did they inspire the new sort of riddles which passed as high wit, such as:

> *J'ai deux trous fort voisins et velus tout*
> *autour,*
> *Je les donne à choisir sans trop avoir d'honte.*
> *Les membres les plus froids y trouvent bien*
> *leur compte,*
> *Puis qu'il y fait tout chaud ainsi que dans*
> *un four.*

> I have two holes that are close and furry
> Which I offer for choice with no thought of shame.
> The coldest of members will find there pleasure
> For either will thaw them in a hurry.

The answer, of course, was a muff.

Sex had always been a major preoccupation at the Valois Court, but it was the example of Henry and his *mignons* that guided it into new channels of license. Their public behavior was a constant source of gossip and trouble, for their effeminacy only served to make more passionate their allegiance to the King. This, along with the ridicule heaped on them, led to spectacular mass duels. L'Estoile notes one of these in which three of the *mignons* challenged three of the Duke of Guise's followers, "to unravel a quarrel begun the previous day over some light trifle." Two of the *mignons* were killed. The third, Quélus, "received nineteen blows and lingered for more than a month until he died. The great favor of the King did him little good, though His Majesty sat all day by his bed and promised 100,000 *écus* to the surgeons if they could save him, and another 100,000 to his favorite to hearten his will to live. In spite of these promises, he passed from this world, saying with his last breath 'Oh, my King, my King,' without mentioning either God or his mother. . . . The King ordered him shorn and took away his blond curls, and removed the earrings which he had formerly put on with his own hands."

As the ranks of the *mignons* thinned out, two emerged as commanding figures. One of them, a much-traveled soldier of fortune named Bernard Nogaret, was successively promoted to Colonel of Infantry, Governor of Lyons, Boulogne, and Provence, and finally raised to peerage as the Duke of Épernon. The other, Anne d'Arques, received even more generous treatment. Named Governor of Normandy and Admiral of France, he became the Duke of Joyeuse. One of his brothers, twenty-two years old, received a cardinal's hat; another, only seventeen, was named Master of the Household; their father was given the baton of a Marshal of France. As crowning recognition, Henry married Joyeuse off to a younger sister of the Queen, making him his own brother-in-law. The wedding, because of its ruinous extravagance, and because it is the subject of one of the Louvre's most popular paintings, has become one of the high points of Henry III's reign. The ceremony was preceded by seventeen different parties, festivities, and masquerades, at which none of the guests appeared twice wearing the same clothes. The Tuscan ambassador summed them all up when he estimated that the marriage, and the gifts made to the young couple, cost Henry "two million in gold."

XV

Through it all, Catherine continued to work tirelessly. Her trip home from Nérac had been a nine-month exercise in personal diplomacy during which she rallied back to loyalty four provinces that had declared themselves for the *Politiques*. No sooner had she returned than she was off again, to Picardy this time where a new Reform coalition was forming. After the taking of Cahors by Navarre, it was she who had directed the counteroffensive, holding her generals in check because an all-out war could only benefit the Guises, the Holy League, and Philip of Spain.

She even found time for a new project which revealed that, for all she had done and accomplished, the relative humbleness of her origin still festered in a corner of her mind. The death of Don Sebastian, whom years earlier she had considered as a bridegroom for Margot, left the Portuguese throne vacant. Philip immediately claimed it for himself, in part by heredity—as a Hapsburg, he could so claim virtually every crown in Europe—and in part by sheer geographic propinquity. Outdoing the Guises in genealogical zeal, Catherine advanced a claim on her own behalf, basing it on the marriage of one of her mother's ancestors, Mahaut, Countess of Boulogne, and Alphonso of Portugal. That the Countess had been repudiated by her husband, and that the marriage itself had taken place in 1235, did not deter her. If she could establish her legitimacy as Queen of Portugal in her own personal right, who would still dare call her the daughter of a Florentine grocer?

Philip did not take the claim seriously, so she determined to give him something to think about—and herself something to bargain with. In one of the lesser-known episodes of European history, a French fleet was slapped together and sent to invade the Azores, which were even then a Portuguese possession. Her old friend, Filippo Strozzi, was put in charge of the operation and given the title of Viceroy of Brazil—intimation that France's ambitions reached to encompass Portugal's transatlantic empire as well. Strozzi was a loyal and skillful general, but unfortunately his entire experience, as well as that of the six thousand-odd men who accompanied him, had been gained on dry land. His little fleet of fifty-five ships sailed westward on June 16, 1582, and held together long enough for Álvaro de Bazán, the Marquis of Santa Cruz and Philip's naval commander, to catch up to them. Half of the French fleet turned for home after the first Spanish broadside; the rest remained to be cut to pieces and the crews, including Strozzi himself, captured. Accustomed to dealing with pirates, Santa Cruz ordered all the captives killed—the gentlemen by decapitation, the rest by hanging— as "enemies of the public peace, disturbers of commerce, and fomenters of rebellion against my King."

If Henry felt any sympathy for his mother at this disastrous end to her personal ambition, he kept it to himself. Instead, he used the opportunity of her preoccupation to dismiss the Marshal de Retz—her old friend Gondi—as First Gentleman of the Bedchamber, a post he had occupied under Charles IX and, at Catherine's request, had been permitted to retain after Henry's return from Poland. In Gondi's place, he named one of his own *mignons*.

To the injury he had dealt the heads of the old nobility by advancing Épernon and Joyeuse above them, Henry now added the insult of demanding higher taxes. The answer was prompt. As L'Estoile noted: "The nobles and people of Brittany, Normandy, Burgundy, and Auvergne joined together and resolved never to pay any more imposts, aids, subsidies, loans, taxes, or any other charges which had not been in force at the time of King Louis XII. They cried out loudly against the King for his daily exactions. . . ." But exactions were necessary to pay for weddings and other royal diversions. Since he could not raise money in any other way, Henry turned to the wholesale traffic of offices. L'Estoile, who was employed as clerk-in-chief of the Paris Parlement, was in excellent position to observe the commerce. His *Journals* enumerate some of the transactions, and add, "I leave it to be imagined what the people of France can expect in the way of justice from these officers."

Observing the rising tide, the Princess of Conti wrote to her friend, the Duke of Nemours: "I have never seen this Court more full of trouble, envy, and hard feelings and the chief nobles more aroused. . . . There are so many malcontents that the number is infinite."

Among them was Henry's sister, Margot. Upon her return, her brother had been the soul of cordiality. Navarre, he told her, had treated her shamefully over the Fosseuse episode. He agreed wholeheartedly with the sentiments Catherine expressed in a letter to Navarre—one of her most self-revealing letters: "You are not the first young and foolish husband," she wrote to the son-in-law she left a few weeks earlier, "in such matters, but certainly the first and only one who after such an occurrence treated your wife as you have. I had the honor of being married to the King, my lord and your sovereign, whose daughter you have wedded. When Madame de Flemming's fault was found out, he thought it very right and proper that she should be dismissed. With Madame de Valentinois, things were conducted as they had once been with Madame D'Étampes—in all honor. It is not the way to treat well-born women, and of such a great House, and to insult them at the whim of a public prostitute, for the whole world knows she bore you a child. You are too well born not to know how you should behave toward a daughter of your King and sister of the one who governs this whole realm and yourself, and who, apart from that, honors and loves you as a noble lady should."

For its scolding, maternal tone—indeed, it was signed

"Your good mother, Catherine"—the letter was intended to goad Navarre into coming to Paris. Henry's cordiality was similarly motivated. Margot, however, had other ideas. Her current lover, Chanvallon, was in Paris. As soon as she decently could, Margot moved out of the Louvre and established herself in a town house on the Rue Culture Sainte-Cathérine, in the Marais quarter. Here, with not a single long Huguenot face in sight, she threw herself into the social whirl of the capital.

Unfortunately, she was by temperament unable to abide by her mother's views regarding the distinction between public behavior and private morality. Within weeks, her parties had become so notorious that the Tuscan ambassador, Giulio Busini, referred knowingly to the house on the Rue Culture Sainte-Cathérine as *"un gran bordello."* It was her further bad fortune that she had, as might have been predicted, developed an instant dislike for Épernon and Joyeuse. Nothing pleased her more than to lure into her circle those members of the *mignon* fraternity who were not irretrievably homosexual. The others repaid her by spreading calumnies about her deportment. She had begun to put on weight, so the rumor arose that she was pregnant by her lover. Further, knowing of her partiality to Alençon, the two *archimignons,* as they were called, reported to Henry that she was secretly soliciting aid for her younger brother's perennial, disastrous scheme to invade the Netherlands.

This, along with the scandalous parties, the affront to his *mignons,* and especially her unwillingness or inability to bring Navarre back, was too much for Henry. Emerging from one of his religious cycles, he arranged a banquet at which Margot, in the Queen's absence, was required to preside. There, according to one account, he interrupted the meal to turn viciously on his sister and denounce her as a whore and public prostitute. "In presence of the full Court, he hurled a thousand insults at her, naming all the lovers she had entertained before she was married, and all those she was currently favoring. Then he ordered her to leave Paris and go back to her husband. She, in great agitation, immediately retired to her apartments. She packed her own baggage and departed on the following day, taking with her only a few of her most faithful servants." The author of this account is Ogier de Bosbecq, ambassador of the Holy Roman Emperor, and it is possible that he invented the scene, or at least embroidered upon it. Henry may have expressed his sentiments in less public circumstances, but the facts are that there was a banquet at the Louvre on August 7, 1583, which Margot attended, and that on August 8 she departed unexpectedly from Paris, accompanied only by her two favorite ladies-in-waiting. And, finally, it is true that she headed south—toward Nérac.

VI

Catherine accepted this latest family storm with long-tried equanimity and even offered to relieve her beloved Henry of the blame for it. She wrote him: "I have preserved and guarded this realm from being divided into several parts. God granted it to me that I might see it entirely obedient to yourself. Whatever evil or hatred toward myself this may have occasioned never came from people of position nor your good servants, but from those whom I prevented from carrying out their own plans. . . . I know that in doing this I did so for myself and partly in satisfaction of the obligation I bore toward the Kings your father and grandfather by preserving what they themselves ruled. . . . That is why I never feared nor ever shall fear to say and do what I think able to serve to maintain everything as nearly as possible according to their intentions."

Among the many plans Catherine had never abandoned

was the notion of marrying one of her sons to Elizabeth of England. She had first proposed Henry for this enterprise while he was still Duke of Anjou, but the subsequent events of St. Bartholomew's and his election to the crown of Poland had caused negotiations to break off. She tried again with Alençon. Concerned lest he make a fool of himself, she had in 1579 sent a courtier named Jean de Simier to plead his case by proxy. Simier's continental friskiness shocked the English Court—he pilfered Elizabeth's nightgown, then confessed he had sent it as a token to his master—but amused the Virgin Queen enough to invite the prospective bridegroom himself for a visit. Alençon arrived and, despite his mother's foreboding, proceeded to charm the Queen. He spent twelve days in England, during which she seemed pleased enough with him to nickname him her "Little Frog," and departed full of hope. But if Elizabeth had any serious matrimonial intentions, they were inhibited by Alençon's religion, nationality, and parentage. Sir Philip Sidney summed up the view of English Protestants by warning the Queen that "the hearts of your people would be galled" by such a marriage, and that furthermore even "the very common people know he is the son of the Jezebel of our age." Diplomatically, he did not refer to the disparity in their ages. At forty-six, Elizabeth was exactly twice as old as Alençon.

Undaunted, Catherine continued to push the match. There was nothing she could do to overcome the three basic objections to Alençon, but external events—the rising power of Philip of Spain and England's consequent desire to seek a French alliance against him—came to her aid. In 1580, Elizabeth let it be known that she was disposed to be courted again, and encouraged Alençon to hurry by sending him £30,000 to pay his troops and wind up the campaign he was then waging in Flanders. Within a week of his arrival after an uncomfortable October crossing, she announced that he was "the most deserving and constant of her lovers." He tried to appease religious sentiment by escorting her to services at

St. Paul's Cathedral. She in turn told the French ambassador that "the Duke of Alençon shall be my husband," and ostensibly sealed the match by "kissing him on the mouth, drawing a ring from her own hand, and giving it to him as a pledge." The Duke let it be known that he was "extremely overjoyed."

The game played out for another three months during which Elizabeth paid tender attentions to her betrothed. She brought him beef tea every morning, and gave him a jewel-encrusted toque to wear until she could present him with a proper crown. But it was, on her part, only a diplomatic game. Because she had estimated accurately the opposition of her Council and subjects—and partly because she feared, at her age, to face the hazards of childbirth—she had never intended to go through with the marriage. It was only intended as a warning to Philip of what she might do if it became necessary. When Alençon took his leave, in February 1582, she apologized that the time was not propitious for their marriage, but assured him she would be unhappy until he could return and claim her. That, too, was part of the game. But the tears she wept as he sailed off aboard the *Discovery* were not altogether diplomatic. She was nearing fifty, and she knew that Alençon was her last, if not in truth her most deserving, suitor.

Alençon's disappointment was softened by the boost to his prestige as well as by the pledge of financial aid which his bride-to-be had made. Back in Flanders and invested with the new title of Duke of Brabant, he mounted the most ambitious military campaign of his career: a simultaneous assault on the cities of Antwerp, Bruges, Dunkirk, and Ostende. The result was multiple disaster. Having chosen to take Antwerp himself, he persuaded the inhabitants to permit him to enter the city in order to honor them with a parade. Wise in the ways of treachery, they agreed and, once the last of the troops had entered, slammed the gates shut behind them. Then from windows and rooftops came a storm of stones, rocks, logs, heavy chains. At the same time, the city's garrison opened deadly, point-blank fire. A few Frenchmen, including Alençon, managed to escape, but some twelve thousand were left behind to be hacked to pieces by the enraged burghers.

The "Folly of Antwerp" marked the end of Alençon's military career. Even Catherine was for the moment stunned. "Would to God," she wrote her youngest son, "you had died young. You would then not have been the cause of the death of so many brave gentlemen." But motherly instincts prevailed. In addition to being doubly humiliated, for Elizabeth had formally terminated her engagement to him after the Antwerp debacle, Alençon fell seriously ill with what his physicians diagnosed as "tertiary ague." Catherine went to him and for the last time brought him back to Paris. She even managed, after a year's efforts, to arrange a reconciliation between her two surviving sons. She watched Henry embrace the younger brother whom he had for years publicly referred to as *le petit magot* ("the little ape"), and wrote to the Swiss ambassador, "I praise God with all my heart to see them on such good terms, which can only be for the great good and prosperity of the affairs of the realm. . . . I never knew a greater joy since the death of the King, my lord, and I am sure that had you seen the behavior of them both you would have wept, like me, for joy."

Her joy was short-lived. The reconciliation had taken place on February 11, 1584. Four months later, having caused his mother nothing but problems while he lived, Alençon compounded them by dying. Henry III was childless and there was no doubt in anyone's mind that he would remain so. The new heir to the throne, therefore, was the King of Navarre—not only a Huguenot but the chief of the Huguenot cause in France.

Part Four

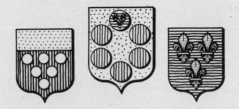

Penumbra

I

Stitched through history there have been men, little known and scarcely remembered, whose special profession has been to serve their own country by undermining the well-being of those of their neighbors. One of them was Don Bernardino de Mendoza, who arrived in Paris in the middle of October, 1584, as the ambassador of His Most Catholic Majesty, Philip II of Spain.

The tenth child of a noble, well-connected family which in his generation produced a Viceroy of Mexico, a political counselor to the Duke of Alva, and a professor of Holy Writ at the University of Alcala, Bernardino originally chose the army as a career. He served in the Netherlands, fought the Berbers in North Africa, and helped to relieve the Turkish siege of Malta. Early on, however, he displayed a flair for diplomacy that caused him to be sent first to Rome, when he was only twenty-six, and then to other sensitive posts. His first tour of duty in England, in 1574, earned him acceptance into the highest order of Spanish knighthood, the Order of Santiago. His second tour began in 1578 and lasted for six years, when his complicity in the Throckmorton plot to overthrow the Queen caused him to be declared *persona non grata,* and he was ordered to leave the country immediately.

Mendoza's official purpose in Paris was to bring Philip's condolences to the royal family on the death of Alençon. Knowing Catherine's weak spot, he also brought her two personal letters from her granddaughter, the Infanta of Spain. The Queen Mother was sincerely grateful but hardly taken in. Sir Edward Stafford, Mendoza's English counterpart in Paris, reported that the Spaniard's audience with Catherine was short and cold. He assumed some of the credit for this by noting that "I was bold to tell her that I was sorry to see the King of Spain had no more respect for the King and her than to send so bad a Spanish relic, retired out of England, to be here, to work as bad effects as he had done with us."

Catherine did not need this warning, for she knew that Mendoza's principal mission was not so much to advance Philip's interests in Paris as in the Château of Joinville, the Guises' family seat 120 miles to the east. There, negotiations had been going on for several months between Spanish agents and the Duke Henry and other members of the family. Initiated after the death of Alençon, they were intended to tighten and formalize the arrangement whereby Philip had been providing financial aid to the Guises and to the Holy League and to set out what he could expect in return. Mindful of his recent experience in England, Mendoza was careful to keep his part in the discussions secret, but he nevertheless was able to bring the parties to agreement.

The Treaty of Joinville, signed on December 31, 1584, specified that Philip would increase his subsidy to 600,000 *écus* a year, payable in monthly installments. In exchange, the Guises agreed that under no circumstances would they recognize a heretic as king of France. Without consulting Henry III, they designated as his heir apparent the Cardinal of Bourbon, brother of the late Antoine and uncle of the King of Navarre. At sixty-four years of age, the Cardinal of Bourbon was vain, weak, empty-headed, and ambitious, and therefore the perfect instrument for both Philip and the Guises, who treated him with elaborate respect in public while scarcely concealing their private contempt. Other provisions of the treaty bound the participants to work toward the complete abolition of Protestantism in France and the Netherlands. The Guises further agreed to help stamp out piracy and other activities that jeopardized Spain's profitable maritime activities, and to help Philip recover French territories he claimed belonged to him.

The death of Alençon, and the spectre it raised, had also served to vitalize public support for the Holy League, particularly in arch-Catholic Paris. Although it was, in 1584, a metropolis of more than 200,000 inhabitants, Paris functioned emotionally and organically—as it still does—as a confederation of *quartiers,* each with its own character and sense of self-identification. Leaders drawn from the bourgeoisie rose spontaneously in one section of the city after another—a lawyer here, an artisan, minor functionary, or priest there. As the Council of Sixteen, one for each of the divisions of the city, they quickly created an underground organization that reached to include every craft and merchant guild in Paris and even such informal groups as the river boatmen of the Right Bank, identified in one document as "five hundred in number, and all of them troublemakers." All would be required to pledge allegiance to the League, to God, His Church, King Charles X—the title to be assumed on his elevation by the Cardinal of Bourbon—and to the city of Paris.

Though he could hardly be unaware of what was happening in Paris, Henry III was occupied with other matters during the early weeks of 1585. In January, he proclaimed new regulations for his household, specifying new uniforms for his personal attendants and for the members of the state Council. In February he entertained—at his own expense, L'Estoile notes—a splendid English embassy led by the Earl of Warwick. Their purpose was to confer upon him the Order of the Garter. The ceremonies of investiture, and Henry's reciprocations, occupied the better part of a month.

Catherine, too, had been observing what was happening, and particularly the role the new Spanish ambassador was assuming. She took advantage of a Court reception to let him know, discreetly, that her son the King was fully aware of the traitorous activities going on in France and of Spain's complicity in them. Mendoza swore innocence and produced letters from Philip showing that Spain had been careful not to take any part in the activities of the Holy League. If that was the case, Catherine then pointed out, His Catholic Majesty could not possibly object if the King of France took measures to eradicate the League.

The gambit was good but the position too weak to sustain it. On March 9, Henry issued an edict that outlawed all unauthorized assemblies within the country and prohibited the formation of armed units. The terms of the edict were intended to apply equally to Huguenots and Catholics, but since the Huguenots had for more than a quarter century ignored similar decrees, it was clear that Henry was addressing himself to the Holy League.

The reply was prompt. On March 31, 1585, the League issued a "Declaration of Causes which had led Monseigneur the Cardinal of Bourbon, and the Catholic Peers, Princes, Nobles, cities, and communities of this kingdom of France to oppose themselves by all possible means to those who would subvert the Catholic religion and the State." The title of the manifesto told most of the story, but for the record, the League rehashed all its old grievances. It complained about Épernon, Joyeuse, and the other *mignons* who "slipped into the favor of our sovereign King to seize his authority and usurp his grandeur." It deplored the fact that faithful, deserving state servants had been dismissed in order to permit the King to sell their offices. It bemoaned high taxes and made the time-honored political promise of reducing their burden while at the same time pursuing with greater intensity the war against heretics. And it ended on a new and defiant note: an appeal to all the towns of France to refuse to admit royal garrisons until the King agreed to meet the League's demands.

Meanwhile, using Philip's money to buy arms and hire troops, the Duke of Guise and his brothers hurried to take over as many of these towns as they could with their own troops. Normandy, Picardy, and Brittany went to the League in their entirety; in Burgundy, Dijon, Mâcon, and Auxonne were seized. Orléans declared for the League on April 7. An attempt to take Marseilles failed, but in Lyons the royal governor surrendered the city. The Duke of Guise himself occupied Verdun, and he intercepted the royal mercenaries tardily summoned from Germany.

Shocked by the unexpected strength of the League and their swiftness to act, Henry withdrew deeper into the Louvre. Not trusting any of the traditional regiments of royal guards, he ordered Épernon to form a force of personal bodyguards. Lest they be already tainted with traitorous contacts at Court, he specified that they should be recruited in the provinces. In addition, each man had to demonstrate his qualities of personal bravery, and each had further to prove his undivided loyalty by agreeing not to marry. They would live in the Louvre, guard the King by day, accompany him everywhere he went, and sleep by his door at night. For this service they would be paid the sum, fantastic at the time for a soldier, of 1,200 *écus* a year. Their formal name was the *Tagliagambi*—literally, cutters of legs—but because of the relatively small number of such paragons that Épernon was able to find, they became better known as the Forty-Five. Then, his own person secure, Henry gave up all concern with state affairs and turned over what was left of his country to Catherine.

She had not waited for him to ask. Early in March after her diplomatic tilt with Mendoza, she had addressed herself directly to Guise: "My nephew, I am as much annoyed as astonished by the news that is going around and the information we have of some new troubles of which it is said that you are the cause. . . ." Guise had not replied to the letter, letting the manifesto speak for him. On the day of its publication, she set out for Joinville uninvited to seek, as she had done so many times before, a formula for compromise and peace. Villeroy, one of her secretaries, noted, "The Queen

Mother, although very indisposed, is having herself taken to meet them . . . in order to endeavor to put out this fire before it spreads any further."

Despite her poor health, Catherine was optimistic and she came armed with several proposals. Her first meeting with Guise, however, persuaded her that a new factor had been introduced which for the first time made it impossible for France to settle her own internal differences. In the long letter she dictated after the meeting, she noted that Guise was very melancholy—"In conversation, he wept"—for a man who clearly held the upper hand. She was struck by his obstinacy in refusing to discuss his plans. "I told him that it was more likely for the purpose of destroying and weakening our religion than for the extirpation of heresy." In vain she tried to make him understand that "our experience has been that peace has weakened the Huguenots more than war." She warned him again and again of the danger—"that this kingdom will become so full of foreigners that we will all be in danger of being thrown out by them." Guise had listened but offered no argument. At the foot of the letter she dictated, Catherine added a notation in her own handwriting: "He could do nothing, he said, by himself."

Mendoza had done his work thoroughly.* In three months of negotiation with Guise and his colleagues, Catherine could extract no substantive concession. The Treaty of Nemours, with which she brought to a halt the threatening conflict between the King and the Holy League, provided for the revocation of all previous edicts of pacification. Further, it forbade the practice of any religion other than the Roman Catholic anywhere in France. Heretics would not be allowed to hold any public office; all ministers of other religions

---

* He even required signed receipts for the monthly subsidies, copies of which survive in the Royal Spanish archives: "We, Henry of Lorraine, Duke of Guise, Peer and Grand Master of France, acknowledge on our own behalf and in the name of all those who comprise our Common League, having received from his Catholic Majesty by the hands of his commissary the sum of 50,000 gold *écus*."

would be banned; and all subjects would have to make profession of the Catholic faith within six months, or be expelled from France.

It was by far the strictest, farthest-reaching expression of intolerance since the start of the civil wars. As he was about to sign it, Henry III turned to the Cardinal of Bourbon, whom he was effectively ratifying as his heir, and said, "My uncle, I made the former edicts of conciliation against my conscience, but willingly, because I knew they would relieve my people. This one is according to my conscience, but I do it most unwillingly, because from it will stem the ruin of my state and my people."

For Henry, it was a rare moment of insight.

II

The brutal, uncompromising provisions of the Treaty of Nemours applied impartially to all inhabitants of France, but they were specifically directed against one man—Navarre.

After having escorted his wife and mother-in-law part of the way to Paris, he had returned home to Nérac where, before long, he found a consuming new diversion. Mme Diane d'Androuin, the widowed Countess of Guiche, was no Rebours or Fosseuse. A well-born, well-educated lady in her late twenties with attractive but not striking features dominated by an unusually high forehead, she became the first of Navarre's serious, semipermanent mistresses. As *La Belle Corisande,* the name they jointly chose for her, she was able for nearly a decade to satisfy his romantic needs while at the same time encouraging and expanding the intellectual interests Margot had first aroused. Doubly smitten, Navarre thus had little personal interest left for Margot—so little that when Henry threw her out of Paris and ordered her to return to her husband, he let it be known that he did not want her back.

Caught in the middle, Margot tried writing conciliatory letters to both her brother and her husband, and to her mother as well. In one of her letters to Catherine, describing her plight and pleading for intercession, she even proposed a way to disprove the rumor that she had brought one or more illegitimate children into the world: "Since my misfortunes have driven me into such misery that I no longer desire to live, may I at least hope that you will take steps to preserve my honor, which is so clearly linked with your own and that of all those to whom I have the honor to be related . . . by providing a lady of quality and worthy of belief, who may testify to my condition and who, after my death, will be present at my autopsy, in order that she may then testify to the state I was in. . . ."

But Margot's honor was not the real issue. The nature of Navarre's relationship with her assumed allowances for flaws in her purity. Such flaws had not prevented the couple from spending companionable years together in the past, nor were they to prevent an even more spectacular reconciliation many years later. Navarre's refusal to take his wife back was in part due to the gross insult her brother had inflicted on her, not as Marguerite of Valois, but as Queen of Navarre. For the rest, it was a tentative invitation to negotiate, for he shrewdly realized that a disgraced and abandoned Daughter of France would prove more embarrassing to the King and the Queen Mother than to him.

Navarre opened by attempting to draw from Henry a concession that he had personally been damaged. "What will Christians say," he asked the King, "if the King of Navarre receives his wife and embraces her after she has been sent back to him so besmirched?"

But Henry was not impressed. "What can they say," he replied, "except that he is receiving his King's sister? What less could he do?"

This, Navarre let it be known, was not satisfactory. Henry waited, then testily and maladroitly wrote him a pacifying letter in which he conceded that Navarre "knew how kings were liable to be deceived by false reports, and that the most virtuous princesses were not exempt from calumny, even including his late mother [Jeanne d'Albret], of whom he knew what had been said and how badly she had been spoken about."

According to L'Estoile, Navarre read the letter, laughed cheerfully, and, before his whole Court, said to Henry's emissary, Bellièvre, "The King does me a great honor with his letters. In the earlier ones, he called me a cuckold, and in this one the son of a whore. I thank him."

The game between the two men dragged on beyond any proportion to the issue at stake—Navarre's demand that Henry return a few strongholds to Huguenot hands. Aware of Margot's plight, Navarre wrote her an encouraging letter: "It is necessary that when we meet it should be of our free will; in my opinion you would do well to tell the Queen your mother so, and I will then make it plain that I cannot be forced to do anything under compulsion. And also I do not believe any of the calumnies. That is all, my dear, I can tell you at present. Without all these complications, we might have had the pleasure of being together by now."

Nevertheless, it was not until April 13, 1584, eight months and a week after her expulsion from Paris, that Margot was permitted to return to Nérac. Navarre went out to meet her and, together, they rode along the same tree-shaded avenues they had traveled on the spring day five years earlier when the Queen of Navarre had made her first entrance into her kingdom. The countryside was as peaceful and lovely as it had been then, but this time there were no joyful crowds or odes of welcome. In the late afternoon, a state dinner was held in the banquet hall of the palace, a graceful and cheerful room for which Margot herself had ordered the decorations. Despite the elaborateness of the occasion, there was little spirit of homecoming. Margot and Navarre had walked together for some time before sitting down to dinner, but one of the guests noted that "I saw the Princess constantly dissolving into tears, so much so that I have never beheld eyes redder with weeping. And I felt a great pity for this Princess, seeing her seated next to the King her husband, who was being entertained by I know not what frivolous conversation with his courtiers, while neither he nor anyone else spoke to her."

To the rest of the world, Margot put on a cheerful face. She wrote her brother that she "thanked God for her happiness" and expressed the wish to be permitted to remain at her husband's side permanently. In a similar vein, she reported to her mother on the splendid welcome she had received from "the King, my husband and friend." But in truth she was neither happy nor especially welcome. Although one of her first actions upon returning was to reconstitute her former Court, both Nérac and her husband had changed during her absence. As heir apparent to the French throne, he was increasingly busy with political matters. The formerly unhurried and pleasure-filled mornings and afternoons were interrupted by discussions of strategy and the comings and goings of foreign emissaries from England, the German states, and other Protestant powers as remote as Denmark. More vexing to Margot, however, was that whatever free time her husband had, he chose to spend with Corisande. Not wholly trusting her royal lover's baser instincts, this lady had at first tried to oppose his taking Margot back. Probably, part of the reason for the eight months which Margot had been obliged to spend in limbo was Navarre's deference to his new mistress's wishes.

Corisande need not have worried, however. Navarre, totally smitten, was in the throes of his first great love. To Corisande, he wrote letters such as he would never have dreamed of sending to La Fosseuse or her predecessors: "I have never seen a place more suitable for you," he reported during one of his trips. "It is an island enclosed by woodland marshes, where every hundred steps there are canals so that you can explore the woods by boat. The water is clear and fast-running, and there are a thousand gardens which can be visited only by boat. . . . One can be tranquil here. One can rejoice in the presence of someone you love, or lament in her absence. . . . My soul, keep me in your grace and believe that my fidelity is pure and spotless. . . . Your slave who adores you madly."

Margot scarcely alluded to her rival in her *Memoirs,* but her feelings showed through in her letters to Navarre. When he was away with Corisande on the Day of the Three Kings —always the occasion for revelry in the past—she wrote him, "If I thought that news from Nérac would be important enough for you to bother reading, Monsieur, I would tell you about our Feast which we have solemnized in the usual way. . . . The occasion would have been very lovely if it had been graced by your presence, for without that nothing seems very pleasant to me."

Judging by the itinerary of her movements, it appears that Margot even resorted to a technique frequently attempted by spurned or ignored wives. She journeyed to the shrine of Notre-Dame-de-Bonne-Encontre, where a miraculous birth had reportedly taken place, and then to Encausse, where she spent nineteen days bathing in the thermal springs known for their therapeutic effect on the lame, the deaf, and the sterile. But the most powerful of cures still require a minimum of human cooperation, and it appears that Navarre was not about to provide it. Diarists of the period apparently could ferret out all manner of information, for one of them noted with authority that "the Queen appears greatly displeased with her husband, who neglected her, having slept with her only on one night since the affront to which the King her brother had subjected her . . . and otherwise cajoling her with fine words and an outwardly friendly manner, but nothing more."

During her previous stay at Nérac, Margot had annually journeyed to the nearby Catholic city of Agen in order to be able to observe Easter, a practice which her Huguenot subjects did not tolerate in their own country. On March 19, 1585, after having as usual secured her husband's consent, she again set out. This time, however, she was not planning to come back.

She had recently entered into her thirties—a most difficult time for women, as the historian Michelet gravely noted. During a life already more than replete with its share of triumphs and reversals, she had accumulated ample reason to detest her mother, her foul brother Henry, all Huguenots in general, and, during the past year, her own husband in particular. In her fertile mind, she conceived a plan that would permit her to extract her revenge from all of them simultaneously.

Agen was her own city, part of her personal possessions as a Princess of France. The townspeople, fervent Catholics all, had become used to her visits, and indeed looked forward to them. The Margot whom they received in 1585 lived up to their warmest memories. She was gay, charming, pious, properly generous with beneficences, sincerely concerned over their welfare. But, she confided to the municipal officials who came to pay their respects, she was also much troubled. During her stay in Nérac there had been an attempt to poison her—an attempt, she intimated, engineered by Corisande, her husband's current doxy. But her personal safety was the lesser of her concerns. What truly frightened her was the possibility, almost the likelihood, that Navarre might make a show of strength by attempting to capture Agen. She proposed, and the townspeople agreed, to strengthen the fortifications of the city and raise two companies of troops.

The many years during which Margot had observed her mother at work had not been wasted. So convincing was her performance that Henry's provincial governor was completely taken in. He wrote reassuringly to Paris that "as regards the said lady, she does not wish to do anything to displease Your Majesty, but has taken refuge here as she no longer felt safe in Nérac, knowing the ill will toward her of the Countess of Guiche and her power over the King of Navarre." Acting on his own, the governor added, he had himself provided Margot with two additional companies of infantry. Even Catherine, to whom Margot also described her plight, interceded with Henry to provide his sister with additional help.

Meanwhile, without telling either her mother or the good people of Agen, Margot had also put herself in touch with her old flame, the Duke of Guise. There is no record of what she wrote to him, but he in turn wrote personally to his good friend, Philip of Spain, requesting him urgently to provide Margot with "a good round sum of money" in order that she, as a good ally, could help them "now that we are most in need of her assistance." Guise also ordered irregular troops of the Holy League to place themselves at her disposal.

Without quite realizing what had happened, the town fathers of Agen found themselves playing host to a motley army of some twelve hundred men. Worse, Margot summoned them together on May 15 and informed them that the King was also conspiring against her. To protect herself, and them, against this new danger, she asked, as their liege lady, that they turn the keys of the city over to her.

Margot had repaid both her brother and her husband. Within less than a month, she had contrived to declare her independence from both of them. Now, still dragging her increasingly reluctant subjects along, she began making preparations for war. To create an impregnable fortress, a quarter of the city was ordered razed. Householders were ordered to pull down their own homes, for which they were told they would be reimbursed when money was available. Peasants from the surrounding countryside were conscripted into digging trenches and moats. Already burdened by having to lodge and feed the soldiers, citizens were forced to pay a tax of ten *écus* a day, or face the prospect of being exposed to pillage. The wholesale destruction of houses let loose thousands of rats which, in turn, caused plague to spread. Immersed in preparations for her campaign, Margot refused to believe the reports, which she dismissed as a Huguenot-inspired rumor. To prevent those men, women, and children who disagreed with her from leaving the city, she ordered the gates shut.

That proved to be too much. Pushed beyond endurance and frightened into hysteria, a mob formed and began marching on the still-unfinished citadel. As L'Estoile reported, "The burghers of the town of Agen, unable to bear any longer the tyrannies and indignities inflicted on them by the League, under the command and orders of the Queen of Navarre, rose against her, beat, drove off, and killed her soldiers, and forced her to leave their city." More precisely, they burst into her quarters as she was sitting down to her midday meal. In the confusion, she raced out into the street where one of her officers scooped her onto the croup of his horse and galloped through one of the gates which had been forced open.

Margot had carried out her plan so successfully that, except for Guise who was too far away to be of any aid, she had not a friend or ally left in France. The troops converging on Agen, both Navarre's and those of the King, had identical orders to find and arrest her. The only prospect of safety was to reach another of her own possessions, the nearest of which was the Château of Carlat, perched on a wild mountain spur in the Auvergne some one hundred miles away. She covered the distance in five days, all of it on horseback and over trails so rocky and jolting that her first act on arrival was to fall bruised and exhausted into bed.

A bed, moreover, was practically the only serviceable piece of furniture in Carlat. Once a richly decorated and appointed residence, the Château had been untenanted since the start of the civil wars and left to fall alternately into the hands of

Huguenot and Catholic marauders. At the time of Margot's arrival, it was a cobwebbed, darkened, and drafty hulk whose damp walls were partly covered with decaying tapestries. One of her first acts, according to her household accounts, was to hire a carpenter in the nearby town of Aurillac to repair the windows and build some makeshift chairs and tables.

In her flight, Margot had left behind all her possessions— jewels, furnishings, plate, books, even her clothing. No one would have blamed the aggrieved citizens of Agen had they decided to keep them as partial reparations for the harm they had suffered but, once again loyal to their Countess now that she was safely away from them, they saw to it that everything down to the last vial of perfume was returned to her. There is indication that, once properly installed in her new home, Margot proposed to begin entertaining on her accustomed scale. The evidence is contained in a letter from Navarre to Corisande, dated December 7, 1585, two months after Margot's arrival in Carlat: "A man came to see me on behalf of the *dame aux chameaux*.* He had a request from her asking me to let pass without duty five hundred barrels of wine. This is guzzling beyond all reason. For fear that she fall lower than the backs of her own beasts, I refused."

Despite her husband's solicitude, Margot did her best. She had never been shy or hypocritical about taking lovers. Until the Agen episode, however, she had been discriminating in her choices. La Môle and Bussy had been professionals at their trade; Margot's embrace was, symbolically as well as palpably, recognition of their unmatched excellence. The others, like Chanvallon, had been handsome, accomplished men—poets, diplomats, courtiers.

In Carlat, where time hung heavy on her hands, Margot's

---

* "The lady of the camels": the reference to an animal best known for its two large humps is in all likelihood an allusion to Margot's celebrated ample bosom. Corisande was, by contrast, proud of her slimness and delicate, understated lines.

choice was more restricted. There were the officers of the garrison, crude soldiers for the most part; there was also a young apothecary's son who had taken care of her during a protracted bout of fever and whose ministrations she rewarded. None of this is important, and much of it still remains unsupported gossip, except that it provided her brother with additional pretext to hound her. The episode with the young man who had nursed her, for instance, assumed the proportions of a gory scandal by the time it had reached Paris, where Mendoza picked it up and relayed it to Philip: "I hear that the Queen Mother was recently lamenting that M de Lignerac [the commandant of the Carlat garrison] had stabbed to death the son of an apothecary in the Queen of Navarre's room, so close to her bed that she was covered in bloodstains, and the worst of it is that his motive was jealousy."

As long as there still remained the remotest chance of reconciling Margot and Navarre, Catherine had been able to persuade Henry not to move harshly against his sister. When that at last was erased by public scandal, she gave up and let him do as he wished. Having waited for the moment, he wasted no time. "The more I examine the matter," he instructed one of his state secretaries, "the more I feel and recognize the ignominy which this wretched woman brings upon us. The best that God can do for her and for us is to take her away." Since he could not rely on this intercession, Henry ordered the next best thing. "Let her be conveyed to the Château of Usson. Let, from this hour, her estates and pensions be sequestered. As for her women and male attendants, let them be dismissed instantly, and let her be given some honest waiting-woman until the Queen my good mother provides such women as she deems suitable."*

Henry had chosen Margot's destination with care. The

* Having thus decreed his sister's destiny, he ended on a characteristically petty, effeminate note: "Give orders that all her rings be sent to me, and with a full inventory, and that they be brought to me as soon as possible."

Château of Usson was the most sinister, isolated medieval fortress left in France. Built as a stone square on the summit of an inaccessible rock, it was protected by three complete sets of walls, each with its own bastions, watchtowers, and battlements. The whole, seen from the distance, looked like a papal tiara, but the fortress was so secure that Louis XI had used it to hold his most valuable prisoners. None had ever escaped. Indeed, it was said of Usson that "even the sun can only enter there by force."

It was to this residence, which ironically also belonged to her by right of inheritance, that Margot was escorted by royal troops on November 13, 1585. She would remain there for nearly twenty years, while the final act of the Valois drama was playing itself out.

III

Henry's hounding his sister, whose marginal political value had vanished with her flight from Agen, was the act of a vicious child afraid to lash out against his real enemies. He had been handed an unexpected opportunity to regain stature by the incautious action of the Pope, Sixtus V. Newly elected and ambitious to regain some of the Church's lost power, Sixtus thunderously excommunicated Navarre by declaring that "the authority vested in Saint Peter and his successors by the infinite power of the Eternal King surpasses all the power of earthly kings and princes. Founded on a firm rock, unmoved by winds and storms, its judgments are irrevocable and thus it zealously guards its duty to see that its laws are kept. When it finds anyone transgressing the laws of God, it punishes them severely, depriving them of their offices, however powerful they may be, and crushing them as ministers of Satan." Having found Navarre a relapsed heretic, the papal bull stripped him of his titles, declared him incapable of succeeding to the throne of France, and absolved all his vassals from allegiance to him.

His own Huguenot subjects naturally ignored the papal sentence, but more surprising was the reaction of the good Catholics of France. Whatever their own feelings about Navarre, they greeted the Pope's action as a gross intrusion into the domestic affairs of France. The Parlement of Paris stated that Sixtus had "no authority over kingdoms established by God before the name of the Pope existed in the world," and refused to publish or register the papal pronouncement. Navarre responded with a series of letters that showed how rapidly he was growing both as a man and as a prince. To the clergy, he wrote: "God caused me to be born a Christian; I desire the affirmation, the growth, and the peace of the Christian faith. We believe in the same God; we recognize the same Jesus Christ. . . . If we differ upon the interpretation of the texts, I believe that if you would consider some of the conciliations I have proposed we will be able to find a ground for accord. I believe also that the war which you pursue so ardently is unworthy of Christians, unworthy between Christians, and especially unworthy of those who profess to be doctors of evangelism. If war pleases you so much, if a battle is dearer to you than a disputation, if you would rather participate in a bloody conspiracy than a Council, there is nothing I can do about it. But the blood that will flow is on your heads." In a similar vein, he wrote to the nobility: "I am of you and I love you all; your losses impoverish me. The foreigner [the Guises of Lorraine] cannot share such sentiment. The foreigner cares not for such losses. I could complain against some of you; I would rather plead your case and complain on your behalf. I am ready to embrace all of you. . . ." To the Third Estate, representing the long-abused and long-suffering people of the nation, he wrote: "I pity myself only because I do not have the power to defend myself without causing innocent people to suffer.

. . . I was born a Frenchman. I sympathize with all your evils. I have tried every means of saving you from civil war, and in order to shorten it I will not spare even my life. . . ."

But it was to Henry himself that Navarre made his most powerful appeal. He pointed out the obvious: that the Pope's right to excuse people from their allegiance to their king had far more dangerous implications for the King of France than for the King of Navarre. In a letter to Catherine, Navarre was even more explicit: "I can foresee the day, Madame, when both you and the King will see, perhaps too late, whose hands you have armed."

Catherine did not need this reminder. As soon as news of the papal bull had reached France, she noted to one of her secretaries, "In all this I see harm only for the King, for if I saw that he had the means to be strong as I wish he were, I would not give a button for all those practices and dealings. . . . I would be sweet to all of them, popes and kings, to win such forces as would enable me to command and not to obey them."

But Henry was not strong. His own reaction to the bull had been petulance rather than indignation or resolve. "It seems," he complained, "that the Pope would like me to act as his provost marshal in France." Honest Catholics who placed their national allegiance above that of their religion heard their king say this and, in large numbers, went over to the side of the *Politiques*. Thus, rather than profiting from the chance offered to him, Henry contrived to turn it into a fresh defeat.

In June, 1586, he received another letter of advice: "Pardon me, but it is my affection which dares me to speak so freely. Before God I have no other motive but my love for you. I am amazed to see you betrayed by your own Council. . . . For the love of God, do not sleep too long a sleep. I understand there is a truce of some days; use this to strengthen your own position and be careful not to agree to their conditions which will only lead to your own disgrace and the loss of your state." The writer of the letter was Elizabeth of England, and if her love of Henry was perhaps less impelling than her fear of France's falling into the hands of Philip of Spain, the urgency of her concern was no less real. Henry did not reply, but L'Estoile noted that the King had found a new diversion: "At this time [he] began to carry a *bilboquet** in his hand and play with it as small children do. Imitating him, the Dukes of Joyeuse and Épernon and many other courtiers took it up, and they in turn were followed by lackeys and young men of all sorts. So great is the weight of the actions of kings, princes, and lords, especially in the matter of folly."

Catherine was sixty-seven years old now. For more than a year she had suffered intermittently from colic and gout, the consequences of her undiminished, hearty appetite. Because frequent attacks of rheumatism had crippled her right hand, she taught herself to sign letters with her left. Unable any longer to indulge in her pastime of riding, she took long walks instead; once, when obliged to stay for some time in a strange château, she ordered a wooden bridge built over a small stream so that she could take the air in an adjoining park. But bodily ills did not affect her mental energy or her spirit. Even after Navarre's excommunication, she did not give up her long-standing hope of persuading him to return to the Church and to the King's side. With the Guises and the League under Mendoza's watchful eye and committed to Philip of Spain, there was no other course open. In the fall of 1586, she again left Paris for what was to be her last meeting with her son-in-law.

She journeyed first to Chenonceaux, and then to the jewel-like château at Azay-le-Rideau. Navarre, however, found reasons to postpone the meeting until Catherine waived all prerogatives of age, sex, and position and agreed to see him

---

* The ancient game of cup-and-ball, consisting of a stick to which a ball with a hole in it is attached by a short length of string. The object of the game is to toss the ball a few inches into the air and catch it on the stick.

at Saint-Brice, deep in Huguenot territory near Cognac. Here, in an isolated manor guarded by exactly fifty Catholic and fifty Huguenot men-at-arms, the two came face to face. According to an observer, the Queen Mother greeted Navarre by embracing him and "covering him with infinite caresses," to which he responded by undoing the buttons of his doublet, baring his chest, and announcing, "You see, Madame, I keep nothing covered."

This set the tone for the discussions. Catherine had, as usual, brought the *escadron volant* along, and she assured Navarre that he could have "anything he wanted." He politely replied that he saw nothing he wished. The Queen Mother then tried to bring the issues down to the level of a family misunderstanding. Why, she asked, did Navarre insist on bringing ruin to the kingdom; why would he not obey the orders of the King? "Have I not," she asked him, "always been a good mother? . . . You used to be so friendly and agreeable, but you have changed so." Navarre pointed out, "Yes, you were a good mother in my youth, but not for the past six years." To a complaint of Catherine's that he was causing her unnecessary hardship, he replied, "It is not I who keep you from sleeping in your bed, but you who keep me from sleeping in mine." Finally, after a long afternoon of fruitless discussion, he permitted himself to voice a perceptive observation, "Madame, you grow strong on this trouble; if you had peace, you would not know how to live." There had never really been any serious prospect for agreement because only Navarre's conversion could solve Catherine's problem, and this he was unwilling to do. "I cannot," he insisted, "change religions as I would my clothes." Nevertheless, he dragged out the verbal fencing with his mother-in-law while his agents were busy raising money and troops in every Protestant corner of Europe.

It was news from England which finally put an end to the charade. On February 18, 1587, Mary Stuart had been beheaded at Fotheringay Castle. Although Catherine, for ample reason, had no love lost for her daughter-in-law, she was shocked and dismayed. Regicide, even of a powerless, long-captive Queen was an alarming portent. "It only requires a beginning," she wrote, "to give much boldness to those who desire to reign." She also foresaw that the execution could only help Henry's opponents—Navarre, because Elizabeth would now be obliged to come to his aid; and the Guises because they would exploit the tragedy to its full worth.

She was right on both counts. A chronicler noted that "at the news of this death, a great show of mourning was put on at the court of France, especially on the part of the members of the Houses of Lorraine and Guise, to whom this Queen was closely related (too close for her good, according to many). . . . The King and Queen and members of the House of Lorraine all put on deep mourning, and on the 13th of this month a solemn service was held in the great church of Paris, with ecclesiastics, nobles, and representatives of the Parlement participating. Her death was infinitely regretted and mourned by the Catholics, principally by the League, who cried aloud that she was a martyr to the Roman, Catholic, and Apostolic religion and that the Queen [Elizabeth] had put her to death on this account no matter what the pretext was. In this opinion they were carefully and cleverly supported by the preachers, who canonized her every day in their sermons."

To impress more forcefully upon Parisians the tragic lot of their Catholic brethren in England, the Duchess of Montpensier, sister of the Duke of Guise, commissioned an immense painting showing in full detail men and women being arrested, tortured, and dismembered, priests being beaten and stripped naked, soldiers breaking into houses to pillage them and butcher their occupants. Displayed at the cemetery of Saint-Séverin, the painting attracted huge crowds who were told that what they were seeing was only a sample of what they could expect if ever a heretic should gain the throne of France.

At the same time in London, reports were being received of a massive undertaking by Philip of Spain, whom Mary Stuart had named as her successor. Walsingham wrote to Lord Burghley: "There is no way so apt to stop the Spanish expeditions against this realm, as the upholding of the King of Navarre and the keeping under of the House of Guise, whom Spain seeketh to advance. If Her Majesty shall lose this opportunity, either by long delay in resolving or by not sending such a portion of treasure as may do good, she shall have cause to say, 'Farewell my days of peace.' "

As German and Swiss mercenaries marched westward to join the Huguenot forces, and as Mendoza urged the Guises to earn their Spanish stipend by taking the field, war on French soil again became inevitable. In the turmoil, Henry saw an opportunity for a master stroke. Using every *écu* Catherine could collect or borrow, he raised three royal armies. One, under the Duke of Guise, was sent to intercept the invading mercenaries. Another, under the Duke of Joyeuse, was to march south and engage Navarre. The third, which he himself undertook to lead, took up a position between the other two, on the Loire. Henry's plan, borrowed from the Bible, was to permit his enemies to avenge him on his enemies. After having inflicted heavy losses on them, Guise would succumb to the Germans and Swiss. The loyal Joyeuse would defeat Navarre and send him scurrying back into his own insignificant kingdom, where he could be dealt with later. And Henry himself, having stoutly held the center, would finish off the foreigners and return to Paris in triumph.

It did not work out that way. Joyeuse's army, "all of gold, with feathers, embroidered scarves, and velvet cloaks," met Navarre's forces at Coutras on October 20, 1587. The Huguenots went into battle singing one of David's Psalms—"This

is the day the Lord has made; let us rejoice and be glad in it."
Within two hours, Joyeuse was dead and his army annihilated. Six days later, Guise engaged the invaders at Vimory, beat them roundly, and proceeded to chase them out of France. Henry, with no one to fight, returned to Paris where he ordered church bells to be rung and a *Te Deum* to be celebrated at Notre-Dame. The priests did as they were told, but six days prior to his return, the Faculty of Theology of the Sorbonne handed down its judgment that, despite its divine source, "one could remove the power of government from the hands of incapable princes just as one could dismiss tutors found to be suspect."

IV

Thus far, Don Bernardino de Mendoza's mission to France had been a series of successes. France, which he had been sent to divide, was bleeding from its self-inflicted wounds. Henry III, whose authority he had been instructed to undermine, was king in name only. The Paris Holy League, an animal he had helped train and whip into anger, was straining at the leash. The Guises, whatever secret plans they were harboring on their own behalf—and Mendoza was not fool enough to believe they were acting only out of affection and respect for Philip of Spain—were for the present safely bought. Henry III had tested the firmness of their loyalty to Spain by offering Henry of Guise material benefits and unprecedented honors. The Duke had reported the offer to Mendoza, comparing it to that used by Satan to tempt Jesus in the wilderness. "And I trust," he added, "that I, too, shall be supported by good angels."

All had gone well, but all had been prologue, for Philip was now engaged in the most ambitious and riskiest enterprise of his entire cautious life. All his energies and much of the wealth of his possessions had been committed to the construction and equipment of an unthinkably massive fleet that would gain him England. Nothing, not the smallest detail affecting the success of this venture, was to be left to chance. France, because her long coast line would in effect represent the Armada's right flank during its voyage, was of capital importance. Mendoza had been instructed to secure from Henry III a guarantee that friendly treatment would be extended to any of the Armada's ships that might be obliged to make port in French harbors and the promise that no difficulty would be put in the way of providing supplies for Spanish vessels. The ambassador was also to obtain from the French King the complete loyalty of some ports near the coast of Flanders, such as Boulogne and Calais, to prevent any possible French Huguenot aid from reaching England.

Mendoza had not been able to secure anything firmer than generalized promises from Henry. Furthermore, he did not feel confident that even a formal treaty would adequately bind the irresponsible, vacillating French monarch. How much simpler and safer it would be if Henry were out of the picture altogether.

There is evidence that Mendoza did more than just muse over this happy prospect. Early in 1588, as preparations for the sailing began to accelerate, so did the activities of the Paris League. New grievances were drawn up and presented to the King; individual acts of defiance of royal ordinances multiplied; political pamphlets attacking the personal habits of the King reached new heights of daring and scurrility. The atmosphere in the capital prompted Filippo Cavriana, the Florentine ambassador, to warn his master of "one of the largest revolts and rebellions ever heard of, which will, I fear, compel me within a month to write you of most extraordinary events."

Guise himself was central to Mendoza's plan. At the conclusion of his victorious campaign, he had been expressly forbidden by the King to come to Paris and instead had joined the rest of the family at Joinville. From there, they composed and issued still another arrogant manifesto. Among other new demands, these Eleven Articles of Nancy required the King to establish Courts of Inquisition in every province, to confiscate all Huguenot property and put to death all Huguenot prisoners of war who refused to recant their heresy, to return to the Church all lands and property it had been forced to cede by earlier edicts. Mendoza applauded the spirit of the words but insisted that the time for demands and rhetoric was past. In March, he prevailed upon Philip to send the Duke an additional sum of 300,000 *écus,* with orders that it be used to do something which would occupy Henry III's attention during the month of May. That the "something" was either suggested or approved by Mendoza is confirmed by a secret message he sent to Philip on April 14: "If the project in question is carried out as planned, the King will have his hands full so that it will be impossible for him, either by words or deeds, to give aid to the English queen. It is for this reason that I have thought it wise to delay the execution of this project until the moment Your Majesty's Armada is on the point of departure."

On noon of May 9, 1588, the Duke of Guise defied the King's orders and appeared in Paris. He came quietly, accompanied by only seven attendants, and started to make his way to the Hôtel de Soissons, the residence of the Queen Mother. Although wearing a great cloak and a large slouched hat, he managed to allow himself to be recognized as soon as he had ridden through the Porte Saint-Martin. According to an eyewitness, one of the young men who had accompanied him pulled down the cloak and shouted, "Monseigneur, show yourself to us!" Whereupon a woman shouted *"Bon Prince!* Here you are! We are saved." Immediately a mob gathered, to kiss his boots, rub their rosaries against him, throw flowers in his path. To the shouts of *"Vive Guise," "Vive le pilier de l'Église"* ("Long live the pillar of the Church"), a crowd of thirty thousand Parisians formed and followed its hero as he rode through the Rue Saint-Honoré to his destination.

At the Hôtel, where Catherine was busy dictating letters, the first person to catch sight of Guise was her favorite dwarf, who had been standing by the window and who rushed into her study to announce the arrival. Thinking it a poor joke, the Queen Mother lost her temper and ordered the dwarf whipped. Moments later, the two antagonists were facing each other. Nervous and frightened, a white-faced Catherine temporized by greeting him, "I am very happy to see you, but I would have preferred you to come at another time." Equally nervous in her presence now that he had committed himself, Guise showed himself "full of respectful humility and profound submission." He had come to see her, he explained, to defend himself against those who were blackening his name and to justify his conduct to the King in person. That he had come to see her and, in effect, seek her help rather than proceed directly to the palace was mute recognition of her position. Catherine immediately sent a messenger to warn Henry, then set about preparing to accompany Guise to the Louvre.

The messenger arrived as the King was sitting with his Privy Council. He read his mother's hastily scribbled note, covered his face with his hands, and looked up: "Monsieur de Guise has come. If you had given him his orders, and if he had taken no notice of them, what would you do?" As Bellièvre, Villequier, La Guiche, and the other state secretaries paused to frame a reply, it was Alphonse d'Ornano, the fiery Corsican commander of the King's chosen Forty-Five, who spoke first. "Sire, if you will honor me by giving me this charge, I will, without causing you any further trouble, this day lay his head at your feet. Not a soul shall give a sign of disturbance, I pledge my life and honor upon it." Immediately, the others spoke up to raise objections: the mutinous crowds, the sorry state of the royal treasury, the risk of arousing the Holy League. They were still at it when Catherine, who had been carried over to the Louvre by litter, and Guise, who had dutifully trotted alongside, were ushered in. At once angry and fearful, Henry demanded to know why Guise had disobeyed his orders and come to Paris. The Duke, still pale and aware of the double rank of guards with naked swords he had passed on the staircase to the Council chamber, explained that he had not received any such orders. Henry wheeled on Bellièvre, who had been instructed to convey the order but turned away even as the shaken man started to protest that Guise was lying. Suddenly fearful for his life, Guise forgot the royal presence and sank into a chair. Catherine hurried over to Henry and led him over to a window, where he could see the gathered, angry mob. When he turned back to face the room, the moment had passed. With a bow and a show of respect, Guise took his departure.

"Strike the shepherd and the sheep will be scattered," Ornano had argued. Perhaps they would indeed, but Henry had lacked the nerve to make the move. Some historians hostile to Catherine have argued that it was she, and not her son, who had spared Guise's life—that his coming to see her instead of the King was part of a conspiracy between them, and that her action in calling Henry's attention to the angry mobs was calculated to trigger his natural cowardice. Her motive, they suggest, was that she had given up all hope of his retaining the crown and was thus attempting to ingratiate herself with what she recognized would be the winning faction. Like many other acts of deceit charged against her, this makes little sense in historical or psychological perspective. It is unlikely that a full, tormented lifetime of protective motherhood and desperate clinging to personal power should be cancelled out by one crisis, however desperate. Far more reasonable, it seems, is the simple explanation that Catherine, having just passed through the mobs herself, had assessed their murderous intent and acted, as she had done so many times before, to temporize and hope for some new accommodation. She had given way to panic only once in her life, sixteen years earlier, and it is not likely that she had forgotten the consequences.

In any case, Guise had won. The Hôtel de Guise, to which he returned after leaving the Louvre, quickly turned into a combined fortress-command post as hundreds of his men infiltrated the aroused city and as delegates from the Paris League arrived to receive their battle orders. On May 10, the Duke again called on the King, but this time accompanied by four hundred armed guards. Together, the two men attended Mass, then sat down to discuss future campaigns against the Huguenots as if nothing unusual had happened the day before.

Despite this show of cordiality, Henry, too, was making his preparations. To reinforce the household troops—the traditional Scottish archers and the Swiss guards—he sent orders that an additional 6,000 men loyal to him and stationed in Lagny, some twenty miles east of Paris, be moved into the city. Guise had no difficulty persuading the Papal Nuncio, Morosini, to intercede with the King, pointing out that such action would "ruin the most beautiful city in the world and cause much innocent blood to be shed." Meanwhile, his deputies were busy distributing arms to the League, arms which for the moment were hidden in churches, monasteries, and convents.

Before dawn of May 12, the populace was awakened by the unmistakable sound of approaching drums and fifes: the King's troops were moving toward the city. At this signal thousands of men and women sprang into action. Recording it, even the usually terse and restrained L'Estoile was moved to imagery: "The artisan left his tools, the merchant his deals, the academic his books, the procurators their briefcases, the lawyers their hats. . . ." Heavy planks that had been prepared for the purpose were dragged out and erected across the narrow streets. Massive chains were stretched between facing doorways. Piles of rocks and barrels filled with earth were thrown up at strategic intersections. The Day of the Barricades had begun.

Operations proceeded with a smoothness and speed that eliminated all possibility of spontaneity. The entire scheme had been worked out by Mendoza, using his military experience to attack the tactical problem of how a civilian population could slow down and hobble an advancing force of well-trained troops. The Spaniard's shrewdness became evident as soon as the soldiers entered the city. Forced to halt and break ranks in order to clear the obstacles in their path, they suddenly became the target for stones, bricks, and heavy pieces of furniture thrown down on them from the roofs and upper stories of the houses lining the streets. Scattered, forced to seek shelter only to fall upon another barricade, the troops became a herd of helpless animals prodded into a hostile maze.

Throughout the days of preparation, Catherine had continued to seek a negotiated settlement, but, just as in her final talks with Navarre, she had few cards left. On the afternoon of the 12th, as Paris was running wild, she had herself carried to Guise's hôtel in the Marais, where she was handed Guise's terms for an armistice. They were tantamount to abdication. The King would have to name Guise as Lieutenant-Governor of France and call the Estates General to confirm the nomination. Navarre was to be unequivocally barred from succession to the throne. The Duke of Épernon and all others of Henry's favorites were to be deprived of their offices and permanently banned from Court. The King's private guard, the Forty-Five, was to be disbanded. Administrative regulations were to be established which the King would not have the power to change.

With great difficulty, Catherine made her way back to the Louvre to discuss these terms with Henry and the Council. Students from the Left Bank had poured across the river by the hundreds and erected their barricades within fifty yards of the entrance to the palace. Inside, Henry and the ministers could not decide whether to accept the demands or to reject them as impertinent. After an inconclusive evening's discussion, matters were left in Catherine's hands. She would talk again to Guise. Later during that same night, Henry announced that he wished to take a stroll in the Tuileries gardens and left the palace by a small rear door, accompanied by a dozen friends.

The next day, as Catherine was again closeted with Guise, a messenger brought in a note which caused the Duke to go deathly white. "Madame," he said, "you have betrayed me. While you have kept me talking here, the King has left Paris and gone where he can stir up more trouble for me." The Queen Mother swore, truthfully, that she knew nothing of this. Fearful and bewildered this time, she again returned to the Louvre to discover that Guise had been accurately informed.

Her son had fled, leaving her in Paris. To a degree that even Francis I had not imagined when he joked about it more than half a century earlier, she was, indeed, naked as a babe.

So hasty was Henry's departure that some members of his party did not have time to change out of their Court clothes, and his own flustered groom strapped his spurs on backward. Riding hard and stopping only for a few hours' rest at Rambouillet, the group reached Chartres where Henry, safely surrounded by his Forty-Five, boasted that his escape from Paris was even more spectacular than the one he had made years before from Cracow. That there were distinct differences between the two did not seem to cloud his delight.

He had, indeed, put Guise in an awkward position. The Duke was, for all practical purposes, King of Paris. Within three days, his men had occupied the city's strategic points— the Bastille, the Arsenal, the castle of Vincennes. The barricades had been torn apart as enthusiastically as they had been thrown up. By the 15th, members of the Guise family had descended on Paris like occupying harpies. His sister, the Duchess of Montpensier, took such pleasure at taking over a vacant *hôtel de ville* and opening it to festivities that Catherine could not restrain herself from rebuking her. "What would you have me do, Madame?" the Duchess threw back. "I am like a brave soldier whose heart is swollen with victory." Everywhere he went in public, Guise was greeted with delirious shouts of "To Rheims!" and for the first time in months preachers began to exhort their congregations to obey law and observe order. The League convened and announced the establishment of a new provisional government for the city, answerable not to the King of France but to his soon-to-be successor, the Cardinal of Bourbon.*

But all this, gratifying as it was, was window dressing. The Parlement of Paris, despite pressure from Guise, declared its continued loyalty to the King, and while in a few cities—notably Orléans and Amiens—the local Holy League assumed municipal control and sided with their Paris brethren, France as a nation was still ruled by Henry of Valois. Trivial as this fact may have appeared to the joyous crowds in Paris, it was not lost on Bernardino de Mendoza. He had, beyond anything Philip might have expected of him, given Henry something "to have his hands full." But Mendoza was a thorough man. On May 23, 1588 he requested an audience with Catherine and secured her acquiescence—hardly surprisingly in view of her other preoccupations—to free entry and exit for Spanish ships at all French ports. Six days later, the mighty Armada set sail. As Garrett Mattingly noted in his study, "As far as France was concerned, [it] sailed in perfect safety, just as Mendoza had promised that it should."

In the wake of the uprising in Paris, the British ambassador, Sir Edward Stafford, assessed the mood of the city and reassured his Queen that "the Duke of Guise is not

* In so doing, they revoked the charter under which Paris had been governed since 1380 and set the precedent for the better-known uprising that was to take place 283 years later.

remained full master." For all his physical endowments and his natural ability to quicken both the pulse of ladies and the temper of street crowds, Guise lacked some of the essential qualities of statesmanship. The German historian, Leopold von Ranke, who admired the Duke, conceded as much in this description: "On one occasion he [Guise] was seen to swim against the current of a stream in complete armor. In the game of tennis, in pugilism, and all military exercises, he was unrivaled, and no hardship seemed to fatigue him. He was a tall and fine-looking man, with fair flowing hair and lively piercing eyes. . . . [I]n the judgment of many he presented the very type of a man. Although brought up in the lap of luxury, he cheerfully put up with the privations and difficulties of the camp. He did not think long consultations and reflection necessary, for in war he believed that everything depended upon rapid execution. In the midst of a numerous company, he would formulate his plan, from the accomplishment of which he would not afterward allow himself to be diverted by any objection." Ranke adds details to humanize his man: "He condescended even to those of the lowest rank and seldom refused an invitation to a baptism, a wedding, or any other domestic festivity. He had been seen to cross the street, hat in hand, to salute an acquaintance, sometimes of mean condition." But as a perceptive historian, Ranke also notes: "He was not fond of regular preparation, even in political affairs; he was at home in disorder and tumult; and looked for all success as the result of his popularity and his star."

Disorder and tumult had indeed delivered Paris into his hands, but he had no plan of his own, or even any clear idea of what he should do next. Sensing this, and aware of its own exposed position, the new municipal government backed down and sent a message to Henry asserting its unalterable loyalty to him and assuring him that "in all that has happened in these past days, they [the citizens of Paris] have never had the wish or intention to depart from the true obedience which subjects owe their king." On the contrary, they deplored the unspecified ill-intending counsellors who had persuaded the King to flee the city and thus deprived them of the opportunity to demonstrate their good faith and obedience. And they respectfully asked the King, should he have no plans of returning, to appoint the Queen Mother as arbiter and mediator because she would know how to restore tranquillity, "as she has done on previous occasions."

Old, ailing, heartsick, stripped of all power save that of her will and personality, Catherine again threw herself into the job of saving the realm for what remained of the Valois dynasty. For the six weeks immediately following her son's flight, her collected correspondence contains more than fifty letters, some long and intricate, to friend, foe, and neutral. In addition, she carried on daily discussions with Guise, with members of the Parlement, with the ambassadors. The struggle was not merely between Valois and Guise, for the vultures who had enlisted in the Duke's cause now smelled the end and began to circle. The Duke of Lorraine let it be known that any agreement would have to include the ceding to him of Sedan and its great fortress. The Duke of Savoy demanded the withdrawal of French protection from Geneva, which he coveted. The Papal Nuncio was on everyone's side, striving to delay any settlement until the Armada had landed its troops in England.

Catherine had always played her best game on such a crowded chessboard, but in this instance Henry undercut every move she planned by himself granting all the demands made by the Guises. Twice, she traveled to see him and beg him to return to Paris. After his second refusal, she made a tearful appeal which cut through artifice to sum up and lay bare her whole life's aim: "My son, what will people say of me, and what will they think when they see that I, whom God made your mother, count for so little with you?"

Henry turned the question away with an evasion, but two

weeks later he gave his reply. Without the slightest warning, and by means of curt notes written in his own hand, he dismissed his eight principal advisers.* All of them had served him faithfully and long, and all of them had been appointed by Catherine or approved by her. In their places, he appointed men new to the Court and with no visible qualifications for their jobs. Catherine was too humiliated at this massive affront to raise public objection, but the Papal Nuncio, Morosini, on her behalf diplomatically raised the question of whether it was wise to incur the enmity of such a powerful group of men. Mockingly, Henry replied: "They are all rich men and no doubt will want to enjoy in peace the great wealth they have acquired in my service." Furthermore, he declared that he wished to apply himself directly and uninterruptedly to the government of the kingdom, "in order to see whether, by governing it myself, according to my own ideas, I shall arrive at a better result."

The explanation was an unnecessary and unfair insult, the act of a vindictive, cruel thirty-seven-year-old child. But this child still wore the crown of France, and by his wish Catherine was to be excluded from power as completely as she had been during the years of Diane de Poitiers' ascendency.

Although neither Catherine nor the Guises were aware of it, the nature and timing of Henry's actions during the months after his flight from Paris were being dictated by events taking place on the high seas off the coasts of Portugal and France. He, too, was watching the progress of the Armada, and with an interest that was, if anything, keener than that of Philip II himself. The Spanish monarch had staked his ambitions to conquer England, pacify the Netherlands, and isolate France on the success of his colossal enterprise; Henry, whether as a last desperate resort or an inspired premonition, had staked his survival on its failure. The

---

* The notes, identical, read: "I am very well satisfied with your services, but go at once to your house and stay there until I send for you. Do not ask the reason for this note, but obey me."

concessions he made to the Guises, granting virtual control of the armed forces to the Duke Henry and the governorship of one province or another to his hungry brothers and cousins, were all given as paper promises, with the expectation that without Spanish support they would never be collected.

Mendoza received the first report that, on August 2, the Armada had engaged the British fleet and cut it to pieces. After relaying the glorious news to Madrid he rushed to Chartres in order to have the pleasure of personally announcing the victory to the French King. A chronicler records that he "arrived in the city, dismounted from his horse in front of the great doors of the Cathedral . . . and demanded that a *Te Deum* be sung in honor of the Spanish forces." His orders were carried out, but in the midst of the procession, Henry icily remarked that he had received more recent news from Calais.

In fact, the King had been better informed and continued to receive reports of the Armada's escalating vicissitudes long before a shaken Mendoza could collect and transmit them to Spain. Certainly, Henry knew that the expedition was a total failure well before he dismissed his mother's hand-picked ministers on September 8.

Now it was the Guises' turn to worry. The setback to their Spanish sponsor raised questions about his continued willingness to support them financially or, if necessary, with troops. Of French sentiment, there was no question. As soon as the fate of the Armada became known, posters appeared all over Paris, announcing that "If anyone knows the whereabouts of the Armada of Spain, victorious over England, and will tell the Spanish ambassador, he will give him five francs' reward." It took little imagination to foresee that the same goodwill being shown to Spain would be extended to its secret allies in France.

One of the demands to which Henry had acceded was a convocation of the Estates General—though in keeping with his strategy of waiting out the fate of the Armada he had postponed the date by a month. With the Spanish threat removed, he could now direct his undivided attention to dealing with the Guises. They in turn, after vainly having tried to cancel the meeting on the grounds that it would delay the war against the Huguenots, prepared to load the assembly in their favor. Sensing the temper of the moment, Cavriana, the Florentine who had predicted the Barricades of Paris, wrote: "The day of the dagger will come."

V

Although, through no dereliction on his part, his principal mission to France had failed utterly, Mendoza continued to press Guise into forcing a showdown with the King. The record shows that on September 4, 1588, the Duke Francis reported to the Spaniard that "throughout all France they are trying to arrange the election of deputies who favor [the Crown]. . . . I have left nothing undone on my side, but have sent into the provinces and bailiwicks men whom I can trust to work against their efforts. I believe I have so far succeeded that the majority of the deputies will be for us." He was right. Of the 191 deputies elected to represent the Third Estate, 150 belonged to either the Parisian or the local Holy Leagues. The nobility was split more evenly: ninety-six for the League and eighty-four for the King. The clergy, with 134 delegates, was unanimously in favor of the League, giving Guise a total of 380 out of 505 deputies. All of them were Catholics; the Huguenots, knowing they would be far outnumbered and fearful for their own safety, had not bothered sending any representatives from the regions they held.

Because the choice of where the Estates met was a royal prerogative, Catherine had urged her son to select Blois. More than any other place in France, it was his own ground, where he had been raised and where he had often returned. But more impelling to the old Queen Mother, it was the Valois's home ground. The Loire was their river. Ever since the trembling Charles VII had huddled in Chinon where Joan of Arc came to seek him out in 1429, the Valois had retreated to the banks of the broad river whenever Paris and the rest of their realm had turned against them. Amboise, Chenonceaux, Chaumont, Azay—all within a day's ride of each other—had all seen the dynasty threatened and prevail. Catherine de' Medici was one of the shrewdest, most accomplished, and pragmatic women of her time, but she was also one of the most superstitious.

On October 16, 1588, after the inevitable delays, the delegates gathered at Blois in the great, tapestried Salle d'État with its vaulted roof supported by seven slim gold and violet columns. Dressed in the white satin of Grand Master of France, the Duke of Guise led an honor guard of one hundred gentlemen into the adjoining castle to escort the King to his place on the raised dais, between his mother on the right and the Queen on his left.

Henry began his speech with a tribute to Catherine. Whether out of sincerity or the knowledge that the great esteem for her abilities had survived his dismissal of her ministers, he said, "I cannot pass over in silence the infinite pains which the Queen my mother has taken to meet the evils which afflict the state, and I think it right to render to her in this illustrious assembly, in my own name and in the name of the nation, public thanks. Not only is it true that I owe to her the honor of being your master seated on the leading throne of Christendom, but if I have any experience, if I have been brought up in good principles, above all that zeal I have for the establishment of the Catholic religion—I owe them all to her. What work has she not undertaken to appease all

the troubles which have arisen and to establish everywhere
the true worship of God and public peace? Has her advanced
age been able to induce her to spare herself? Has she not for
this cause sacrificed her health? It is indeed from her that
I have learned to find all my pleasure in the cares which are
inseparable from government."

To Catherine, the words could only have been of passing
comfort, for no sooner had he paid her this homage than
Henry rushed on to ignore not only her advice but the
example of her conciliatory attitude which he had just
finished citing. Looking directly at Guise, he continued:
"The evidence is sufficiently well known . . . as to the zeal
and steadfastness with which I have ever proceeded in the
extirpation of heresy. . . . Do not imagine that I alone am
responsible for the afflictions of the country. I have expressly
forbidden every association formed without my authority;
all raising of troops and of money, both within and without
my kingdom; and I now declare that all those who persist
in such criminal intelligence in spite of my prohibition shall
be guilty of high treason." Lest there be any doubt, he went
on to add: "Certain great nobles in my kingdom have banded
into leagues and associations. As an example of my accustomed good will, I am prepared to overlook what they have
done in the past, but as I am obliged to preserve royal dignity,
I warn that henceforth those of my subjects who persist in
these designs will be charged and found guilty of the crime
of *lèse-majesté*." And he ended by blandly charging the
Estates with the responsibility of supporting his "good intentions."

Since Henry was intelligent enough to be able to count
votes, and had, in fact, insisted on personally greeting most
of the arriving delegates to solicit their views, the speech was
either a bluff or a provocation. But Guise, who had listened
white-faced, would not rise to the bait. Under the leadership
of his brother, who had succeeded to the family's private
fiefdom as Cardinal of Lorraine, the Estates brushed aside

the royal pretensions and instead belabored Henry with complaints about high taxes, royal extravagance, and dereliction of duty. Unschooled and ill-equipped by temperament for this kind of political haggling, and further hampered by the absence of the counselors he had dismissed, Henry was maneuvered into making one concession after another. He agreed to curtail the sales of offices, which he had relied upon to finance his own establishment; he agreed to reduce or eliminate certain taxes. He even consented, at the demand of the outraged Cardinal of Bourbon, to have his remarks about "certain great nobles of my kingdom" expunged from the formal record. He conceded that the elimination of heresy should be the first concern of the state, thus admitting that he had been derelict in his duty. Emboldened by their success, the Third Estate demanded that a special council be appointed to oversee "the due observance of resolutions passed in these Estates." Not until 1789 would such a direct challenge to royal authority again be issued. A face-saving compromise was achieved after Henry humbly promised to reduce the scale of his Court and "make do with one capon where he had formerly served two."

As autumn lengthened into winter, a grimness settled over Blois. The manic energy that had propelled Henry wound down under the weight of the daily assaults upon him. The fulminations of the preachers rose to such a pitch that he could no longer walk the streets of his own town of Blois without risking insult. To one of the ambassadors observing the meetings he announced that he "would sooner die than see his kingly dignity lessened and tarnished." Nevertheless, he was obliged on more than one occasion to ask for Guise's intercession in moderating the demands made upon him by the League.

Catherine, meanwhile, fell ill. The Papal Legate visited her ten days after she had taken to bed and reported that "to tell the truth, I am not content with the condition of the Queen Mother. She has a heavy cold and a troublesome cough and fever every day. She is weakened by her illness and with seventy years on top of that." Despite her ailments, however, Catherine managed to get out of bed on December 18, two days after the Legate's call on her, and even to preside over yet another of the splendid entertainments that, however grim the surrounding circumstances, had punctuated her entire life. The occasion was very close to her heart: the marriage of her granddaughter, Christine, to Ferdinand, the Grand Duke of Florence. It was a match Catherine had nurtured over several years, with the same perseverance she had always found for matrimonial enterprises. For an evening, the great hall of Blois was filled with music and dancing as if the disagreeable Estates did not exist. The Guises and their retinue were in attendance; even the King made his appearance, ashen-faced beneath his pomades and kohl. And as always, it was the *escadron volant* that drew all eyes, performing their well-practiced coquetries for what was to be the last time.

For days, rumors of impending violence had been circulating around Blois. The Guises were preparing to seize the King and remove him from the throne;* the King was plotting to do away with the Duke of Guise. Mendoza, who had established himself quietly in Saint-Dié, a small village not far from Blois, was sufficiently concerned to warn the Duke. Others of his followers also proposed that he should leave until the Estates had completed their work. Guise brushed off the warnings, reputedly by asserting that "he who gives up the game has lost it." He reassured Mendoza that he had many friends and that "if an enterprise is begun against me, I shall end it more roughly than I did in Paris."

Henry's intentions are more difficult to document. During the sessions of the Estates, a proposal had been made to go

* The spiteful female of the species, Mme de Montpensier, gave credence to these stories by ostentatiously wearing a pair of golden scissors at her waist. They were intended, she would tell one and all, to give Henry of Valois his new crown—the tonsure of a monk.

over his head and nominate Guise as Constable of France, by the authority of the Estates to "save religion and to reform the government in spite of the King and his ministers." Whether such a measure, tantamount to superseding the divinely ordained monarchy, could have been adopted is questionable. Some historians point to it, however, as the threat that moved Henry to act. An equally likely, and psychologically more intriguing hypothesis, is that Henry had known all along what he would have to do in order to safeguard his crown, that he had turned down the opportunity to deliver himself once and for all of the Duke of Guise in Paris because he feared the retaliation of the crowds, and that he had stage-managed the meeting in Blois in order to draw his enemy away from the capital and on to his own grounds. If that was Henry's plan all the intervening scenes —the show of independence, the imperious opening speech— were just the playing-out of a heroic performance for which the author-actor had already, in his mind, written the ending. In the absence of documents, this can only be a supposition, but it hangs convincingly on the frame of Henry of Valois's character.

However long the plan had been nurtured, it was put into execution after the nuptial ceremonies. Under pretext of making religious preparations for Christmas, Henry suspended the meetings of Estates, which had become a daily humiliation, and retired to his apartments. There, it appears that on the night of December 20 he held a secret council with his most trusted servants—not his new ministers, but the chiefs of the royal guard regiments and the Forty-Five. The sole question under discussion was what to do about the Duke of Guise. A proposal was advanced that, since he had openly defied the King's proscription against forming illegal associations, he should be charged with treason and tried. But who would dare press the charges? How could the crime be proved? And what tribunal could be trusted to pass sentence? In the silence which ensued, Crillon, the com-

mander of the French guards, spoke up. He would volunteer
to challenge Guise to a duel and do his best to wound him
mortally. Again there was silence. Henry turned to Loignac,
the head of the Forty-Five. "And what do you say?" he
asked. "Let him come here," was the reply. "Do not even
think of it," Henry said, "they will all call me another Nero."
Loignac knew his master, however. "There is no question of
Nero," he said. "You are the first judge in your own kingdom. Declare him guilty of treason now and that will be
the end of it."

The rest was easy, and it had already been planned for.
Some time after taking up his residence at Blois three months
earlier, Henry had ordered certain minor structural changes
made to the royal apartments. Two doors had been walled
up so that anyone proceeding from the council chamber on
the principal floor to the royal rooms upstairs would have
to ascend a circular staircase and pass through a narrow
passage in order to reach the King's study, which lay beyond
his bedroom. The trap had been made; all that remained
was to fix a time.

When they encountered each other at Mass on the morning of December 22, Henry told Guise that he planned to
make a pilgrimage to the Valois shrine at Notre-Dame de
Cléry, some twenty-five miles from Blois on the opposite
bank of the Loire. Later that afternoon, however, the Duke
received a message requesting his presence at an extraordinary meeting of the royal Council at eight o'clock on the
following morning. Again the rumors flew that something
was afoot. At dinner that evening, Guise found a note under
his napkin. He read it, crumpled it up, and threw it under
the table, announcing *"Il n'oserait"* ("He wouldn't dare").
Then he proceeded to spend the night with his current
mistress—none other than the durable Charlotte de Sauves.

Meanwhile, the King had retired early, leaving orders to
be woken up at four o'clock. When the knock came, he
called for his robe and candle and proceeded to his study.

One by one, the chosen members of the Forty-Five joined him there and then took up their positions in small rooms off the staircase.

Guise arrived promptly at eight. Because the morning was cold and raw, he asked that a fire be kindled in the chimney that dominated one wall of the Council chamber. Warming his back, he chatted with members of the Council while they waited for the King to make his appearance. Finally the door leading from the staircase opened, but instead of Henry it was Revol, his secretary, who came in. "Monseigneur," he said to Guise, "the King is asking for you. He is in his study."

Despite his show of unconcern, Guise had taken precautions to safeguard himself during his stay at Blois. He never ventured out alone, and in particular he was careful not to be lured into anything that could be a trap. This summons, however, caught him off guard, as Henry had hoped it would. Guise could not very well refuse, nor could he ask any of his colleagues on the Council to accompany him to a private meeting with the King. With a bow, he excused himself and started up the staircase.

As he reached the top and entered the narrow passage, the first of the assassins stabbed him in the breast. Guise tried to grapple with him, but others closed in. Though there was no question of the outcome, Guise put up a ferocious, bloody fight, dragging his assailants into the royal bedroom and to the foot of the bed, where he finally fell.* When the noise had subsided, a frightened Henry, who had been waiting in the study, entered the room and walked over to the body which had fallen face down. With a slippered foot, he rolled it over, looked down, and exclaimed, "My God, he is bigger dead than alive." A search of the body produced only one

---

* Guides at Blois still point out the exact spot to visitors, even though the entire bedroom and study were demolished to make way for the addition of a new wing in the seventeenth century.

The Murder of Henry Duke of Guise. Contemporary print shows the Duke being hacked to death by members of the Forty-Five as Henry III watches from the safety of an adjoining chamber.

item of interest: a note hidden in a sleeve and bearing the words, in Guise's own hand: "To prosecute the war in France, 700,000 *livres* a month is necessary."

VI

Catherine's bedroom was almost directly below that of her son. Hearing the noises upstairs, she asked several times what was happening but received no reply until Henry himself, still dressed in his bathrobe, entered. The only witness to what passed between mother and son was her physician, but his account has been preserved at second hand by the Florentine, Cavriana. Henry asked after her health, to which the physician replied that she had just taken her medicine. Then he drew near to the bed and said, "Good day, Madame, I beg you to forgive me. Monsieur de Guise is dead. I have had him killed, having got ahead in what he planned to do to me. . . . Now I am King again. The King of Paris is dead." The rest of the speech the Florentine puts into Henry's mouth—a long, measured recital of his grievances against the Guises and the League and a detailed catalogue of what he now proposed to do—is inconsistent with Henry's at his most rational and could not possibly have been made at the time under the circumstances. Catherine's reported reply—or replies, for there are several versions—is equally questionable. According to one account, she is supposed to have said, "I only pray God that the result may be what you hope." In another, more fanciful, it is "Well cut, my son, but will you now be able to sew?" In still a third, it is "My son, I am pleased to hear it, so long as it is for the good of the State."

The likelihood is that, stunned by the implications of Henry's act, she said nothing, or at least nothing of moment. There was, moreover, another shock in store for her. On hearing the shouts and commotion upstairs, the Cardinal of

Lorraine had tried to rush to the aid of his brother, but was stopped and put under arrest. After a day of debating what to do with him, Henry ordered him killed as well. Both bodies were then carried to the cellar of the castle and buried in quicklime.

On the day following this second murder, Catherine was visited by an Italian Capuchin monk, Bernardo d'Osimo, to whom she said, "What has he done? Pray for him, who needs it more than ever, for I can see him hastening to his ruin, and I fear that he will lose his body, his soul, and the kingdom." The news from Paris seemed to bear out her worst apprehensions. The entire town had risen. There was talk that Henry would himself now be excommunicated for the crime of having given the order to kill a prince of the Church. The Estates were for the moment shocked into inactivity, but it would not take long for the forces of the League to press for whatever punishment they deemed appropriate. Some attempt at a start toward reconciliation had to be made. Despite the bitterness of the weather, Catherine had herself carried to the Cardinal of Bourbon, who was being held under house arrest. She assured him that he was henceforth at liberty, but the old man was too distraught to understand. "Madame," he reproached her, "if you had not tricked us and made us come here with good words and a thousand assurances, these two would not be dead, and I should be free." The accusation was not only unjust but supremely ironic. Had she only been able to prevent them, the useless killings would never have taken place. A witness noted, "Both of them began to make fountains of their eyes, and suddenly afterwards the poor lady returned to her chamber."

Catherine's condition had been improving somewhat, but the visit, undertaken against the order of her physician, caused a relapse. "She has a great fever," the Papal Legate wrote on January 4, "and although the doctors say it is merely a feverish cold and there is no danger, the advanced age of the patient is causing great anxiety." Fever no doubt was a factor, as was the patient's age, but another, invisible affliction had stricken her as well. After the decades of activity, the plans and schemes and feints and thrusts, there was nothing left for her to do.

She took pains to dictate her will. Her principal legatee was her granddaughter, Christine, whom she had only a few days earlier seen married. Henry's wife, Louise, of whom she had always been fond, was to receive her favorite retreat, Chenonceaux. Her grandson, Charles of Valois, the natural son of Charles IX, was to inherit her properties in the maternal line—the comtés of Auvergne and Clermont, the barony of La Tour. There was a long list of bequests to those who had served her over the years—ladies, officers, attendants, and the Sisters of the *Murate* in Florence. The remainder was to go to "the King, her son, whom she appoints and institutes as her sole heir." Of her other surviving child, her daughter Margot who was still captive in the fortress of Usson, there was not a mention. At one o'clock on the afternoon of January 5, 1589, according to her physician, "she confessed, took the communion, and received extreme unction so contritely and devoutly that she has left us much consolation in the hope of her glory." Half an hour later, she died.

She received the formal honors dictated for the sovereigns of France. Her body lay in state in a room hung with black velvet while Franciscan friars recited prayers. In an antechamber, her plaster effigy was served at table morning and evening for forty days, and the food afterward taken away and distributed to the poor. But she could not be taken to Saint-Denis to be buried under the stately monument where her husband lay, and where she had already ordered her own statue placed. Asked for permission, the Council of Sixteen, which ruled Paris, said that if her body were brought to the city it would be thrown into the Seine.

On the Sunday following her death, a preacher in one of

the Paris churches—appropriately, that of Saint-Barthélemy —offered a funeral oration: "She has done much good and much evil in her day; more evil, I think, than good. I make no doubt of this. Today, gentlemen, a difficulty presents itself. Ought the Holy Catholic Church to pray for one who has lived as badly as she has done, who has so often upheld heresy, though she ended by supporting our Holy League? Gentlemen, to this question, I reply that if you will, of your charity, give her now and then a *Pater* and an *Ave,* you may do so. If not, it does not much matter. I leave you a free choice."

Part Five

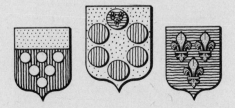

Postscript

I

In the rash of diplomatic reports and assessments that followed Catherine's death, the most prophetic was, again, that of Cavriana: "We all remain without light," he wrote, "without counsel or consolation, and to tell the truth, with her died what kept us alive. From now on we must turn our thoughts elsewhere and find some other support. The kingdom will suffer more than is believed, and the King remains without the most faithful and necessary support that he had."

Paris was in full, vengeful revolt. Royal arms and emblems were torn down and trampled; the tombs of the *mignons* were desecrated. Roused by the preachers, thousands took to the streets, marching barefoot and sometimes fully naked, chanting hymns and carrying torches which they extinguished at the entrance to Notre-Dame in symbol of the eclipse of the Valois race. The Duke of Guise was raised to the rank of "tutelary God," and the baptism of his posthumous son, born on January 20, 1589, was the occasion of a great public celebration at which the city assumed the sponsorship of the child, who was named François-Paris. The Faculty of Theology of the Sorbonne excised the King's name from the prayers of the Church and declared him a "most execrable tyrant who has injured the Catholic faith." They further absolved all his subjects from their oath of allegiance to him and urged them "with a free conscience to wage war on him." The Council of Sixteen seized full control of the city and called on other local Leagues for support. Favorable replies poured in from Rouen, Amiens, Chartres, Rheims, Angers, Marseilles, Le Mans, Toulouse, Lyons—every corner of France not held by the Huguenots.

The one missing factor was a leader. The Guises had so

effectively shaped the Holy League into an instrument of personal power that it was unthinkable to look outside of the family for a successor. But with the death of the Duke Henry, the leadership of the house had passed to his brother Charles, Duke of Mayenne, a fat, slow-witted, and slow-moving man given to aristocratic pretensions and strenuous womanizing. Mayenne was established in Lyons when news of the murders reached him, but it was not until February 15 that he could bestir himself to Paris. There, he condescended to accept the freshly coined and ambiguous title of Lord General of the Royal Estates and Crown of France and settled down in proper style. Even Mendoza, who had returned to Paris for the specific purpose of stirring Mayenne into action, could do no more than persuade him to call for a national assembly which would meet in July to "create a new king and establish a definitive government."

Meanwhile, an unnatural calm settled over Blois. Stunned first by the murders, then by the arrest of some of the League's leaders, and finally by the death of Catherine, the Estates General went through the motions of completing its sessions until Henry dismissed them on January 16. A bold, decisive move might yet have allowed him to exploit the initiative he had gained, but he chose instead to shut himself up in his rooms and compose long, confused justifications for the acts he had ordered. No one bothered to read them.

With the drama suspended as two of the principals took themselves out of action, attention inevitably focused on the third. Navarre had profited from the struggle between Valois and Guise to improve his own military position by seizing a number of towns for the Huguenots. In the wake of the events at Blois and their consequences in Paris, however, he recognized both a great danger to the country and an opportunity for himself. On March 4, 1589, he published a declaration that asked: "Is it not a pity that there is in this kingdom no person so great or so small that he cannot see its misery, that he cannot name the fatal fever which is attacking our state? . . . Yet no one has raised his voice to call for the remedy. No one in that entire assembly at Blois had dared pronounce the single sacred word of peace, the word in which is contained the well-being of our kingdom. . . . We have all done enough harm and suffered enough for it. We have, for these years, remained furious, insensate, drunk. Is it not enough?" Spanish support of the League was now an open secret throughout France; Navarre alluded to it in his appeal: "What will become of the face of this state if this evil continues? What will become of our nobility if our government is changed as it will undoubtedly be? . . . What will happen to those citizens who hold from the crown positions in finance or justice, police or soldiery? All this is lost if the monarch is lost. Who will guarantee their possessions? Who will hold the authority for justice? Who will command the armies? And you, the people, when the nobility and the cities are divided, what security will you have?"

In Paris, the League and Mendoza read the proclamation but were powerless. Anticipating that Henry would grasp at Navarre's offer of conciliation, they excoriated him in advance for this final example of the "treacheries, perfidies, sacrilege, exactions, cruelties, and deeds of shame of the arch-hypocrite of France." Mayenne, who might yet have intervened, refused to commit his troops. Undoubtedly, he was not as ambitious or politically motivated as his late brother; possibly he was also a better Frenchman, unwilling to play the Spanish game. A cease-fire was signed on behalf of the King and Navarre on April 2, and it was informally ratified by royal and Huguenot troops in the province of Poitou. Upon hearing the news, they threw down their weapons and broke lines to fraternize. Four weeks later, the event for which Catherine de' Medici had worked so long, tirelessly, and unsuccessfully at last took place.

Navarre knew his erratic brother-in-law well enough to mistrust him completely. Against the objections of his fellow Huguenots who suspected another Valois trap, he insisted on cementing the truce and alliance with a personal meeting. Escorted only by a few gentlemen, he rode to the outskirts of Tours, passed the night at the Château de Maillé, and on the next day had himself rowed across the Loire to Plessis-les-Tours, where Henry was staying. Wearing a doublet worn thin at the shoulders by his cuirass, he stepped ashore and started walking through the tree-shaded park toward the royal residence. As soon as he was recognized, throngs of soldiers and onlookers "incredible with joy" surrounded him, tried to touch him, to lift him to their shoulders. Henry meanwhile had walked out into the park as well, but so dense was the crowd that for a quarter of an hour the two men, who had not met since Navarre's escape from Paris thirteen years earlier, could only look at each other and stretch their arms out. At last, at shouts of *"Vivent les Rois,"* the mob parted to permit them to approach each other. Navarre, with "tears as big as peas rolling down his cheeks," fell to his knees before Henry and proclaimed: "After today, I care not by what death I die; I shall be content since God has granted me to look upon the face of my King." Afterward, the two men retired alone to speak for more than an hour, and later still Navarre, in less histrionic vein, sent a message back to his camp: "The ice has been broken. As I passed over the water I commended myself to God who in His goodness has not only preserved me but has made the King's face radiant with joy. As for the people, there was unparalleled applause, which made me very happy. . . . Please send me my baggage and have all the troops advance."

Well might Henry have radiated joy, for he had enlisted as his ally the most effective soldier in France. The truce brought fresh maledictions from both the League and the Vatican, which ordered Henry to appear in Rome and explain why he should not be excommunicated and deposed. But the merged armies under Navarre's command had already set off to march on Paris.

Joined by *Politique* volunteers who could at last see the

end of the slaughter, the troops advanced so rapidly that the English legate in Paris wrote: "The King of Navarre is thought to do what he does by sorcery, for all places yield to him."

On July 31, the two kings established camp in Saint-Cloud, overlooking a terrified Paris choked with Catholic refugees. The subject of their fears, whom they had called the "Valois monster," paced his room and mused aloud: "It would be a great pity to ruin and lose such a fine city. All the same, I must get the better of the mutineers inside it."

Henry was spared the need to make this decision. Early on the morning of August 1, as he was dressing, word was brought to him that "a monk from Paris" wished to see him. Reluctant to antagonize the clergy unnecessarily, the King ordered his visitor brought in. He was a young man of twenty-four, a Dominican Brother named Jacques Clément, who approached the King and handed him a letter. L'Estoile records the story: "The King, not thinking that any harm could come from this little monk, told those who were near to retire and opened the letter and began to read. When the monk saw him absorbed, he pulled a knife from his sleeve and struck him right below the navel. . . . The King, reeling from the blow, struck the monk on his left side and cried, 'Ah, the wicked monk, he has killed me! Someone kill him!' At this cry the guards rushed in, those who were nearest massacring the little Jacobin at the King's feet. He was at once removed . . . and stripped naked because some thought he must be a soldier in disguise, as it was too bold an act for a monk. But he was soon seen to be just what he was. . . ."*

---

* In their haste to execute Clément, the guards left a small mystery unsolved. The Duchess of Montpensier immediately took credit for the assassination, letting it be known that it was she who had inspired Clément to the deed, with the promise not only of a cardinal's hat but of more immediate, palpable reward. Scholarship, however, suggests that she did not even know of his existence prior to the event, and that he had acted alone upon the command of "an angel with a great light and a naked sword" who had appeared to him during the night.

Although bleeding heavily, the King seemed to rally after the initial shock, and he vowed that he would be on horseback within ten days. He spent an hour with Navarre, wrote a letter to his wife, and dictated another to the British ambassador: "I am sure the Queen your mistress will be sorry for this but I hope it will be quickly healed and so I pray write unto her from me." By evening, however, it was clear that the wound had caused massive internal bleeding, and by early morning the last of the Valois, not yet thirty-eight years old, was dead.

As a man and a monarch, a son and a brother, he had been such an abysmal failure that his only affirmative act was to die. In so doing, he prevented Spanish dominance of France by taking out of the hands of the Holy League the choice of a successor. As he lay dying, he named Navarre as his heir, and commanded his officers' allegiance to him. The son of Jeanne d'Albret and Antoine of Bourbon, the Gascon hayseed bridegroom, the willing captive of Mme de Sauves, the prince who had been slow to start growing up, was now on the throne as Henry IV of France and Navarre.

There was still more growing up ahead of him, for on August 2, 1589, as he himself ruefully observed, he was "a king without a kingdom, a general without a treasury, a husband without a wife." Five-sixths of France was still in the hands of the League; Mendoza was still in Paris and now openly attempting to move the lethargic Duke of Mayenne. Because Henry IV was a Protestant and under the ban of excommunication, the League proclaimed the senile Cardinal of Bourbon as the legitimate King of France and struck off some medals commemorating him as Charles X. More ominously, Philip II advanced a personal claim on the throne of France through the person of the elder daughter of his own marriage to Elizabeth, the daughter of Catherine de' Medici and Henry II. With the ready concurrence of the Pope, Philip also proposed that, until the question of succession was resolved, he be appointed "Protector of the State and of the Religion of the Kingdom of France."

The details of Henry IV's response to those challenges belong in another narrative. Town by town, he set about reconstituting his kingdom. When it became at last clear to him that his capital would never accept a heretic as king, he applied for conversion and was readmitted to the bosom of the Church in 1593—though it is doubtful that he ever uttered the famous, cynical "Paris is worth a Mass" which is attributed to him. In any case, it required another five years until Philip at last gave up and consented, by withdrawing his support, to let the fighting stop. Eight months later, internal peace was secured, after nearly forty years of civil war, by the Edict of Nantes, which granted unconditional freedom of religious conscience in every part of the kingdom. At last, Henry IV had reached full stature.

II

When Henry complained that he was "a husband without a wife," he had not been wholly accurate. Not only did he have a wife, but she was now Queen of France, even if circumstances did not permit her the full enjoyment of her new position.

Margot had entered the fortress of Usson in November, 1586, as a captive with neither hope nor prospective savior. Henry III had personally chosen as her jailer the Marquis of Canillac, a young noble who was commended to him for both his ambition and his loyalty. But Margot, at thirty-three, was still a handsome, extremely desirable woman of wit and imagination. Within less than a year, the inevitable had happened. As one of her biographers writes: "This lord of a very illustrious house saw himself the captive of his prisoner. He thought to have triumphed over her, but the mere sight of her ivory arms triumphed over him, and henceforth he lived only by the favor of the victorious eyes of his beautiful captive." And Brantôme adds: "Poor man! What could he do? To wish to keep prisoner her who, by the power of her eyes and her beautiful face, could rivet her chains upon the rest of the world, as though they had been galley-slaves!"

Despite this testimony from her admirers, it appears that Margot had learned something about the inconsistency of men, for there is a document in the archives of Clermont-Ferrand in which, over her signature, she "in consideration of the very signal and very acceptable services which she has received and hopes to receive from Jean de Beaufort, Marquis of Canillac, gives, cedes and transfers to him all the rights that she may possess over the county of Auvergne and other estates and lordships . . . also the sum of 40,000 *écus,* payable as soon as it will be possible to discharge it." For good measure, Margot also managed to win over the Marchioness of Canillac by persuading her that her personality and charm were wasted in rusticity and truly belonged in Court where they would assure her of immediate success. In preparation for this debut, Margot ransacked her own wardrobe for suitable dresses and began to give the dazzled woman lessons in proper etiquette and deportment. There is no telling how long a *ménage à trois* based on such interlocking interests might have lasted, but unfortunately the Marquis was summoned to military duty and perished in April, 1589, while directing a battery of artillery.

During her stay at Usson, events had moved rapidly: her husband's victory at Coutras; the rise of her former lover, Guise; the humiliation of her brother during the Day of the Barricades; his bloody revenge at Blois; the death of her mother, followed within a few months by that of her brother. In principle, Margot was now a free woman, but in fact she had no place to go and enjoy her freedom. As long as civil war raged on every side of her mountain top, she could hardly take the chance of being captured by any of the contending parties, for she had during her own brief military fling made enemies of all of them. The news of the execution of Mary Stuart, her sister-in-law, frightened her and caused her to order her food tasted before she would touch it. Beyond this precaution, however, it appears that she settled down to make the best of her situation. In the absence of reliable witnesses or testimony of her own—her *Memoirs* end abruptly with the start of her troubles—there is a choice of accounts of her life style. According to Père Hilarion de Coste, her earliest biographer, Usson became "a Tabor for devotion, a Libya for retirement, an Olympus for the arts, a Parnassus for the Muses, a Caucasus for the afflictions. . . ." It was, he continued, a "sweet hermitage, where Majesty meditated . . . [an] earthly paradise of delights, where sweet and harmonious voices combine to soothe—the only place where Royalty enjoyed the repose and contentment which blessed souls find in another world." Another writer compared it at once to Noah's Ark, a sacred temple, and a devout monastery.

Less admiring accounts paint a picture of Usson which more nearly resembles the Capri of Tiberius and concede that its mistress was possessed of "a temperament too ardent not to yield to temptation." The *Divorce Satirique* lists some of the objects of this temptation: an itinerant tenor named Pomini; a young carpenter from Arles whom Margot ennobled; a village shepherd; the son of a local coppersmith. Because the tenor, Pomini, was of a characteristically roving nature, it is told that Margot ordered the beds of all her household women raised higher off the ground in order that she might be able to look under them without suffering the embarrassment and discomfort of stooping down. There are undoubtedly elements of both truth and exaggeration in

only satisfied these requirements, but another one as well. Her name was Marie de' Medici—a remote cousin to Catherine, descended from the cadet branch of the family—and her father, the Duke of Tuscany, had let it be known that she would bring with her the staggering dowry of one million *écus* in gold.

Henry was still far from persuaded, and Margot still adamant, when Gabrielle resolved the problem by dying, while giving birth to a stillborn child, on April 10, 1599. The annulment proceedings now could move rapidly. Nine witnesses were rounded up to testify that Margot had been coerced into marriage by her mother and her brother Charles.* With no evidence to the contrary and no objections from the principal parties, judgment was handed down on December 17, 1599, declaring the marriage null and void. Twelve days later, Henry confirmed that his ex-wife should continue to bear the title of Queen of Navarre, to which he added that of Duchess of Valois. He also agreed to pay her debts and see to it that she received the full revenues from the estates which had been part of her marriage settlement.

His own second marriage, to Marie, was celebrated by procuration, much to the disappointment of the bride who had yet to see him, on October 5, 1600. In commissioning Sully to find him a wife, Henry had laid down three requirements: that she be pretty, that she be complaisant, and that she bear him sons. After first meeting her in Lyons on December 9 he could determine for himself that, with allowance for a bit of excessive chubbiness and shortness of leg, his faithful minister had satisfied the first two requirements. The third took a little more time, but hardly any more than necessary. On September 21, 1601, Marie was delivered of a boy—the future Louis XIII.

---

* One of them was the ubiquitous Charlotte de Sauves, who stated that Catherine had threatened Margot that "if she did not consent to this marriage, she would make her the most miserable woman in the kingdom."

III

During their final negotiations, Henry had written Margot: "I shall have more care for you than ever . . . being very satisfied with the ingeniousness and candor of your behavior and hoping that God will bless our remaining days by our fraternal friendship and the general happiness of the people. . . ."

He lived up to his promise. When Margot finally left Usson to return to Paris, Henry sent a splendid delegation headed by the Duke of Vendôme—his own elder son, César —to greet her and accompany her to temporary quarters in Francis I's Château of Madrid, which Catherine had converted into a royal silk-weaving factory. Within the week, Henry himself came to call and stayed for more than three hours. It was the couple's first meeting since Margot had left Nérac twenty years earlier. Both had changed in appearance since then. Henry's hair had turned white, and his face had acquired deep lines that testified to the unceasing labor of pulling a country together. Margot had grown so obese that her breasts, which she still fashioned to display, oozed out like great mounds from above her tight corsets. Her blond wigs now looked foolish, and the fair complexion of which she had been so justly proud was daubed and rouged. But temperamentally, neither of them had changed. On the occasion of Marguerite's first formal visit to the Louvre, she struck the perfect blend of graciousness, friendship, and deference. It was the younger, reigning Queen who stood awkwardly still and ill at ease until Henry nudged her to come forward and greet her predecessor.

The return of the Duchess of Valois was a major social event, commented upon by all the chroniclers. L'Estoile wrote: "The arrival of Queen Marguerite in Paris, where she had not been seen for twenty-four or twenty-five years, and her appearance at Court, so suddenly and hurriedly that it seemed she could not get there fast enough . . . caused a great deal of talk. It was said that on her arrival the King asked two things of her: firstly, that for the sake of her health she should no longer turn day into night and night into day; secondly, that she should restrain her generosity and practice a little economy. She replied to him that in the former case she would find it very difficult; but regarding the latter, that would be quite impossible, as she could never live otherwise, having acquired the habit from her mother. . . ."

In fact, Margot quickly tired of her quarters in the Château of Madrid and built herself a new establishment on the Left Bank of the Seine, on a site which presently is bounded by the Rue de Seine, the Rue Visconti, and the Rue des Saints-Pères. The principal mansion faced the river, and from its upstairs windows Margot enjoyed a splendid view of the Louvre and the Pont-Neuf, newly completed on her husband's orders.

To compensate for the lean years at Usson, Marguerite decorated her new house in Medici style. Her household accounts list the purchase of "eighteen tapestries from Flanders, twelve paintings on wood representing philosophers, and twenty-four of large size showing historic scenes," just to decorate the principal salon. The list of her personal effects —"*robes de grand apparat, robes de moindre cérémonie, manteaux de chambre*" ("robes of state, less ceremonial dresses, housecoats") to say nothing of scarves, furs, coats, skirts of every color and material—cover more than twelve pages. Because no corset however rigid could nip her waist to fashionable slimness, Margot took to padding out her thighs in order to make them look larger by comparison. In consequence, a visitor noted, there were doors in her own house through which she could not pass. Nevertheless, neither her mind nor her wit had suffered. Her nightly banquets attracted the leading poets, musicians, philosophers, and writers of the day. At the same time, she continued to entertain an unending chain of progressively younger semi-permanent house guests of no particular intellectual distinction.

Despite the unsavory and thoroughly deserved reputation these guests earned her, she remained a great and good friend of the royal family. Young and relatively provincial in up-bringing, Marie often sought out Margot's advice on the arrangements for a ball or consulted her on the proper up-bringing of the children. Henry himself, when not occupied elsewhere, took delight in being seen entering the notorious den of iniquity presided over by his former wife.

As has happened more than once since, their divorce became far more successful than their marriage had ever been. Margot was a doting aunt to the royal children, legitimate and otherwise, and especially to the young Dauphin who, to her delight, called her *"Maman-fille"* ("mother-girl"). Upon his birth, she had written Henry: "Monseigneur, Like the most grateful of all those in the humble service of Your Majesty, you will allow me to rejoice with you that by His Grace He has given you a son. Every good Frenchman will rejoice with you; but the happiness gives me particular pleasure, since I imagine that no one, excepting those to whom it matters most, can share it as completely as myself. . . ." The happiness and pleasure never wavered, for in her will the young Dauphin, by then King, was named as her heir.

In some ways, Henry IV never changed. The reason he had been obliged to marry his second wife by procuration and not in person was that his mistress of the time, Henriette d'Entragues, threatened to make his life unbearable if he left her for so trifling a reason. Only by establishing her in the Louvre as his new bride's Mistress of the Robes, and by fathering a child to match each one produced by the Queen, was he able to maintain a tenuous domestic harmony.

Nevertheless, he found time to be an excellent king—seen across the centuries, perhaps the best France ever had. He ended the butchery of the civil wars which in their first twenty years alone had claimed some eight hundred thousand lives, the razing of nine cities and two hundred villages, and began the slow process of healing the wounds they had inflicted. He reformed a national system of finance, which had descended to the level of an open auction for offices. He built roads and ordered them lined with trees—elms, for they made the best gun carriages. He created industries, from lead mines and iron mills to the Gobelin weaving shops and the Savonnerie carpet works. He instituted reforms in education and dispatched Samuel de Champlain to establish a fur-trading establishment in Quebec. Largely at the urging of Sully, he set in motion the first scheme to unify the most important of the national states of Europe. But above all, he put into practice his genuine concern for the simple peasant who, he recognized, was the abiding backbone of the nation. On one occasion, when told that royal troops had in time-honored style pillaged a district in Champagne, he sent for the guilty officers and dressed them down: "Give the orders to leave at once or you'll answer for it. If you ruin the people who supply the needs of the state, who then is going to pay your pensions, gentlemen?"

Certainly, Henry IV was France's most popular king, in his own time and now. After the feverish, lurid procession of the last Valois, he was a breath of fresh mountain air, and no one minded that it carried a waft of garlic. Every Frenchman could identify with a monarch who could fight well, whose heart was in the right place, who could tell a story on himself, and, of course, who could distinguish himself in bed —although on this last qualification there is dissenting opinion: Mme de Verneuil, one of Henry's last mistresses, called him Captain Good Intentions.

But all things have a term. On the afternoon of May 14, 1610, while Henry was on his way from the Louvre to pay a visit to Sully, who was ailing, the royal coach was stopped by traffic in the Rue Saint-Honoré. In what can only be described as the insensate act of a lunatic, for no political or personal motives were ever unearthed for his deed, a man named Jean-François Ravaillac, who had followed the coach from the palace, jumped upon a small stone pillar on the side of the narrow street, reached through the window and twice stabbed the King, the second time fatally.

Margot lived on for another five years. As a close friend of the widowed Queen, she was invited to be one of the young Louis XIII's sponsors when he was crowned at the cathedral in Rheims, and later, in one of her last public appearances, to attend his wedding to Anne of Austria. Always, it had been she who had set the style by what she had chosen to wear. This time, her gown of silver brocade with huge sleeves covered with pink diamonds, the rows of pearls and diamonds that stretched across her wide bosom, the jeweled wig, appeared a silly costume out of the past. Not long after, she contracted a chill she could not shake off, which eventually caused her death, at the age of sixty-one, on March 27, 1615. With her, this narrative ends, as did an era.

IV

A crypt had been prepared for Catherine de' Medici in the tiny church of Saint-Sauveur in Blois, but so inadequately had her body been embalmed that it was necessary to remove it and bury it in the soil of the common graveyard. There it rested for twenty-one years while, in L'Estoile's words, "No more notice was paid to her than to a dead goat." In the first years of his reign, her son-in-law had too much else on his mind to concern himself about finding a more suitable burial site. Later, when peace was restored, he chose to leave well enough alone and not rekindle old hatreds. After his death, it was the Duchess of Montmorency, the daughter of Henry II by Mary Stuart's companion, Lady Flemming, who quietly arranged for Catherine's remains to be brought to Paris and laid to rest at the side of her husband.

Historians have, with rare exceptions, not been kind to Catherine de' Medici. Those of her time, writing with the stench of blood still in their nostrils, imputed every foul treachery and vile motive to her. In the passion of their own Catholic or Huguenot partiality, they could find horror and guilt enough to condemn her to their respective hells. The Venetian Correro wrote: "The Huguenots say she has deceived them by fine words, and by her air of mendacious kindness; while, all the time, she was weaving their destruction. On the other hand, the Catholics declare that if she had not encouraged the Huguenots, they would never have dared to go so far." This can be taken as a working description of duplicity, but in another light it is also the formula for compromise.

A later age, personally removed from events and enriched with the documentary fruits of scholarship, recognized that religion had had little to do with the tragedy of the wars, that it had served as a convenience for personal ambitions and international designs. Catherine, reared in the frescoed chambers of Roman and Florentine palaces, had perceived this situation from the beginning. Moreover, it is clear that she herself never was preoccupied with theological differences; though her letters are replete with pious expressions, it is impossible to tell from them, except for her references to attending Mass, whether the writer was a Catholic or a Protestant. After a conversation with her, the Venetian ambassador once noted, "I do not believe the Queen Mother understands what the word 'dogma' signifies."

Yet even in this better-informed historic construction, it is still Catherine who personifies the great evil, the guiltiest ambition. Everyone else, Huguenot and Catholic, is conceded to have treated with the enemies of France, yet it is she who is damned as the intruder, the foreigner. Paradoxically, her crime is that she sought to defend the monarchy, to preserve it intact as it passed through the fatally inept hands of her sons.

Still closer to our own day, the charge against Catherine changes again, but not the verdict. Now, it is not what she did which damns her, but what she failed to do. "Catherine," writes Edith Sichel in what is otherwise a masterful evocation of her life, "was all means and no ends. She walked as the moment prompted, with no big centre to focus her outlook. . . . There was nothing to give unity to all her scattered efforts, hopes and fears."

Of course there was. In a century molded by extraordinary women, she was a woman of infinite industry and patience, of lively intelligence and shrewd calculation, of outstanding personal courage and fortitude. She was also as unalloyedly cynical as a brothel-keeper—a role, moreover, that she assumed whenever it served her purpose. But first and always, she was the fiercely protective mother, the substitute for the dead father, the trustee of her children's inheritance. The further charge has been made that even this concern was only a mask behind which she hid her own personal ambition for power. The Venetian Cavalli, who was both a sympathetic observer and an admirer, noted the high degree to which she revealed *"un affetto di signoreggiare"* ("a passion to rule"). Perhaps, had her sons grown into men, she would have been satisfied, or have been obliged, to recede into the background. But then, perhaps it was the intensity of her own possessiveness that stifled and warped them.

On balance, one of the fairest, most acute judgments of Catherine de' Medici was rendered, in his own fashion, by Henry IV, the man who had the greatest reason to be grateful for her labors. When it became known that he was to marry Marie de' Medici, a courtier tried to compliment him on having found the cure for France's ills in the very same city where all its troubles had begun. Henry listened, paused, and replied: "Someone has already said this to me. But let me ask you, what could a poor woman do, left alone by the death of her husband with five small children on her arms, and with two families in France, ours and that of the Guises, striving to take away the Crown? Was it not necessary that she play strange parts in order to deceive the one and the other and yet, as she did, to protect her children, who reigned in succession by the wisdom of a woman so able? I marvel that she did not do worse."

Bibliography

Alberi, Eugènio. *Vita di Caterina dei Medici.* Florence, 1838.
—— ed. *Relazioni degli ambasciatori veneti al Senato durante il secolo decimosesto.* Florence, 1830–1862.
Armstrong, Edward. *The French Wars of Religion, Their Political Aspects.* Oxford, 1904.
Aubais, Charles. *Pièces fugitives pour servir à l'Histoire de France.* Paris, 1759.
Aubigné, Agrippa d'. *Mémoires.* Paris, 1854.
Babelon, Jean. *La Reine Margot.* Paris, 1965.
Bardon, Françoise. *Diane de Poitiers et le mythe de Diane.* Paris, 1963.
Baschet, Armand. *La Diplomatie Vénitienne.* Paris, 1862.
—— *Les Comédiens italiens à la cour de France.* Paris, 1882.
Battifol, Louis. *Le Siècle de la Renaissance.* Paris, 1911.
Batut, Guy de la. *Henri III.* Paris, 1931.
—— *Les Amours des rois de France racontées par leurs contemporains.* Paris, 1929.
Belleval, René. *Les Fils de Henri II.* Paris, 1898.
Bidou, Henri. *Le Château de Blois.* Paris, 1931.
Bloch, M. *Les Rois thaumaturges.* Strasbourg, 1929.
Bouchet, Henri. *Catherine de Médicis.* Paris, 1899.
—— *Les Femmes de Brantôme.* Paris, 1890.
Bouillé, René de. *Histoire des ducs de Guise,* 4 vols. Paris, 1850.
Boulé, Alphonse. *Catherine de Médicis et Coligny.* Paris, 1913.
Bourciez, Édouard. *Les Moeurs polies et la littérature de Cour sous Henri II.* Paris, 1886.
Bourilly, V. L., ed. *Journal d'un bourgeois de Paris sous François Ier, 1515–1536.* Paris, 1910.
Brantôme, Seigneur de, Pierre de Bourdeilles. *Oeuvres complètes,* 11 vols. Paris, 1864–1882.
Braudel, Fernand. *La Méditerranée et le monde méditerranéen à l'époque de Philippe II.* Paris, 1967. (*The Mediterranean and*

the Mediterranean World in the Age of Philip II, tr. Sian Reynolds, New York, 1974.)

Buchon, J. A. C., ed. *Choix des chroniques et mémoires sur l'histoire de France* (XVIe siècle). Paris, 1836.

Burnand, Robert. *La Cour des Valois*. Paris, 1938.

Busbecq, Ogier Ghislain de. *Letters to the Holy Roman Emperor Maximilian II*. New York, 1962.

Capefigue, J. B. H. R. *Diane de Poitiers*. 1859.

Castelnau, Jacques. *Catherine de Médicis*. Paris, 1954.

Castelot, André. *Les Grandes Heures des cités et des châteaux de la Loire*. Paris, 1951.

Castries, duc de, René de la Croiz. *Henry IV, roi de coeur, roi de France*. Paris, 1970.

Catalogue des Actes de François Ier, 10 vols. Paris, 1887–1908.

Catherine dei Medici. *Letters*, 10 vols. Ed. Hector de la Ferrière and Baguenault de Puchesse. Paris, 1880–1907.

Cerceau, J. A. du. *Les Plus Excellens Bastimens de France*. Paris, 1870.

Cerf, Léon Dr. *L'Histoire vue par un médecin: Héritiers et bâtards des rois; les Valois*. Paris, 1951.

Champion, Pierre. *Catherine de Médicis présente à Charles IX son royaume*. Paris, 1937.

—— *Charles IX*, 2 vols. Paris, 1939.

—— *La Galérie des rois de France*. Paris, 1934.

—— *La Jeunesse de Henri III*, 2 vols. Paris, 1934.

—— *Paris au temps de la Renaissance*. Paris, 1936.

Champollion-Figeac, A. L. *La Captivité du roi François Ier*. Paris, 1847.

Chéruel, A. *Marie Stuart et Catherine de Médicis*. Paris, 1858.

Chevallier, Casimir. *Archives royales de Chenonceau*. Paris, 1864–1869.

Cook, Theodore A. *Old Touraine*, 2 vols. London, 1912.

Croze, Joseph de. *Les Guises, les Valois et Philippe II*, 2 vols. Paris, 1966.

Davila, H. C. *The History of the Civil Wars in France*, 6 vols. London, 1801.

De Crue de Stoutz, Francis. *La Cour de France au seizième siècle*. Paris, 1888.

BIBLIOGRAPHY

Defrance, Eugène. *Catherine de Médicis, ses astrologues et ses magiciens.* Paris, 1911.

Denieuil-Cormier, Anne. *La France de la Renaissance.* Grenoble, 1962.

Desjardins, E. *Anne de Pisseleu, duchesse d'Étampes et François Ier.* Paris, 1909.

Dickerman, Edmund H. *Bellièvre and Villeroi: Power in France under Henri III and Henry IV.* Providence, 1971.

Dimier, Lucien. *Le Château de Fontainebleau et la Cour de François Ier.* Paris, 1930.

Dodu, Gaston. *Les Valois.* Paris, 1934.

Doucet, Roger. *Les Institutions de la France au XVIème siècle,* 2 vols. Paris, 1948.

Erlanger, Philippe. *Diane de Poitiers.* Paris, 1955.

—— *Henri III.* Paris, 1935.

—— *Le Massacre de la Saint-Barthélemy.* Paris, 1960.

Estienne, Charles. *Le Guide des chemins de France,* 2 vols. Paris, 1936.

Estienne, Pierre. *Discours merveilleux de la vie, actions et déportemens de Catherine de Médicis, Royne Mère.* 1575.

Estoile, Pierre de l'. *Mémoires-journaux,* vols. 1–3. Paris, 1885–1896.

Febvre, Lucien. *Au Coeur religieux du 16ème siècle.* Paris, 1957.

—— *Autour de l'Heptameron: Amour sacré, amour profane.* Paris, 1942.

Ferrière, Hector de la. *Le XVIème Siècle et les Valois.* Paris, 1879.

—— *Trois Amoureuses au seizième siècle.* Paris, 1885.

Forneron, H. *Les Ducs de Guise et leur époque.* Paris, 1877.

Franchi, Anna. *Caterina de' Medici, regina di Francia.* Milan, 1933.

Franklin, Alfred. *Paris et les Parisiens au XVIème siècle.* Paris, 1874.

Funck-Brentano, Frantz. *Ce qu'était un Roi de France.* Paris, 1940.

—— *La Renaissance.* Paris, 1935.

Gaillard, G. H. *Histoire de François Ier, roi de France,* 4 vols. Paris, 1819.

Galzy, Jeanne. *Catherine de Médicis.* Paris, 1936.

Gebelin, François. *Les Châteaux de la Renaissance.* Paris, 1927.

Godefroy, Théodore. *Le Cérémonial Français,* 2 vols. Paris, 1619.

Guérard, Albert. *The Life and Death of an Ideal: France in the Classical Age.* New York, 1956.

Guiffrey, Georges. *Lettres inédites de Diane de Poitiers.* Paris, 1886.

Habesque, F. *La Vie en province au XVIème.* Agen, 1887.

Hackett, Francis. *Francis the First.* London, 1934.

Haldane, Charlotte. *The Queen of Hearts.* New York, 1968.

Hamel, Frank. *Fair Women at Fontainebleau.* New York, 1909.

Haton, Claude. *Mémoires contenant le récit des événements accomplis de 1543 à 1582.* Paris, 1862.

Hauser, Henri. *Les Débuts du capitalisme moderne en France.* Paris, 1902.

—— *Ouvriers du temps passé.* Paris, 1927.

—— *La Prépondérance espagnole (1559–1660).* Paris, 1948.

Hay, Marie. *Madame Diane de Poitiers.* New York, 1900.

Henry-Bordeaux, Paule. *Louise de Savoie, "roi" de France.* Paris, 1954.

Héritier, Jean. *Catherine de Médicis.* Paris, 1940.

Imbart de la Tour, P. *Les Origines de la réforme en France.* Paris, 1935.

Jackson, Catherine Charlotte. *The Court of France in the 16th Century,* 2 vols. London, 1886.

Jensen, De Lamar. *Diplomacy and Dogmatism, Bernardino de Mendoza and the French Catholic League.* Cambridge, 1964.

Jouvenel, Henri de. *Huit Cents Ans de révolution française.* Paris, 1932.

Jusserand, J. J. *Les Sports et jeux d'exercises de l'ancienne France.* Paris, 1935.

Lacombe, Bernard de. *Catherine de Médicis entre Guise et Condé.* Paris, 1899.

Lacroix, Paul. *Moeurs, usages et costumes au Moyen-âge et à l'époque de la Renaissance.* Paris, 1872.

—— *Les Secrets de beauté de Diane de Poitiers.* Paris, 1857.

La Noue, François de. *Discours politiques et militaires.* Geneva, 1967.

Lauzun, Philippe. *Itinéraire raisonné de Marguerite de Valois en Gascogne.* Paris, 1902.

Lavisse, Ernest, ed. *Histoire de France,* vols. 4–6. Paris, 1903–1911.

Lefranc, Abel. *La Vie quotidienne au temps de la Renaissance.* Paris, 1938.

Le Gras, Joseph. *Tour de France de Charles IX (variété inédite).* Paris, 1931.

Lenient, Charles. *La Satire en France,* 2 vols. Paris, 1886.

Lesueur, Frédéric et Pierre. *Le Château de Blois.* Paris, 1927.

Lévis-Mirepoix, duc de, Antoine. *François Ier.* Paris, 1931.

—— *Les Guerres de religion, 1559–1610.* Paris, 1950.

—— *Henri IV, roi de France et de Navarre.* Paris, 1971.

Livet, Georges. *Les Guerres de religion.* Paris, 1970.

Lucinge, René de. *Lettres sur les débuts de la Ligue (1585).* Geneva, 1964.

Luzatti, Ivo. *Caterina dei Medici.* Milan, 1946.

Macchetta, Adriana. *Il regno tempestuoso di Caterina de' Medici.* Milan, 1967.

Madinier, Renée. *Amours et destins des reines de France.* Paris, 1969.

—— *Amours royales et impériales.* Paris, 1967.

Mahoney, Irene. *Royal Cousin; the Life of Henry IV.* New York, 1970.

Major, J. Russell. *Representative Institutions in Renaissance France: 1421–1550.* Madison, 1960.

Mandrou, Robert. *Introduction à la France moderne: Essai de psychologie historique 1500–1640.* Paris, 1961.

Marguerite de Valois. *Mémoires et Lettres.* Ed. M. F. Guessard. Paris, 1860.

Maricourt, A. de. *Les Valois; hérédité, pathologie.* Paris, 1937.

Mariejol, J. H. *Catherine de Médicis.* Paris, 1920.

—— *La Vie de Marguerite de Valois.* Paris, 1928.

Martin, Henri. *Histoire de France,* 8 vols. Paris, 1833.

Mattingly, Garrett. *The Armada.* Boston, 1959.

—— *Renaissance Diplomacy.* Boston, 1955.

Maulde de la Clavière, R. de. *Louise de Savoie et François Ier.* Paris, 1895.

—— *Les Origines de la Révolution Française.* Paris, 1889.

BIBLIOGRAPHY

Mayer, Marcel. *Le Château d'Anet.* Paris, 1952.

Merki, Charles. *L'Amiral de Coligny.* Paris, 1909.

—— *La Reine Margot et la fin des Valois.* Paris, 1905.

Michaud, Joseph-François et Poujoulat, Jean-Joseph, ed. *Nouvelle Collection des mémoires sur l'histoire de France,* 32 vols. Paris, 1836–1854.

Michelet, Jules. *Histoire de France,* vols. 6–12. Paris, 1856.

Mignet, F. A. M. *La Rivalité de François Ier et de Charles Quint,* 2 vols. Paris, 1875.

Monluc, Blaise de. *Commentaires et Lettres.* Paris, 1901.

Mouton, Léo. *Un Demi-roi, le duc d'Épernon.* Paris, 1922.

Neale, John E. *The Age of Catherine de Medici.* London, 1943.

Noell, Henri. *Henri II et la naissance de la société moderne.* Paris, 1944.

Noguères, Henri. *La Saint-Barthélemy, 24 Août 1572.* Paris, 1959.

Oman, Sir Charles. *History of the Art of War in the Sixteenth Century.* New York, 1937.

Orliac, Jeanne d'. *Diane de Poitiers, grand' sénéchale de Normandie.* Paris, 1930.

Palm, Franklin Charles. *Politics and Religion in Sixteenth-Century France.* Boston, 1927.

Pardoe, Julia. *The Court and Reign of Francis the First,* 3 vols. New York, 1901.

Paris, Paulin. *Essai sur François Ier, roi de France.* Paris, 1885.

Pasquier, Étienne. *Lettres historiques pour les années 1556–1594.* Geneva, 1966.

—— *Recherches sur la France.* Paris, 1951.

Petitot, Claude-Bernard, ed. *Collection complète des mémoires relatifs à l'histoire de France,* 130 vols. Paris, 1818–1829.

Picot, Emile. *Les Italiens en France au seizième siècle.* Paris, 1901.

Planche, Regnier de la. *Histoire de l'état de France sous le règne de François II.* Paris, 1836.

Prudhomme, Louis-Marie. *Les Crimes des reines de France.* Paris, 1791.

Quicherat, J. *Histoire du costume en France.* Paris, 1875.

Rain, Pierre. *Les Chroniques des châteaux de la Loire.* Paris, 1932.

Ranke, Leopold von. *Civil Wars and Monarchy in France in the 16th and 17th Centuries.* New York, 1854.

Reumont, A. de. *La Jeunesse de Catherine de Médici.* Paris, 1866.

BIBLIOGRAPHY

Rival, Paul. *La Folle Vie de la reine Margot.* Paris, 1929.

Robin, Gilbert. *L'Énigme sexuelle d'Henri III.* Paris, 1964.

Roeder, Ralph. *Catherine de Medici and the Lost Revolution.* New York, 1964.

Roelker, Nancy Lyman. *Queen of Navarre; Jeanne d'Albret, 1528–1572.* Cambridge, 1968.

Romier, Lucien. *Catholiques et Huguenots à la cour de Charles IX.* Paris, 1924.

—— *La Conjuration d'Amboise.* Paris, 1923.

—— *Les Origines politiques des guerres de religion,* 2 vols. Paris, 1913.

—— *Le Royaume de Catherine de Médicis,* 2 vols. Paris, 1922.

Ruble, A. de. *La Cour des enfants de France sous François Ier.* Paris, 1884.

—— *Le Traité de Cateau-Cambrésis.* Paris, 1889.

Russell, Jocelyne G. *The Field of Cloth of Gold: Men and Manners in 1520.* London, 1969.

Saint-Armand, Imbert de. *Les Femmes de la Cour des Valois.* Paris, n.d.

Sauval, H. *Les Amours des rois de France.* Paris, 1792.

Sedgewick, Henry D. *Henry of Navarre.* Indianapolis, 1930.

Seely, Grace Hart. *Diane the Huntress; the Life and Times of Diane de Poitiers.* New York, 1936.

Seward, Desmond. *The First Bourbon: Henry IV, King of France and Navarre.* Boston, 1971.

Sichel, Edith. *Catherine de Medici and the French Reformation.* New York, 1969.

—— *The Later Years of Catherine de Medici.* New York, 1969.

—— *Men and Women of the French Renaissance.* New York, 1969.

Sizeranne, Robert de la. *Les Masques et les visages.* Paris, 1913–1927.

Slocombe, George. *The White-Plumed Knight.* New York, 1931.

Smith, Pauline D. *The Anti-Courtier Trend in 16th Century French Literature.* Geneva, 1966.

Sutherland, N. M. *Catherine de Medici and the Ancien Régime.* London, 1966.

—— *The French Secretaries of State in the Age of Catherine de Medici.* London, 1962.

Terasse, Charles. *François Ier, le roi et le règne,* 3 vols. Paris, 1950.

Thompson, James W. *The Wars of Religion in France.* Chicago, 1909.

Tommaseo, M. N. *Relations des ambassadeurs vénitiens sur les affaires de France au XVIème siècle,* 2 vols. Paris, 1838.

Tortorel, Jacques et Perissin, Jean. *Les Grandes Scènes historiques du XVIème siècle.* Paris, 1886.

Trollope, Thomas A. *The Girlhood of Catherine de Medici.* London, 1856.

Vaissière, Pierre de. *Gentilshommes campagnards de l'ancienne France.* Paris, 1904.

—— *Henri IV.* Paris, 1928.

—— *Le château d'Amboise.* Paris, 1935.

—— *Récits du temps des troubles: De quelques assassins.* Paris, 1912.

—— "Reine sans couronne: la reine Margot à Paris," in *Revue des Études Historiques,* January–March, 1938.

Van Dyke, Paul. *Catherine de Medici,* 2 vols. New York, 1922–1927.

Vanel, Charles. *The Royal Mistresses of France.* London, 1695.

Varillas, Antoine. *Histoire de Charles IX,* 2 vols. Paris, 1684.

Vivent, Jacques. *La Tragédie de Blois.* Paris, 1946.

Waldman, Milton. *Biography of a Family: Catherine de Medici and Her Children.* Boston, 1936.

Weill, Georges Jacques. *Les Théories sur le pouvoir royal en France pendant les guerres de religion.* Paris, 1891.

Weiss, Nathaniel. *La Chambre ardente.* Paris, 1890.

Whitehead, A. W. *Gaspard de Coligny, Admiral of France.* London, 1904.

Wiley, William Leon. *The Gentlemen of Renaissance France.* Cambridge, 1954.

Williams, H. Noel. *Henry II, His Court and Times.* New York, 1910.

Yates, Frances A. *The Valois Tapestries.* London, 1959.

Zeller, Gaston. *Les Institutions de France au XVIème siècle.* Paris, 1948.

Index

INDEX

INDEX

INDEX

INDEX

INDEX

INDEX

INDEX